The Debt I Owe

ISBN: 978-1-947319-78-3

Cover and text layout design: Kristi Yoder

Printed in the USA

Published by:

TGS International
P.O. Box 355
Berlin, Ohio 44610 USA
Phone: 330.893.4828
Fax: 330.893.2305
www.tgsinternational.com

TGS001742

JOHNNY MILLER

The Debt I Owe

A memoir of 1-W Service
in Zanesville, Ohio

Dedication

I dedicate this book to the memory of those faithful pioneers whose keen spiritual insight and tireless labors of love produced a structured haven where Christian youth could safely work. Without the sacrifice of these devoted brothers and the voluntary service unit they built, our pathway would be strewn with more spiritual causalities.

I further dedicate this book to those of this generation whom God is calling to surmount present difficulties to provide a structured, godly atmosphere where youth can safely serve in Christ's kingdom.

Table of Contents

Introduction

The world's focus in 1965 was riveted on the Vietnam War, where soldiers were dying in the jungles and rice paddies of the Mekong Delta. Here in the United States, the Selective Service System was drafting men at ever-younger ages, sending them off to kill and be killed. However, the Selective Service also cooperated with church leaders to allow conscientious objectors an alternative: twenty-four months of 1-W service.

COs could choose from a number of accepted locations. The majority worked in hospitals or old people's homes as orderlies, maintenance workers, and kitchen or laundry staff. The 1-W program influenced the lives of thousands of participants over a twenty-year period. Some young men were ill-prepared for the temptations they faced, and lost out spiritually. Others had support from their home churches, and their experiences were positive.

I received my draft notice at nineteen years old, but as a follower of Jesus Christ, I knew I could never take human life or assist those who did. I filled out those life-altering forms and wrote across the bottom of the first page, *I am a conscientious objector to war*. The Selective Service sent me a second set of forms that requested details of my religious beliefs and church affiliation. After review, I was granted 1-W status, which gave me sixty days to find an approved job.

With limited construction experience in my hometown of Virginia Beach, I wondered how to find a qualifying job. A friend suggested an agricultural experiment station in nearby Maryland where the pay was good and workers had weekends off. Was that the place for me?

As the weeks passed, I earnestly prayed for direction. I enlisted my special friend, Ruth Overholt, who was teaching in our church school, to join me in fasting and prayer. Through this experience, I learned that God's wisdom is indeed marvelous and His ways past finding out! His answer was a major steppingstone in my life.

—Johnny Miller

CHAPTER 1

Decisions

"Say, aren't you about draft age?" the visiting minister asked after we exchanged greetings. I had been deeply impressed by his sermon, and following the benediction, I moved up the aisle to thank him. I waited while William McGrath finished his conversation with another brother before turning toward me.

He hurried to explain. "A new voluntary service unit has just opened in Zanesville, Ohio, under the Conservative Mennonite Mission Board. They have an understanding with Bethesda Hospital to receive 1-W applicants, and I highly encourage you to consider serving there."

I had already received my draft notice, so I weighed his words. A church-sponsored voluntary service unit provided room and board, but very little pay. How would I pay my share of the car my father and I had jointly purchased? I also had a special friend, Ruth Overholt. The conviction that God was leading us toward marriage was growing in my heart. How would I support her financially?

While working alone that week, I told God all the reasons why I couldn't join the VS unit in Zanesville. I needed to prepare for a future with Ruth, and that didn't seem possible on a meager VS allowance. A calmness settled over me, but it was soon shattered. I sensed God's still small voice saying, "But I want you to go." The battle in my heart returned with a vengeance as I tried to argue with God. After a long struggle, I finally surrendered. "Lord, if you want me to go, I will go!" A deep peace flooded my soul.

Further confirmation came the next Sunday when I approached another visiting minister at church. I asked Brother Willie Wagler about the new VS unit in Zanesville. Any lingering doubt was dispelled when he enthusiastically responded, "I highly recommend it!"

I made the necessary phone calls, and in January 1966 I bid Ruth and my parents farewell and headed from Virginia to Ohio. There I met two other 1-W workers, Levi Schrock from Wisconsin and Earl Nisly from Kansas. The two years of life-changing experiences we would share would make us lifelong friends. One by one, we were interviewed by a panel of three ministers and accepted into the Zanesville Voluntary Service Unit. Little did we grasp what God had in store for us as we began serving Christ by serving people.

I had stepped out of my familiar rural life of church, family, and friends, and into the unfamiliar world of hospitals and medical professionals. How would I fare? My work experience so far had been in construction, and I realized that I had much to learn. As a conscientious objector, I was determined to do well with the privilege of working at Bethesda Community Hospital instead of being inducted into the military. I wanted to pay the debt I owed to my country.

I was thankful to have experienced Messiah Bible School. The Biblical truths, stringent rules, and dorm life had prepared me for the close interaction with others in the Zanesville VS Unit.

However, those thoughts were forced out as I concentrated on our orientation from Mrs. Vann,[1] the nursing supervisor. "I will

[1] Throughout the book, names of doctors, hospital personnel, and patients have been changed to protect privacy, except where permission was obtained to use the actual names.

The Bethesda Community Hospital.

be training you for your duties in patient care in various departments," she began. "One of the first things you need to learn is the layout of the hospital. There are four floors and the basement. The hospital is laid out in a T-shape with three wings. Each wing on its respective floor is set up for a particular purpose. For example, 1-West is our orthopedic surgical floor, 3-East is our medical surgical unit, 4-North is our psych ward, and so on.

"I will teach you how to care for patients, how to change bed sheets, and how to bathe a bedfast patient," Mrs. Vann continued with a reassuring smile. "You will learn to make a bed with the patient lying in it. We will take this one step at a time. You are bright young men, and I am sure you will learn quickly. Here is a list of abbreviations I want you to learn. Study them well because we use them a lot in the hospital. For example, you will hear *TPR* for temperature, pulse, and respirations. We say *IV* for intravenous, *IM* for intramuscular, and *CPR* for cardiopulmonary resuscitation." She handed us three sheets of paper filled with a confusing array of abbreviations and definitions. "The sooner you can master these, the sooner I can integrate you into our workforce. And we do need you," she said, smiling again to dispel our apprehension.

"Now," Mrs. Vann continued as she rose and glanced at her watch, "it's past twelve, and I will show you the cafeteria where you will have your meals while on duty. Just follow me." Her crisp white uniform and decisive manner suggested she was used to being respected and obeyed.

A steady hum of conversation greeted us as we entered the huge cafeteria. Mrs. Vann explained that the hospital would provide food while we were in training, but we would be responsible for our own meals once we became employees. The daily menu had two kinds of meat, a selection of vegetables, and dessert. Employees were allotted a half hour for meals, and one fifteen-minute break during the eight-hour shift.

We made our selections, keenly aware of the curious glances in our direction as Mrs. Vann led the way to an empty table. Mrs. Vann introduced us to Dr. Shuman, who was seated nearby, and explained that we were joining the hospital staff as conscientious objectors in the government's 1-W program. He welcomed us, and we learned that he was a pediatric surgeon specializing in nose and throat surgeries.

Hoping to prevent embarrassment as we began our first meal in the cafeteria, I said, "We usually pray before we eat. Would that be all right?" Mrs. Vann nodded respectfully and waited as we bowed our heads and silently asked God's blessing on our meal and this new chapter in our lives.

As we ate, our nursing supervisor asked about our families, our job experiences, and our beliefs. She seemed genuinely interested as Earl Nisly described his farming family from the Mennonite community of Hutchinson, Kansas. I talked about my family and experience working for a plumber in my church community of Virginia Beach, Virginia.

We began feeling more comfortable as we followed Mrs. Vann through the hospital. We learned that the regular elevators were for public use while the larger ones were reserved for hospital carts, beds, and employees. "And here," she said, waving her hand, "is the staircase in the very center of the hospital connecting all floors. You will find other stairs at the far end of each wing."

Mrs. Vann pointed out the dumbwaiter that ferried supplies and utensils between the floors. "Each floor and nurses' station is also connected by our pneumatic tube system to the central supply room, emergency room, blood bank, and surgery. With this," she explained, holding up a bullet-shaped tube, "we send and receive written messages, requisitions, small items, and even medication throughout the entire hospital!" She showed us the programmable dial on the tube which directed it to the desired destination.

Names of doctors, departments, medical terms, and procedures filled our waking hours and our dreams. Over and over, we practiced "gloving up" with sterile technique to assist ER doctors. We took each other's blood pressures and temperatures while learning to read the results. During training, we practiced CPR on medical mannequins and studied body mechanics for lifting heavy patients. Nurse aides were also in these classes, and we took turns playing the part of a patient, lying completely limp so the other students could practice working together to properly support and carry an unconscious person.

While the rest of us were taking this training, Levi Schrock was becoming acquainted with the inner workings of the storeroom where all goods were stocked and catalogued. Lee, as we came to know him, was naturally gifted at organization, so his job fit him like a glove. From the storeroom, needed materials were delivered to the central supply room and then to the respective departments all over the hospital.

Our weeks of orientation were packed as we struggled to absorb mountains of new information, but we loved it. This was voluntary service at its best, and we were eager to become hospital employees.

CHAPTER 2

Hard Lessons

I felt exhilarated as I jogged across the open field and entered the back of the hospital for my first day as an employee. My path wound through basement corridors where overhead steam pipes carried heat to the far reaches of Bethesda Hospital. An elevator took me to the first floor, and I entered 1-West. I was thrilled to be here!

With two weeks of orientation behind me, I was ushered into a world of new challenges. I intended to do my duty diligently in appreciation to our government for allowing me to work with a free conscience in a civilian hospital. I was grateful to have an alternative to military service. This was exactly why I had come to Zanesville, and I would do my best.

After clocking in, I received a list of patients for the day. I was responsible for the men in the four-bed ward at the end of the hall. The incoming shift of nurses in white and the student nurses in striped uniforms lounged about the nurses' station while the departing shift engaged in a flurry of last-minute details. I headed for Room 124 with determination. *They can stand about if they like, but I'm going to get to work!*

Greeting my patient with a cheery good morning, I began the routine temperature, pulse, and respiration check (TPR). I took his personal thermometer from the antiseptic solution on the night-stand. With several well-practiced snaps of my wrist, I adjusted the mercury and placed the thermometer carefully into the patient's mouth. I counted his pulse and respirations and recorded them in my pocket notepad. With smooth efficiency, I moved on to the next bed and repeated the process. Noting elapsed time, I reminded myself that the thermometer had to remain in the patient's mouth for three minutes. All my practice certainly was paying off. I took a thermometer to the man in Bed 3, and realizing the three minutes were up, turned to retrieve the thermometer from the patient in Bed 1. I had taken only a few steps when I was interrupted by a student nurse who suddenly appeared in the doorway.

"Mr. Miller!" She gestured urgently. "Come!"

"I'll be right back," I informed my patients.

"What's up?" I asked as I stepped into the hallway.

The student nurse looked at me incredulously and sputtered, "Re–report! Hurry!"

I followed her to the nurses' station wondering, *What in the world is "report"?* I quickly learned that report was given at each shift change on every floor. It consisted of a thorough update on every patient and took half an hour. Everyone was required to be present to be informed of all new admissions, dismissals, doctors' orders, patients' prognoses, assigned treatments, or newly developed complications.

Oh no! I thought as I visualized my poor patients with thermometers still stuck in their mouths, waiting for my return. The minutes ticked slowly by, and I panicked. *What if they fall asleep, roll over, or bite and break their glass thermometers? What if they choke on them?* Pulling my bewildered thoughts back to report, I listened to the description of the paralyzed lady in Room 105. Glancing at the serious faces of the staff, I suppressed the rising urge to sprint down the hall and remove those languishing thermometers.

The moment report was over, I rushed for Room 124. My first patient had given up holding the thermometer under his tongue and had laid it on his night stand. The second had fallen asleep, and the thermometer lay harmlessly on his pillow. The third, however, had dutifully held his thermometer in his mouth for a full thirty minutes! With a sigh of relief, I apologized and started over with taking temps, a more sober but better-informed orderly than I had been a half hour before.

Some patients were ambulatory and could use the showers, while those with severe injuries were asked to wash up at their bedsides. After distributing a towel, a washcloth, soap, and a basin of warm water to each of my patients, I pulled the privacy curtains so they could bathe. Thankfully, I had been taught these tasks during orientation, and they felt natural even on my first day on the job.

A cart filled with breakfast trays arrived just as I cleaned and replaced the last of the basins on the rack. I headed for the rolling clothes hamper to drop my load of wet towels and washcloths, making a mental note to scrub my hands again before distributing the breakfast trays. Three of my charges were sitting on the edges of their beds waiting for me. I rolled their bedside stands into position and delivered their trays. However, my fourth patient was suffering from severe back strain and needed to eat his breakfast in a reclining position. Thankfully, the bedside tables were made to swing over the bed and accommodate such patients. While they enjoyed their breakfast, I hurried to the nurses' station to register my TPRs.

Mrs. Stevens, the head nurse of 1-West, was speaking with a

doctor who appeared to be in his mid-fifties. He was of medium height, balding, and he had a kind face. He spoke slowly and deliberately as they discussed a new admission suffering from severe whiplash incurred in an auto accident.

"I have set him up with seven pounds of cervical traction," the doctor was saying, "and I want that traction attached except when he uses the restroom."

"Yes, Dr. Lance," Mrs. Stevens responded as Dr. Lance turned to leave. "Excuse me, Doctor, I would like you to meet our new orderly, Mr. Miller." I shook the doctor's extended hand and murmured a greeting.

"Dr. Lance is the head surgeon in partnership with Dr. Crown," Mrs. Stevens explained. "They are an orthopedic surgical team, and their patients are often admitted to our floor. You will be working with many of Dr. Lance's patients."

Dr. Lance asked me to follow him, as he had something to show me. He led me to the last room on our floor. "This," he said, swinging the door wide, "is the cast room. As you can see, it is unorganized right now. I am making you responsible to bring order to this room." He waved his hand toward a huge pile of hexagonal aluminum pipes dumped against the far wall. They varied from two to eight feet in length, and the shorter ones had a clamping device on either end. My confusion must have been obvious as I viewed this jumbled mess. I had no idea what these pipes were nor how they were used.

Dr. Lance, seeing my consternation, said, "Come. I'll show you how we use these." He led me across the hall to a patient's room. "Mr. Smith," he said as we entered, "how are you feeling this morning? How is that back strain coming? Are you still experiencing a burning sensation in your legs? Is it as severe as it was last week?"

"Well," replied Mr. Smith, "as long as I lie still, my back pain is tolerable, but if I move about, it flares up again. This morning, just walking to and from the restroom got my legs burning and tingling. But as long as I'm in traction, I don't feel anything."

"Good!" exclaimed Dr. Lance. "That shows us the traction is taking the pressure off your back, and hopefully the inflammation will diminish if we give it a little time."

"Mr. Smith," he continued, "I want you to meet one of our new employees, Mr. Miller. He is going to be working with traction, and I want to show him your setup."

"Nice to meet you, Mr. Miller," the patient replied. "Go ahead," he said, nodding to the doctor.

Dr. Lance showed me how the head and footboards of the hospital beds were designed with sockets to receive the rods supporting the horizontal hexagonal bar. He explained Mr. Smith's pelvic belt and demonstrated the straps, spreader, and weights easing the pressure from his injured back. We thanked Mr. Smith and headed back to the cast room. I liked the doctor's fatherly, down-to-earth manner.

I hurried back to my patients to pick up their breakfast trays, but the carts had already been taken back to the kitchen, loaded with dirty dishes from the other patients. The tedious task of sending each of my patients' trays down the dumbwaiter was a firm reminder to place the trays on the carts before they were returned to the kitchen. I was learning the hard way.

Next came the fresh linen and bed making for my men. All went well with the patients who could sit in their bedside chairs while I creased the corners of the sheets and bedspreads as I had been taught. But I had to make Bed 4 with the patient in it. I followed the steps I had learned and helped the patient roll to one side. Loosening the dirty linens, I replaced them with fresh ones, carefully smoothing out the freshened half of the bed. Then I assisted the patient as he rolled over both soiled and fresh linens to the clean side of the bed so I could remove the used linens and complete the process on the other side.

These duties quickly became routine for the 1-W orderlies working the 7:00 to 3:00 shift. Soon we were assigned as many as seven patients per shift, and several of those could be full bed patients. This meant that I would bathe them while they were lying flat in bed. I found myself nearly running at times to complete my work before the shift ended.

After eight hours of relentless walking on concrete floors, my feet were screaming for mercy. When I mentioned this to a nurse, she looked at my regulation white shoes, noticed the hard leather soles, and recommended I purchase shoes with soft soles like the rest of the staff wore. My small stash of cash was dwindling fast, and another pair of shoes would nearly consume my monthly VS income of $25! What was I to do? After two weeks of constant pain, I gave in and purchased shoes with soft soles. To my relief, my pain began to diminish.

On Sunday, we gathered in the garage of our pastor, Brother Clyde Wagler. Along with his wife Miriam and their two children, he had moved from Hillsdale, Michigan, to become our voluntary service unit leader. He was under the direction of the mission board of the Conservative Mennonite Church.

We set up chairs, passed out song books, and began our worship service. We were a small group, but we enjoyed a lively Sunday school discussion and an inspiring message by Brother Clyde.

Coming from numerous churches and blending into a smoothly functioning unit took a bit of humble submission and respect. I found the experience rewarding and spiritually strengthening.

Following our church service, we ate lunch right where we had taken our spiritual food. Soon, however, a three-room bungalow

Unit leaders Clyde and Miriam Wagler, with Myra and Brian.

across the street was converted into a dining hall where we shared meals when not on duty at the hospital.

The small houses and property we occupied had been purchased by the hospital for future expansion and were in various stages of disrepair. Each member of the unit was required to work a minimum of four hours per week on repairs and upkeep. We enjoyed doing remodeling, painting, carpentry, and plumbing together during our off hours.

We fellows were assigned sleeping quarters in the little white, asbestos-shingled house just behind the dining hall. The green ceramic floor tile was cracked in places, and several rooms were barely large enough to accommodate a bed and dresser. We fellows immediately dubbed it the White House.

On one of our days off, Mrs. Vann asked Earl and me to come to her office. Feeling a bit apprehensive, we arrived at the specified time.

"Welcome, fellows. Take seats, and I will explain our mission for today," began Mrs. Vann. "How are you getting along with your new work? Do you like it?"

"I like it," I answered. "But I do wish I were more knowledgeable. I sometimes feel at a loss because everything is so new to me."

"That's understandable," she acknowledged. "However, with a few more weeks of experience you will feel more competent. And you, Earl, how have you found hospital work?"

"It's very different from what I am used to," Earl told her. "There is so much to learn that I wonder if I will ever know enough."

"Earl," smiled Mrs. Vann, "I've been here for a long time, and I am still learning as well. Your experience is totally normal."

"I do like the work," Earl assured her.

"Good," she said briskly. "I know this is your day off, so I will keep this brief. Besides the two of you, there is only one other orderly working in our entire hospital. He works the night shift from 11:00 to 7:00. During the night, if a male patient needs an enema or a urinary catheter, he is the one called on to administer them. What we are proposing is to train you to perform those duties while working morning and afternoon shifts. That would relieve our nurses and help us provide better comfort for our patients. What do you think?"

"We are here to serve," I said. "If you are willing to teach us, we are willing to learn."

Mrs. Vann continued. "We will temporarily reduce your workload to fit in the necessary training. The most important factor is to understand that the urinary tract is considered sterile. Therefore, you will have to perfect your sterile technique to avoid introducing infectious agents. I will arrange your schedules so you can both come at 9:00 on Monday morning. Will that be satisfactory?"

"Yes, that will work for us. Where would you like us to meet?"

"Just tap on my office door. I will be here," she concluded.

On Monday, our training began in earnest. Sterile technique was first explained in class, then hands-on tests ensured that we understood the concepts and could perform them flawlessly. We later watched our supervisors perform these procedures, and then progressed to doing them ourselves under a supervisor's watchful eye. Then we would be on call to render this service throughout the hospital.

My first experience of administering a urinary catheter alone was with Mr. Bradley, who was suffering from a weak heart, fluid build-up, and lumbar back strain. His doctor had ordered complete bed rest, which meant he was not to get out of bed at all.

I tried to allay the patient's anxiety with friendly conversation as I pulled the privacy curtain about his bed and opened the sterile tray. I was careful to glove up without touching any unsterile surfaces. To my relief, I completed the procedure without difficulty. Connecting the tubing to the bedside bag, I explained how this new "plumbing" was going to help him comply with the doctor's orders to remain in bed.

"Thank you, Mr. Miller," my patient said. "That wasn't bad at all, but I suppose you have done lots of them before."

I smiled reassuringly as I gathered my tray and opened the curtain, but I didn't bother to mention that this was my first solo urinary catheter experience!

Four days later, I was shocked to receive an order to remove Mr. Bradley's catheter. He had passed away from a massive heart attack during the night, and the men from the funeral home would be arriving shortly to remove his body. It was sobering to handle Mr. Bradley's lifeless body after working and chatting with him so recently. He looked just like he had four days earlier, but now he was dead!

Observing life and death in this manner gave me a much deeper sense of life's values and the awesomeness of eternity. I was deeply moved.

CHAPTER 3

Grasping

Remembering Dr. Lance's orders to organize the traction equipment, I continued working on it whenever I had a spare moment. It took time to separate all the pieces, identify their uses, sort them by type and size, and hang them on hooks on a pegboard, but I enjoyed the challenge. When I finished the job, it was easy to locate the needed pieces at a glance.

I was so absorbed in organizing the cast room that I needed to be reminded when we were nearing the end of our shift. Mrs. Stevens noted that my afternoon TPRs had not been registered and asked for my whereabouts. I was embarrassed, as I had completely forgotten to write them in! Rushing to the nurses' station, I entered the information from my pocket notebook into the desk registry so the nurses could complete their charting before our shift ended.

I respected Mrs. Stevens, who was even-tempered and fair with everyone under her command, and I certainly wanted to please her. The extra patients assigned to me, coupled with occasional interruptions to help someone else's male patients, might have been irksome except for the fact that I loved my work. I felt amply rewarded when Mrs. Stevens smiled and said, "Dr. Lance was here while you were on break, and he is very pleased with the new organization in the cast room! It will save him time when he needs a traction setup."

Knowing that men my age were dodging bullets and land mines in the rice paddies and jungles of Vietnam while I was working in a protected environment was humbling. Occasionally, I was reminded that not everyone shared my sentiments. Many young American men were taking a different route. Although not opposed to fighting in general, they were adamantly against the Vietnam War. Thousands avoided military service by slipping across the border into Canada. American newspapers referred to them as draft dodgers. We sometimes heard snide remarks placing us in the same category, but our deep-rooted nonresistance helped us to patiently endure this unjust criticism without retaliation. We hoped our Christ-like character and willing service would eventually win their understanding.

"Mr. Miller, the light is on for Room 117," the ward secretary announced over the intercom. "Could you check that out for me?"

I pushed the intercom button. "Sure, I'll be right there." I strode down the hall and entered the doorway by the blinking call light. "May I help you?"

"Yes, I do need help," explained the patient, who was lying in bed with his hands grasping his neck. He was supposed to be in cervical traction. I gently slipped the soft muslin harness over his head and reattached its cords to the spreader. Slowly, I allowed the traction to exert its seven pounds of pull to relieve the pressure from his neck injury.

"Mr. Henderson," I said, "the next time you need to use the restroom, please hit the call button, and I'll be right here to assist you. Do not take the traction off by yourself again. We want you to get well, but jarring that whiplash will just prolong the healing process. Remember, it's not a bother. I'm happy to help, okay?"

"Okay," he responded with a sigh of relief and a feeble smile. "I didn't want to bother anyone, but I will remember." Poor man, he was obviously in pain!

"Is there anything else I can do for you?" I asked.

"Yes," he said, waving his hand toward the night stand. "Some fresh water would be appreciated."

"Certainly. And how about yours?" I asked the patient in the other bed.

"Yeah. It could use some ice too."

As I returned from the kitchenette with the carafes of fresh ice water, Mrs. Stevens called my name from the nurses' station.

I paused and gave her my full attention. "Yes?"

"Dr. Lance just admitted Mr. Sellers into Room 111 and ordered thirty-five pounds of pelvic traction with the bed in a William's position. I would like you to set up that traction before taking your lunch break, okay?" She nodded her head; this was more a command than a request. "Dr. Lance will be making rounds in about an hour, and he would like to inspect the traction on his visit."

"Certainly," I responded. "I'll get right to it."

"I've ordered the pelvic belt, and it should be on the dumbwaiter shortly," Mrs. Stevens added as she smiled my dismissal and stepped back to her desk. I hurried down the hall and delivered the fresh water. Then I opened the drapes at the giant picture window so my patients could enjoy the sunlight and the expansive, well-kept lawn and shrubbery of the hospital grounds. They murmured their thanks, and I was off to the dumbwaiter to retrieve the pelvic belt.

Selecting the needed traction equipment and carefully weighing out the thirty-five pounds of weights, I placed them on a small cart and rolled them into Room 111. Firmly compressing the mattress, I passed the pelvic belt under the small of Mr. Sellers' back without causing more pain to his lumbar injury. I tried to fasten the belt firmly enough to keep it from slipping over his pelvis, but not too tightly for comfort. Adjusting the straps to the desired length and placing the bed in a reclining position with the feet elevated, I slowly applied the weight.

"Wow!" Mr. Sellers exclaimed. "That really pulls!"

"That's exactly what it's supposed to do," I said with a smile. "Dr. Lance will be seeing you shortly, and he will make any needed adjustments. Here is your call button." I clipped it to his sheet within easy reach. "Don't hesitate to call if you need anything."

I reported to Mrs. Stevens that the job was complete, then headed for the cafeteria. After filling my tray, I joined the group of student nurses and aides from 1-West. I thanked God for my food and began eating. Conversation flowed around me about patients, doctors, and difficult experiences. The topic drifted toward our head nurse, and Miss Andrews asked, "Johnny, what do you think of Mrs. Stevens by now? Don't you find her a bit severe at times?"

I chewed thoughtfully before answering. "I'll admit that she is demanding, but I believe when she sees anyone doing his best, she's quite fair. I've made my share of mistakes, but she has been more than gracious with me."

"Well," replied Miss Gerhart, rising with a glance at the clock, "you better stay on her good side, because if you ever get on her naughty list, you'll be in trouble!"

Miss Watson picked up her tray, looked kindly toward me, and said, "Johnny, I don't think you'll have any trouble with Mrs. Stevens. You are naturally conscientious, and that's what she appreciates." I felt a bit uncomfortable with her praise, but received it in the honest spirit in which it was given. I truly desired the Spirit of Christ to be evident in my attitudes and actions.

When I returned to the floor, Dr. Lance was making rounds and asked me to step into Room 111. "Miller," he began, "do you see how the weight of the traction tends to pull the patient toward the foot of the bed? We need to shorten these straps to keep the spreader from hitting the pulley. Two things—keep the pulley adjusted farther out on the riser, and shorten the straps to give the spreader more room."

"I–I'm sorry," I stammered. "I should have figured that out myself."

"No problem, young man," he said reassuringly. "You'll learn. I've ordered a trapeze bar to be added to the headboard so Mr. Sellers can pull himself up comfortably to counteract the constant pull of the traction. This is a new apparatus we've just gotten in, and you will need to follow instructions to figure out how to attach it to the bed. You got that?" he asked, clapping me on my shoulder in a friendly gesture as he moved toward the door.

"Sure," I responded. "I'll do my best."

That afternoon, I carefully read the instructions for the trapeze bar. I placed the large metal hook over the bottom of the bed frame as directed, while firmly tightening the rubber-padded clamps to the headboard. However, when I lowered the bed back to its normal position, the vertical beam of the trapeze bar hit the floor. The weight of the heavy hospital bed slowly pushed the clamps up and disengaged the hook from the bedframe, rendering the trapeze bar useless.

I raised the bed and crawled under it to see what could be done. Realizing that the new trapeze bar needed adjustment from its factory settings, I told the ward secretary I was leaving for a few minutes to obtain the needed tools from maintenance. Soon I was back under the bed with a set of wrenches. Loosening the yoke on the trapeze frame, I raised the main beam and was tightening the last set of bolts when I heard Mrs. Stevens and a doctor enter the room.

They began reviewing the prognosis of Mr. Charles in Bed 1, who was recovering from a knee operation. I recognized Dr. Morgan's voice asking Mr. Charles to lift his leg. "No, don't bend your knee," he instructed. "Just keep your leg straight and lift from your hip. Lift it higher if you can."

"Wow, Doctor. My leg feels like lead, and the pain is pretty intense," Mr. Charles said.

"I understand, but until you can do that repeatedly, you have not recuperated well enough to be released. Keep working at it, and I'll check in on you tomorrow. Mrs. Stevens, make a note to have an assistant help this patient do these exercises three times per shift. Okay?"

Just then, Mrs. Stevens caught sight of my legs protruding from under the other bed. "Mr. Miller!" came her surprised voice. "Just what are you doing under that bed?"

I slid out quickly, explained that I had just completed the necessary adjustments, and then lowered the bed to its normal position. All went well. With a quizzical grin, Mrs. Stevens followed Dr. Morgan to check on his patient in the next room, and I returned the borrowed tools.

Earl and I worked alternating schedules. Every two weeks, we switched from morning to evening shifts. We were also gradually being trained to work in the emergency room, which we loved. I was in the ER when a mother brought in her eight-year-old daughter. The girl was wearing a pink party dress and a tear-stained face. They were gingerly cradling the daughter's right arm in a towel. A tumble from the sliding board at her friend's birthday party had resulted in severe pain and a trip to our hospital.

The doctor was called, and the X-rays he ordered confirmed the radius was fractured just above the wrist. I prepared a bucket of warm water and laid out two rolls of casting material while the nurse prepared a tray with syringe, needle, and Xylocaine.

Dr. Lance arrived and traced the unnatural upward bend of the larger wrist bone visible in the X-ray with jagged bone fibers protruding from the lower portion of the radius. "This is called a greentwig fracture," he said. "This is what would happen if you bent a green twig and it only broke partway through. Everything is in good alignment. However, we do need to reduce that bend and protect it with a cast, and in about six weeks it will be as good as new."

"Oh, I hope so!" responded the mother, placing a tender arm around her little girl. Dr. Lance pulled up a stool and began engaging the little girl by asking what had happened and whose birthday party it was while he filled the syringe.

"Now I will have to give you just a little pinprick and put some medicine into your arm to make it stop hurting." The little girl's eyes grew wide with fear, and she whimpered. "Look over there at your mother," he instructed. "Mr. Miller will hold your arm."

I anchored the arm gently to the board. Dr. Lance swabbed the wrist and expertly slipped the needle through the skin. "It hurts!" wailed our little patient. The arm tightened with a jerk, but I held it firmly. The doctor pushed the needle deeper before injecting the numbing medication. He partially withdrew the needle, then reinserted it in another direction and then another.

"There, that's over," he said, replacing the syringe on the tray. "Now you may sit up."

"Is it fixed now?" wondered our sniffling little patient. She brushed a tear from her cheek and gazed at her wrist.

"It's not completely fixed," Dr. Lance told her. "We must put a cast on your arm so it will heal nice and straight. You don't want your arm to grow crooked, do you?" She shook her head as the doctor fingered her wrist.

"Does that hurt now?" he asked as he squeezed gently. Again, she shook her head. "Okay, I have to reduce the fracture," he explained. "Look at your mama again." The little girl obediently buried her face in her mother's arms. Dr. Lance placed the fractured wrist over his knee and with a quick downward movement, he returned the fractured bone to its natural position.

"Ouch, OUCH!" cried our brave little patient.

"Okay, it's all done! I won't hurt you anymore," the doctor assured her.

I watched in fascination as Dr. Lance slipped a stretchy tube of fabric over the arm and cut a hole for the thumb. He wrapped the arm in wide cotton bands, soaked a roll of casting material, and squeezed until just the right amount of moisture remained in the plaster-laced webbing. He wrapped the arm, layer upon layer, while I suspended it, holding the little girl's fingers. Wetting his gloved hand, he smoothed the cast's surface and held it steady as the plaster began to harden.

"Mama, my arm is getting really warm!" exclaimed our little trooper.

"That tells me the cast is curing," explained the doctor. "And that's what I want." Dr. Lance pressed a slight indention over the break to ensure the fracture would be protected from movement. He held it for a few more minutes while the plaster finished hardening.

"Well, there you are, Miss Priss," he said affectionately, "and I want you to be more careful the next time you go to a birthday party, okay?" He smiled down at her as he removed his gloves and was rewarded by the sweet smile she flashed back. To the mother, he said, "See me in the office in two weeks. We just want to make sure everything is progressing well."

They walked out together, and I began cleaning up, rehearsing all I had witnessed so I could be of greater help in the future.

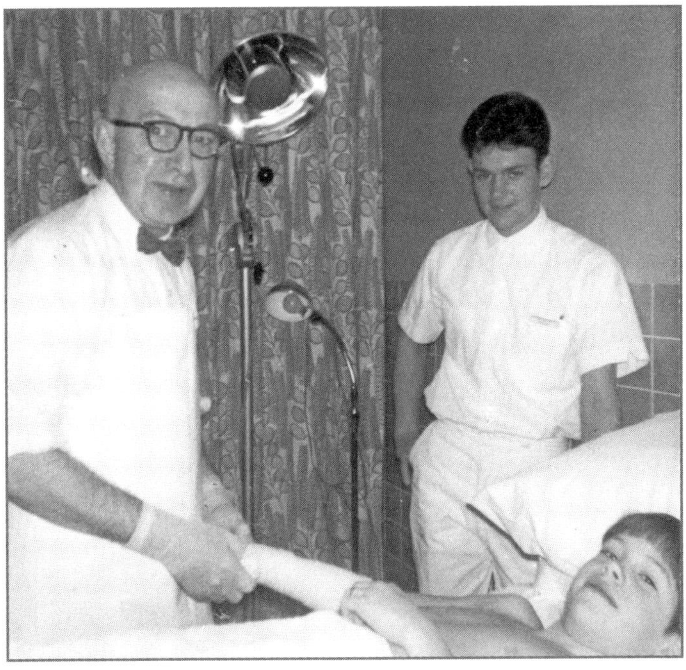

Johnny assists Dr. Lance in casting a fractured wrist.

CHAPTER 4

Teasing and Testing

Between working at the hospital and enjoying life in the VS unit, our days were filled with constant activity. We welcomed several new members to our VS family. Young ladies came as domestic workers to help with cooking, cleaning, never-ending laundry, and the daily pressing of our white uniforms. Others were nurse aides who worked in the hospital.

Our two newest arrivals were sisters from Lebanon, Pennsylvania. Edna and Ruth Zimmerman were licensed practical nurses, or LPNs. They hoped to put their training to use by serving in the hospital as part of our VS unit. They were soon in high demand throughout the hospital.

The VS girls occupied a two-story frame house around the corner from our unit leader and just beyond a vacant lot which became our VS garden. The lot sloped away from the road toward a brush-filled ravine, and no other houses were nearby.

In spite of full schedules, we fellows did find time to tease the girls occasionally. At times we had to be reprimanded by our unit leader when we went a bit overboard with our innocent fun.

One day after our 3:00 to 11:00 shift, six of us headed home across the field while discussing hospital experiences.

"A lady on our floor is dying of cancer, and it is so sad," said Edna. "We also have a little girl who was admitted to pediatrics this evening. She had been playing with a quarter, had popped it into her mouth, and somehow inhaled it into her trachea. You ought to see the X-rays. That quarter is plainly visible at the entrance to her left lung."

"I suppose they will have to operate," replied Ruth. "She's certain to contract pneumonia if that lodges in her lung. Who is her doctor?"

"She's been referred to Dr. Wise, the lung specialist," explained Elmeda. "He is so careful and compassionate with his patients, I've wondered if he is a Christian."

"I know," agreed Edna. "I've never heard him comment on his faith, but he certainly acts like a Christian."

"What are we going to eat?" wondered Earl as we entered the dining hall.

"We're starved!" chorused the three orderlies together.

Within minutes, we had raided the refrigerator and set the table with food for the late shift. Working full tilt until 11 p.m., then trying to get a bite to eat during the lively discussion was not the best preparation for a good night's sleep.

Several of us fellows excused ourselves a bit earlier than usual, claiming we needed sleep. After quickly changing from our white uniforms into darker, less visible clothing, we sneaked quietly from the back of the boys' house. Tiptoeing past the dining hall where the girls were finishing their snacks, we hid below the garden at the lower end of the vacant lot. We whispered excitedly, "This is going to be fun!" Finally, we heard the girls chatting as they came up the street toward their house.

"Are you ready?" asked Earl.

"Yeah," we whispered.

We allowed them to get halfway past the garden before one of the fellows let out a series of very realistic wildcat screams. The girls sprinted to the refuge of their house and slammed the door! We fellows nearly choked with suppressed laughter in our hiding place behind the bushes. After waiting a few minutes to make sure we wouldn't be caught, we skirted the empty shed and quietly made our way past our unit leader's house, the darkened dining hall, and into the back door of our own White House for a good night's sleep.

It was difficult to act innocent at the lunch table the following day. Brother Clyde announced, "The girls think they heard a wildcat last night as they were walking home."

With as much concern as I could muster, I asked, "What did it sound like?"

One of the girls tried to explain. "It sounded like a big cat, and it screamed three times."

"The cries seemed to be right there in the garden!" exclaimed Edna.

"I'm doubtful that it was a wildcat, but I'll tell you what," I offered. "Just to be sure, we'll go check the garden for tracks." We feigned seriousness as we traipsed in vain through the garden, looking for the nonexistent wildcat tracks. Clyde suggested we walk the ladies to their door if they would feel safer that way.

As I was soon to discover, the girls were quite capable of pulling off pranks of their own. After my turn at washing lunch dishes, I was deep in an interesting discussion when I suddenly realized time had slipped away. I would have to hurry to avoid being late for my afternoon shift. I dashed over to the White House and scrubbed up. The rule was that you didn't dare clock in late—ever! If I hurried, I could just make it.

I grabbed my white uniform trousers from the hanger and started pulling them on, but just below the knee, my foot suddenly encountered a blockage with such force that I nearly fell over. Incredulous, I tried again with the same results. Examining the trousers more carefully, I discovered one of the girls had neatly sewn the leg shut. Furthermore, she had shrewdly used white thread so I wouldn't notice until it was too late! *Oh, those girls!* I thought as I grabbed the next pair, but it had suffered the same fate. Thankfully, I had not turned in the pair I had worn the night before, so I made do with those. I hoped no girls were watching as I ran all the way to the hospital. I arrived panting and raced up the stairs two at a time rather than waiting for the slow elevator. I breezed past the nurses' station and clocked in just in the nick of time. As I took my place in report, I had to smile at the ingenuity of the girls in giving me my just due. I was pretty sure more would follow.

As fellows living together in the White House, we discussed many things. In our previous jobs, we had not been required to work on Sunday, and we had always enjoyed it as a day of worship and rest. But now that had changed. We were required to work our Sunday shifts at the hospital like all the other employees working in patient care.

Our VS unit guidelines stated that if we were required to work on Sunday morning, we were to respect the remainder of the Lord's Day and attend our evening service. Although this worked well, we all thought there could be a better way. Since we were privileged to work in this hospital helping to *save* lives instead of being in Vietnam *taking* lives, why not go the extra mile?

Following much discussion of many ideas, we proposed a change. We would work all the shifts assigned to us, but whenever we worked on Sunday, we would not clock in and track our hours. This would keep our consciences clear about working on the Lord's Day, and it would provide an extra benefit to the hospital. But more importantly, it could enhance our testimony for the Lord.

All of us VS workers received a paycheck from the hospital, but we simply endorsed the check and gave it to the VS unit. In return, we received room, board, and a monthly allowance of $25. Our unit leader had to approve our Sunday work plan, because operating revenue for the VS unit would decline if we worked without pay on Sundays.

Brother Clyde gave his blessing after due consideration, but the hospital strongly objected to the idea at first. The administration was concerned that unpaid volunteers would be less time-conscious or less dedicated than when they were earning pay. We never learned what the hospital administration discussed behind closed doors, but we eventually gained permission to try our plan. The dedicated VS workers soon demonstrated that they were equally committed to doing an excellent job whether they were being paid or not.

Back on 1-West, I listened carefully to report. "In Room 112, Bed 1," Nurse Brenda was saying, "is Mr. Warren, a patient of Doctors Capp and Magill, transferred to us from Dover Hospital."

A quick glance at my assignments confirmed that Mr. Warren would be among my charges for the day, and I listened more intently.

"His diagnosis," she continued, "is crushed lumbar vertebrae five and six with extensive spinal cord damage resulting in back pain, paralysis to the lower extremities, and impaired intestinal action causing repeated bowel impactions. Dr. Capp has ordered all bowel action charted, and enemas administered following every 48-hour period of inaction."

Three months before, Mr. Warren had been working on a ladder when it began to topple over backwards. He crashed onto his back across the end of a heavy picnic table, smashing several vertebrae in his lower spine. Dr. Capp and Dr. Magill were doing a battery of tests to determine whether surgery could reverse his paralysis. But in the meantime, we orderlies would be caring for Mr. Warren.

Not only were we to care for the physical wellbeing of our patients, but we had been trained to care for their emotional health as well. Mr. Warren was dealing with life-changing effects from his injury, and he needed our encouragement. Although our training never mentioned helping patients spiritually, we were not forbidden to do so. As a follower of Jesus Christ, I was continually looking for opportunities to extend God's grace to those facing suffering or even death.

How would Mr. Warren cope with the possibility that he would never again be able to provide for his family, stand on his own feet, or even control his body functions? Lesser men would wish to die, but Mr. Warren had a faithful wife who stood by her husband, and together, they had God. My heart was filled with compassion at Mr. Warren's plight, and I shared spiritual encouragements with the couple whenever possible. Since I was often assigned to care for Mr. Warren, I enjoyed chatting with him about his family and experiences.

I used the hydraulic lift to move him from his bed to a wheelchair, but kept the sling under him as I disengaged the lift. This would make it easier to lower him into the large whirlpool in physical therapy for his 1 p.m. appointments. The action of the water encouraged circulation in his lower limbs.

Lunch trays arrived, and I set up Mr. Warren's tray over his wheelchair and changed his bed while he was eating. By 2 p.m., he had returned from physical therapy, and I transferred him back into his bed with the lift. He was pleased to be out and about, but exhausted from all the activity. I took his TPR and asked, "Did you have a bowel movement yesterday?"

"Yes," he responded. "It was the result of the enema you gave me, remember?"

"Oh yes, I do remember. Any today?"

"Nope, not today."

"Okay, be sure to tell us when you do," I encouraged him. "With your condition, we must be very careful to prevent impaction."

We received additional training as we began to work in the emergency room. There, we admitted patients and wrote up their general information and symptoms whenever the charge nurse was assisting another patient. We needed to identify the patient's family doctor and complete the information on the chart.

We soon learned the prescribed ways to chart injuries. For example, if a child fell from a swing and was brought in with an obviously broken and misshapen wrist, we were forbidden to write that the wrist was broken. To do so would be making a diagnosis, and only doctors were qualified to diagnose. When we explained to the doctor by phone that the wrist appeared to be *disfigured,* he would usually order an X-ray. We would then prepare the items needed for cast application.

The hospital had sterile trays preassembled with the instruments for each procedure, and we became familiar with their uses and storage locations. We were taught how to open these sterilized packs and add suture material and antiseptic solutions without contaminating the additional materials or the tray. In this way, we could have everything ready for the doctor's arrival. Each doctor had his preferences and was displeased if we failed to prepare his tray accordingly.

One day, two friends in their mid-twenties were brought by ambulance from the scene of their accident. They were heavily intoxicated and had suffered multiple face, hand, and arm lacerations.

Dr. White was on call, and I carefully set an ER tray on each of the bedside stands and prepped them for the doctor.

In their inebriated state, our patients were quite boisterous. One of them, Tom, called loudly to his friend, "How ya doing over there, Jimmy old man? You all right?"

"Yeah, I'm doing just fine," the other one replied. "Scraped up a little, that's all. When's that doctor gonna get here?"

"Man, you gotta be blind," Tom laughed. "He's over here by me, can't ya see?"

"Actually," I interjected, "I'm an orderly, not a doctor."

"What's an orally?" Tom slurred, raising his head and trying to focus his alcohol-blurred gaze on me. "What did you say you was?"

I moved across the room to add Zephyrin chloride to the first tray and ignored his question. I was just finishing Jimmy's tray when I heard Tom curse and exclaim, "Look here, I knew something wasn't right!" With that, he extracted a filthy shard of broken Coke bottle from under his shirt and dropped it right in the middle of my sterile tray! My patience was sorely tried as I prepared a fresh tray and discarded the contaminated one. I set the new one well out of the patient's reach. I finished the setup and laid out a pack of sterile latex gloves just as Dr. White arrived.

The boisterous chatter continued as the doctor examined their injuries. I could tell by his quick movements and sharp commands that he was irked by their drunken behavior. He ordered an unusually large quantity of suture packs placed on the trays. Then he scrubbed, gloved, pushed a stool into place with his foot, and set to work.

I was adjusting the light for him when he said, "Miller, glove up." I did so and presented myself at his side. He rapidly swabbed out the lacerations, injected Xylocaine, picked up the needle holder, and began suturing the deep laceration in Jimmy's upper arm. I was awed by the speed with which Dr. White sewed. The fingers of both hands interacted with the suture like a well-oiled machine.

"Cut," he ordered, and I moved in swiftly and snipped the suture just below his fingers. Moments later, he had another stitch ready and halted his flying fingers as he barked, "Cut!" I quickly snipped again. "A little shorter next time," he said. Our stitch and cut routine went on for twenty minutes, and Tom began to snore loudly as we finished closing Jimmy's wounds.

When the last of their lacerations had been closed and bandaged, Dr. White stood, stretched, ripped off his gloves, and dropped them onto the tray. He smiled at me, and said, "Thanks." With that, he turned on his heel and walked out. He was among our best surgeons, and his wife, Dr. Arlene White, was a respected pediatrician. I considered them a model couple.

The following afternoon on 1-West, our head nurse, Mrs. Stevens, approached me. "Miller, were you assigned to Mr. Warren on Tuesday?"

Pausing a moment to reflect, I replied, "Yes, I was. Did I miss doing something?"

"Did you ask Mr. Warren whether he had a bowel movement on Monday?"

"Yes, I did."

"And do you recall his response?"

"He told me he had one on Monday, but not on the day he was assigned to me. Why?"

She ignored the question and asked, "So you are sure he had no bowel movement the day you worked with him?"

"I asked him when I took his TPR and explained that since he had no feeling in his lower extremities, his bowel action must be charted to prevent impaction. Is there a problem?"

"I was simply checking. Thank you," she said as she started away.

"If he needs an enema, I'd be glad to administer it," I offered.

She paused for a moment. "Would you?" she asked. "This is his third day. Yes, please do, and chart the results." With that, Mrs. Stevens headed for the nurses' station, leaving me wondering why there was such concern for Mr. Warren.

I found Mr. Warren feeling a bit restless. He was also complaining of a headache. I administered the enema, achieved rather spectacular results, and charted them accordingly.

The following day, Mr. Warren's paralysis was being discussed among several student nurses during break time. I listened, wondering what it was all about.

"You know," said a student nurse, "Mrs. Stevens is determined to make real nurses out of us, and she absolutely doesn't tolerate cutting corners!"

"True," responded another, "and she really let Sandra Andrews have it! Wow, I wouldn't have wanted to be in her shoes!"

"You know what?" chimed in someone else. "If you don't want to be in Sandra's shoes, then make sure you are perfectly honest with Mrs. Stevens. She really hates when someone lies to her. There was a discrepancy in Sandra's charting. I mean, Mr. Warren was nearly impacted, and Sandra charted that he had a bowel movement while he was in her care. That's just not possible."

"I heard Mrs. Stevens say as she took off down the hall, 'I'll ask Johnny. I know he'll tell me the truth.' And you did, didn't you?" she asked, turning to me.

Embarrassed, I shrugged and said, "I certainly had no idea *why* I was being questioned by Mrs. Stevens, but of course, I had to tell her the truth. Truth is always right, isn't it?"

CHAPTER 5

Warnings and Shocks

Once a month, we received a weekend off from the hospital. With permission, I could then visit Ruth and her family. Following the 7:00 to 3:00 shift on Friday, I left for Minerva, where I enjoyed a wonderful time with Ruth's large family. I never experienced a dull moment sitting at the table with Ruth's parents and her ten lively siblings. I soaked up their company along with the home cooking.

One Saturday, there was a work bee for a brother from church who was building a house, and I joined in laying up the block basement. It was strenuous work, but it felt good to be working outdoors again. I especially enjoyed the interaction and fellowship with the brothers who exhibited a quiet, steady faith.

Lunch was quite a spread as the church sisters supplied us with a delicious meal. A young brother asked me to share some of my hospital experiences, and I soon had a small group asking questions. When the lunch break ended, we returned to work.

As we wrapped up the day's tasks, the deacon of the church

approached me and asked, "So, did I understand you work closely with nurses and student nurses?"

"Yes," I replied. "I am under the authority of the nurses on my floor, and there are about eight student nurses who are getting their hands-on experience by rotating on several floors. Because our specialty on 1-West is orthopedic surgical, the student nurses must work there to gain experience."

"Could I share a warning with you?" he asked.

"Sure."

"You know, in our church environment we are used to seeing the women dressed modestly, as well as wearing the devotional head covering to honor God's Word. In working closely with your female coworkers, they may appear somewhat like the women in our churches, because they also wear modest dress uniforms and nurses' caps, right?"

"Yes, that is correct," I confirmed.

"Well, I just want to point out that when you're away from your family and church, the lines can easily become blurred. You could assume those nurses hold the same spiritual values as our Mennonite sisters do. But most often, that is not the case. I just felt led to share this warning: Guard your heart as you work in the hospital."

I thanked him for his concern and gladly received his advice. I felt his warning would strengthen me, and I appreciated his insight.

The weekend passed all too soon, and I headed back to Zanesville and the hospital with a glow in my heart. I was refreshed and looked forward to being on 1-West again.

Back on duty, I scurried about the ward with fresh linens, making beds as the patients finished their breakfast. First the under sheet, then the draw sheet, followed by the top sheet, and finally the bedspread, with its corners tucked and pleated. The dirty linens had to be dropped down the linen chute to the laundry department in the basement.

My concentration was broken by a voice on the overhead television set. I paused, struck by what I heard. The TV showed U.S. soldiers in training. The drill sergeant was gesturing dramatically as he shouted, "And you will see the enemy, and you will point your weapon at the enemy, and you will fire your weapon at the enemy, and you will *kill* the enemy!"

The picture on the screen showed fifty recruits about my age with their attention riveted on their sergeant. They closely followed his every move and word. A chill shot up my spine as I realized what this officer was doing. He was indoctrinating the young men to suppress their natural revulsion against taking human life. Their responses would become automatic, without compassion or thought. Over and over, the sergeant said, ". . . and you will see the enemy, and you will point your weapon at the enemy, and you will *kill* the enemy!"

He hung on to the word *kill*, making it sound lethal as he strung it out in two syllables, ". . . and you will *ki-yill* the enemy!" His fierce grimace as he mouthed the word left no room for hesitation or contemplation about the value of human life. His job was to turn these young Americans into killing machines! I felt sickened.

The intercom clicked, and a voice asked, "Johnny, can you come to the nurses' station, please?"

"Sure, I'll be right there." I quickly emptied the bedpan I was carrying and washed it before replacing it on the rack beneath the sink. I scrubbed my hands and headed for the nurses' station.

"Dr. Capp is sending a patient over from ER to have a cast removed. Can you do it?" asked our charge nurse.

"Y–yes," I responded with a bit more confidence than I felt.

I had watched doctors remove casts with the electric saw and its vacuum dust collector, and I understood the mechanics of the reciprocating blade, but I had never actually used it on a patient. This would be a first for me, and I wanted the experience.

A volunteer wheeled the fourteen-year-old over from ER. His left leg was in a cast from hip to toe, and his anxious mother hovered nervously over him. "Just what happened to you?" I asked.

Without giving her son an opportunity to speak, the mother explained, "He was jumping his bicycle over a ramp when he lost control and sideswiped a tree, breaking his thigh bone. It was a spiral break. That was nearly two months ago, and we are so ready to have Jimmy get back on his feet."

"Well, Jimmy, let's get this cast removed so you can walk again. Are you ready?" I wheeled the cast cutting machine into position and plugged it in. I explained to the volunteer that we would bring Jimmy back to ER as soon as we had the cast removed. I locked his wheelchair and sat on the stool facing Jimmy.

"Will it hurt?" asked Jimmy as he eyed the cutter with obvious distrust.

"Of course not," I responded confidently, scooting closer and flipping the switch. The high-pitched whine of the cutter was too much for the young patient.

"No, no!" he cried in alarm as he pulled his leg away. "Don't do it!" he shouted above the sound of the cutter, and I immediately switched it off.

"You have to be careful!" snapped his mother forcefully. "Don't you hurt my son; he has suffered enough already."

I tried to hide my exasperation. "Jimmy," I said as I held out the cutter so he could examine it. "This is not a rotating blade like a saw that cuts wood. This round blade only vibrates back and forth a fraction of an inch. So even if its teeth contact your skin, it will not cut because your skin is flexible and moves back and forth that short distance with the blade."

"Are you sure?" asked Jimmy's mother skeptically.

"Of course I'm sure!" I declared, turning on the saw and jamming the vibrating blade against the palm of my hand for emphasis. I barely suppressed the urge to wince as I realized I had pressed far too hard, and the teeth of the cutter had given me a painful abrasion. Hiding that fact, I smiled encouragingly. "See," I said, laying my fingers lightly on the vibrating blade. "It won't hurt you."

"Okay," said Jimmy timidly, moving his leg closer so I could begin.

With my stinging hand and a deeper sympathy for Jimmy, I began slowly cutting through his thick cast with increased care. I could feel the resistance of the plaster as the blade ate deeper and deeper. When the pressure lightened, I knew the blade had made it through to the cotton wrapping surrounding Jimmy's leg. Extracting the blade, I began immediately extending the first cut. It was slow, tedious work as the blade ate its way up one side of Jimmy's cast and down the other.

At last the cast was off, the wrapping removed, and we wheeled Jimmy back to ER. His mother thanked me, and I returned to 1-West to clean up the room. My first cast removal was completed, and I had learned a valuable lesson.

"Johnny, I have a message here that you are to assist on the psychiatric ward for the balance of the shift," announced Mrs. Shirley, our ward secretary. I headed for the elevator and my new assignment.

The 4-North charge nurse explained that Mr. Bowden in Room 8 was plagued with manic depression and could potentially become violent. She had demanded that the head office send an orderly if they expected her to remain at her post. I wasn't sure what a conscientious objector was supposed to do if a mental patient turned violent, and I prayed I would never find out. Mr. Bowden was muscular, deeply troubled, and withdrawn.

I also learned he was scheduled for a series of electrical shock treatments that evening, and my assistance was needed. Working with psychiatric patients was entirely new to me, and although I had heard of shock treatments, I had no idea what to expect.

The psychiatrist arrived and explained that we were going to administer shock treatments to four patients. They had been prepped with a mild sedative and were waiting in their beds. We followed Dr. Benning into the first room, where he addressed the patient briefly. He applied a conductive lotion and electrode disc to the temples. The nurse inserted a cushioned tongue depressor into the patient's mouth. Dr. Benning said, "Now just relax, and I'm going to put you to sleep for a few minutes, okay?"

"Uh huh," came the muffled response. The doctor activated the machine attached by wires to the discs, and the patient's body stiffened from head to foot and began quivering all over. Dr. Benning removed the electrodes, and the nurse wiped them clean as the patient's reactions grew into a full-blown seizure. All the muscles of his body seemed to be contracting in spastic, involuntary movements.

Speaking rapidly, the doctor explained this patient's diagnosis and the symptoms of deep, hopeless depression. He thought this treatment might relieve the constant stress for several days, during which the patient would hopefully respond to further treatment.

The convulsing patient exhaled until the seizure was complete, and then took deep, rasping breaths as he relaxed completely and lapsed into unconsciousness. The nurse removed the tongue depressor, and the patient was rolled onto his side, still breathing deeply. Dr. Benning asked an aide to stay with the patient as he moved the machine into the next room.

"Hello, Mary," he greeted the patient, "we are going to put you to sleep for a bit to help you recover. Just relax; this will only take a minute, and it will not hurt." With that, he repeated the process and asked me to stay with Mary as the rest of the crew exited to repeat the process for the third and fourth patients. Mary slowly regained consciousness after seven minutes and looked about the room, obviously puzzled.

"Do you know where you are?" I gently asked. I was rewarded with only a blank stare. Taking her pulse while waiting, I found it to be unusually rapid. "Do you know where you are?"

This time she looked at me and whispered, "Where?"

"You're in the hospital. Do you know which hospital?"

For a long moment, she glanced slowly about the room as though searching for something recognizable. She shook her head sluggishly.

"You are in the Bethesda Hospital," I told her.

Her brow furrowed as though searching for memory. Then she slowly whispered, "Be-thes-da?" as though the name was new to her.

After a few minutes, I asked, "What is your name?"

She looked troubled and gazed into space. I waited and then asked again, "Can you tell me your name?" This time she shook her head slightly. Mary could not recall her own name!

I tried again. "Is your name Helen?" She looked puzzled, but finally shook her head.

"Is your name Rachel?"

"N–no."

"Is your name Mary?"

She looked perplexed for a moment, but then her troubled gaze gave way to recognition, and with a faint smile, she replied, "Yes."

I asked about the year, the month, and then the day. Slowly, we established each of these facts as her cognitive understanding ebbed back into her mind. An aide relieved me, and I went out onto the floor where I engaged patients who were eating their supper. I noted Mr. Bowden was not among them, having chosen to eat alone in his room.

At the 11 p.m. shift change, all patients on 4-North had received their medications and were in their beds. Everything was quiet. The outgoing and incoming nurses retired to the office for report, and I was left alone in the nurses' station. The evening's events absorbed me as I thought of Mary and her emotional struggles. What caused her to lose her sense of wellbeing? What was keeping her from becoming emotionally well? Would that shock treatment actually help her recover?

And then I heard it! A slight shuffling sound broke the eerie silence directly behind me. Startled, I glanced at the glass surrounding the nurses' station and saw the towering reflection of Mr. Bowden right behind me! I froze.

"H–hey," he faltered as I cautiously turned to face him. There was tension in his expression, like a taut string threatening to snap. His face was sweaty, and his fists were clenched. "Can you come and . . . and tie me to my bed?" he asked.

"Sure, I'll be right there," I responded, concealing my shock and acting as though it were a perfectly normal request.

"Thanks," he murmured. He turned and shuffled zombie-like toward his room. I followed, and when he was well situated, fastened the Posey™ belt about his body, turning the key and locking him to his bed. Mr. Bowden stretched his foot toward the heavy leather restraint fastened to the bedrail, and I tightened it firmly around his ankle.

"Is that too tight?" I asked him.

"No," he responded. "You better make it a little tighter." I complied, and then moved to restrain the other foot and both wrists. When he was completely shackled to his bed, I said, "Mr. Bowden, you look tired."

"I can't sleep," he explained. "I haven't slept in two nights."

"Why, what's the problem?"

"It's my mother-in-law. She is trying to get my wife to leave me. I gotta get rid of my mother-in-law!" he hissed through clenched teach.

"You know," I responded, "I have a better plan."

"You do?" he said eagerly. "You know how to get rid of her?"

"Listen, and I'll tell you a plan. I am dating Ruth, a wonderful girl I hope to marry someday. But, you know, she had some doubts about dating me at one point. I had visited their family several times and had won the respect and trust of Ruth's mother. So when Ruth was uncertain about our relationship, her mother came to my rescue. She told Ruth she respected me as a Christian young man, and she encouraged her daughter not to make a hasty decision. She urged Ruth to pray and ask God whether she should continue our relationship. Ruth followed her mother's advice, and now we both sense God leading us together. Here's my advice to you, Mr. Bowden. If you win your mother-in-law's approval and confidence, she will quit trying to break up your marriage. She will actually help your marriage prosper."

"You think so?" he asked hopefully.

"It certainly has worked for me," I responded. "Have you ever studied the Bible?"

"No, not really," he yawned.

"There are many truths in the Bible that would help you. I highly recommend that you begin studying God's Word for answers to your problems."

Mr. Bowden's eyelids were noticeably heavy. He yawned again. "Man, I am so sleepy," he murmured. "Let's talk about this another time, okay?"

"All right," I agreed. "You get some sleep."

"G'night," he said as I turned off his light and headed for the door.

"Good night, Mr. Bowden."

CHAPTER 6

Dead Bones

Stifling a yawn, I made a mental note to get more sleep. I forced myself to listen as the night charge nurse continued report for the shift that was ending. "Room 112, Bed 1." She took a deep breath before continuing. "Ernest Hanson, fifty-two-year-old patient of Doctors Capp and Morgan, admitted yesterday with multiple compound fractures of the right tibia and fibula. External stabilization rods with wires through the knee and ankle for support," she intoned. "The patient is experiencing excessive pain, got very little sleep during the night, and suffers from anxiety."

Glancing at my list of five patients for the day, I saw that this man had been assigned to me. I listened more intently. "Antiseptic solution to be applied to the wound site twice daily, and no operation scheduled until swelling and inflammation are reduced."

"Room 113," she continued, flipping the index to the next patient. I sighed. *This is going to be a full day.*

Following the breakfast and bathing of my patients, I selected fresh linens and headed for Room 112. Mr. Hanson was dozing, but as I entered, he jerked awake with a nervous start. Momentarily wide-eyed, he then sank slowly back in his pillow and relaxed.

"How's your leg this morning?" I inquired, placing the fresh sheets on the bedside chair.

"The pain never lets up, and it kept me awake most of the night," he responded. "But whenever I get a shot, it eases up a little." I helped him roll to the far side of the bed and began changing the sheet under him as carefully as I could. I gingerly lifted his injured leg by the bars that were holding his leg rigid.

"How did this happen?" I asked as he lay back on the fresh sheets and gazed at the ceiling.

"I am a welder and was working on a commercial building," he began. "A large steel I-beam was protruding from its gable end and had to be cut off. I was cutting it with an acetylene torch on a twenty-foot extension ladder. When the piece I cut off dropped to the ground, it bounced back and knocked the ladder out from under me. My right leg pushed through the rungs and was folded under me when I hit the ground. I must have been numb with shock. All I could think of was to get away from that acetylene torch, so I tried to run on my broken leg. I guess I did more damage in doing so, because the bones were sticking out."

"Wow, you can thank the Lord you are alive!" I said while arranging the sheets around his injured leg.

That afternoon, a nurse taught me how to apply the antiseptic solution to Mr. Hanson's wound by soaking the bandage with the prescribed medication. This became a daily routine for the next ten days. During that time, I became fast friends with Mr. Hanson and his wife, who spent every possible evening with her beloved husband.

A week passed, and I came into his room one evening for his regular treatment. After carefully sliding a plastic sheet under his leg, I loaded a syringe with the antiseptic solution and dribbled it onto the bandage.

"You said you are from Virginia. How did you wind up working in a hospital here in Ohio?" asked Ernest.

"I am a conscientious objector to war, and I'm working here instead of being in the military," I replied.

"I see," he said thoughtfully. "And the government is okay with that?"

Completing the application and replacing the syringe, I responded, "Why, yes. In fact, Bethesda Hospital specifically qualified under government guidelines to receive workers like myself."

"That other orderly, is he here for the same reason?" asked Ernest.

"You mean Earl? Yes, there are actually six of us living together in a small house." I stepped to the large picture window and pointed. "Our house is the little white one on the next street, just across the open field. You can see it from here. But not all of us serve as orderlies," I explained. "One works in the cafeteria, another works in inhalation therapy, some work in the maintenance department, and one works in shipping and receiving. We are from different states, but we are all members of Mennonite churches and share the same belief that we cannot take human life since Jesus taught us to love even our enemies."

"Hmm, that's quite interesting," he mused.

On Friday evening, our entire VS unit gathered on a street corner in downtown Zanesville and sang familiar hymns: "What a Friend We Have in Jesus," "The Old Rugged Cross," "Jesus Signed My Pardon," and several others. Then Brother Clyde began to preach a short sermon calling people to repentance. He challenged them as he exalted Jesus, the only means whereby we can be cleansed from our sins.

Most people only heard small segments of the message as they went about their business. Some drove by slowly with their windows rolled down so they could hear. One driver circled the block and came back to hear another portion of the sermon.

Our group also handed out Gospel tracts to folks passing by on the sidewalks. Whenever people showed interest, we talked with them and gave witness to the saving knowledge of Jesus Christ. One man said, "There are good people of different faiths all around the world. I believe the important thing is that we are sincere in what we believe."

"True," came the ready response from one of our group. "Sincerity is important, but only if it works in the end."

"What do you mean by that?" asked the man.

"We can be ever so sincere in what we believe, but in the end, if our beliefs do not save us from sin, our sincerity about them won't do us any good."

The man walked on, contemplating deeper thoughts of salvation and eternity.

For the next two weeks, I was back working on 1-West, where my duties included caring for Mr. Hanson. On Saturday, I had a day off from hospital duties. By early afternoon, I completed my required four hours of weekly VS unit maintenance making plumbing repairs at the dining hall. After cleaning up and changing, I enjoyed writing a letter to my girlfriend, Ruth, who was now teaching school in Minerva, Ohio. She had written about her fond memories of frequent weekends spent with my family when she taught in Virginia. I smiled as I reread her description of waking up to my dad's singing early Saturday morning as he fried pancakes for the family. I felt a momentary pang of homesickness.

Ruth wrote how wonderful it had been that my parents had made her feel like a daughter.

In my reply, I detailed the events of my week and my work at the hospital. I wrote of my growing respect for Dr. Lance, and how he was teaching me the ins and outs of traction. I described our head nurse and Mr. Hanson's injuries and explained that I had been entrusted with applying the solution to his injured leg. I asked about her students, church events, and youth group activities. I loved hearing about her life.

Sitting there for a few moments, I savored our growing relationship, our love for God, and our future. Looking ahead, I thought of marriage. Although it was still distant, the thought was becoming more distinct. The big question was, just how could one support a wife on $25 a month? I brushed these thoughts aside, knowing marriage was a long way off. However, I did wish Ruth could share my 1-W and VS experience. I completed my letter, sealed and stamped it, and headed for the hospital where I would mail it.

I gazed at the flow of visitors moving through the main lobby and briefly visited the personnel on 1-West. For a moment, I wished to be working instead of visiting. Not feeling exactly ready to head back to the White House, I started up the staircase, but stopped on the landing half way between the first and second floors. There I sat soaking up the throb of life as though the hospital were a living entity with its own personality. The faint murmur of nurses and patients from the first floor below were punctuated with the distinct tapping of a visitor wearing high-heeled shoes on the floor above.

Then came the sound of a vacuum tube. It sounded like a mini train, making a soft thud each time it barreled over the joints in the tubing through which it carried important messages. These impressions soaked into my soul, and I savored the feeling of loving and belonging. I could only thank God for having led me into this great work and opportunity. Here I experienced the soul-satisfying fulfillment of serving God by serving others.

Before leaving the hospital, I felt led to visit the emergency room to see what might be going on. ER was mostly quiet, but as I passed the open door of Room 3, Dr. Capp looked over his shoulder and asked, "Say, Miller, can you help me a minute?"

I entered, and he said, "You will need to scrub." I quickly washed my hands with the germicide soap, wondering if he had noticed I was wearing black trousers instead of the regulation white pants of an orderly on duty.

Then I saw the patient. "Well, hello there," I said to Ernest Hanson. "What's up with you?"

He smiled in recognition and explained, "They brought me down to ER. The doctor wants to change the bandage and see how things are progressing."

I moved to the foot of the bed, grasped the rods stabilizing his leg, and raised it off the bed so Dr. Capp could cut the soggy gauze away. The waste can was soon filled with wet, smelly bandages. When the leg was bare, I was aghast! There was no living skin or flesh, just a gaping wound of gray, decaying tissue from below the knee to just above the ankle.

Dr. Capp began swabbing out the wound with sterile gauze pads. All was silent as he worked. My back was crying for mercy from supporting the weight of the leg in so awkward a position. Looking at Mr. Hanson, I was relieved to see he was lying flat and unable to see what was going on at our end of the cart. I handed Dr. Capp the necessary items from the tray as needed until Mr. Hanson asked, "Can I see it?"

Dr. Capp was silent for a moment, then shrugged and said, "If you want." There was a long pause, and then he added, "Miller, help him sit up."

I moved to the head of the bed and gently slid my arm under Ernest's shoulders, thinking, *Oh, this poor soul!* Supporting his shoulders, I gazed with him into the depth of his wound as Dr. Capp continued working. We surveyed the blackened, broken bone segments and the dead, gray muscle. My heart bled for Ernest, and I felt him push back against my supporting arm to signal that he had seen enough. Easing him back onto the cart, I laid my hand reassuringly on his shoulder. He didn't respond, but his eyes darted around the room as though seeking an escape from this terrible predicament.

The minutes slid by in slow motion as Dr. Capp continued swabbing out the dead tissue from the wound.

"We can save it, right, Doc?" asked Ernest, breaking the silence. His voice betrayed a hint of fear mingled with a note of pleading. Dr. Capp made no reply, and I wondered if he had heard. He kept cleansing the wound deeper and deeper without saying a word. I considered repeating the question, but quickly discarded the idea. *He* was the doctor, and *I* was the orderly.

After several minutes had ticked by in complete silence, Dr. Capp finally replied, "We're going to try."

I held the leg by its rods again as Dr. Capp wound roll after roll of gauze over the non-sticking Telfa™ placed over the wound. It was tedious even for the doctor's deft hands to work the bandage around the leg and under the support rods.

We called a volunteer to wheel Ernest back to his room. I began cleaning up while Dr. Capp filled out an ER form. When he had finished, I said, "Dr. Capp, I noticed Mr. Hanson's leg has broken sections of bone that are black. What does that mean?"

"Well," he began, carefully choosing his words. "Bone cannot live unless it is covered with flesh, and flesh cannot live unless it is covered with skin. So what you saw was dead bone. And as you know, once bone dies, it never heals or becomes alive again." I thanked him for his explanation, and he thanked me for my help.

Dr. Capp went on to see other patients in the hospital, and I walked slowly across the field, sobered by what I had witnessed.

I came to work on Monday evening, refreshed from my weekend off, to find I had been assigned to work in ER. It was a quiet evening with only a few patients coming in before supper. I was to work the shift with Nurse Janet White. She was a calm, easygoing person who knew what she was doing.

Dr. Leonard was the on-call physician that evening. Suddenly, the wail of a siren grabbed our attention, and flashing lights headed for our emergency room entrance. The attendants wheeled in a man groaning with pain, and we directed them to Room 1, where he was transferred into our bed. He grimaced as he pointed to his left foot, and there, protruding from his shoe, was a double wire about four inches long. We took his information and called Dr. Leonard, but while we waited, Nurse Janet went to work with a heavy bandage scissors, gingerly cutting the shoe from the man's foot. Each time the wire moved the least little bit, the poor man clenched his fists and gritted his teeth with pain.

By the time we had the shoe off, Dr. Leonard arrived and said, "Tell me what happened."

"I was pushing my mower," the man gasped. "There must have been a coat hanger lying in the grass. I didn't see it, but suddenly I heard a terrible noise from the mower. The next thing I knew, I was on the ground in terrible pain with a coat hanger sticking out of my shoe."

"Were you able to cut the wire?" asked the doctor, carefully fingering the big toe.

"The ambulance attendants cut most of it off so they could transport me more easily."

"I see," said Dr. Leonard. Turning to me, he continued, "Miller, bring me Xylocaine, a 5-cc syringe, and an 18-gauge needle."

"Yes sir," I responded, and I was on my way.

He called after me, "Set up an ER tray also."

I returned with the requested items, and Dr. Leonard went to work injecting the toe with pain-numbing Xylocaine. I opened the tray and adjusted the light as he gloved up. "Look at this," he said, and pointed out a whitened bump on the inside edge of the injured toe. "That's the wire! See how close the wire came to punching all the way through his big toe? It appears that it just grazed the bottom of the bone. We'll take an X-ray just to confirm no bone damage has occurred."

Nurse Janet returned from surgery with sterile pliers that looked just like the kind used by electricians. "Okay, here goes," said Dr. Leonard. Firmly grasping the toe with one hand and gripping the wire in the pliers with the other, he began to pull. Lightly at first, then increasing the pressure, he pulled harder, but nothing happened. The wire had not budged.

"You all right?" he asked, glancing at the patient.

"As good as can be expected," came the response, but I noticed beads of sweat forming on the patient's forehead.

Dr. Leonard braced his knee against the heel of the patient's foot, and grasping the wire again, he held the toe more firmly and began to pull in earnest. Still nothing budged until he twisted the pliers while he continued pulling.

"Ouch!" cried the patient, and with a mighty wrench, out came the wire! Dr. Leonard held it up in triumph. The mower had folded the coat hanger wire sharply together before slinging it out with enough force to penetrate the shoe leather and pierce nearly through the man's toe.

Dr. Leonard ordered a bandage and an X-ray before writing a prescription for a tetanus booster and an antibiotic. He released his patient with instructions to see him in his office in a week.

I passed the entrance to 1-West on my way to take my break, and impulsively decided to go see my friend Ernest Hanson. "Do you know what?" said his wife as I entered the room. "Dr. Capp was here this afternoon and told us they are going to amputate Ernest's leg on Thursday."

"Really!" I exclaimed.

"But I told that doctor, 'Oh no, you're not! If you are going to cut my husband's leg off, then you're going to do it tomorrow. You cannot put him through the torture of lying here for two days thinking about having his leg amputated!'"

"What did Dr. Capp have to say about that?" I glanced at my watch, relieved to see I still had a few minutes.

"He said I just didn't understand, and that the surgery schedule is made out ahead of time."

"And then?" I queried.

"Well, I told him that he is the doctor so he can change the schedule!" Mrs. Hanson grinned. "He walked out of here shaking his head, but he came back an hour later and told us Ernest's surgery is re-scheduled for 7 a.m. tomorrow."

"Mr. Hanson, I have to leave in a moment, but how do you feel about this?" I asked.

"At first, I was pretty downhearted, but I'm beginning to think this really is the best decision," said Ernest.

I eased toward the door. "Sorry I have to go now, but I'll be praying for you."

"Thank you," they said in unison. I headed back to the ER.

CHAPTER 7

The Voice of Conscience

Brother Clyde rented a sizable room in the YMCA for our worship services. We fellows often arrived on Sunday mornings to find several men seated comfortably in our rented room, smoking and reading. We set up chairs and invited the men to stay and enjoy the service. Sometimes one or more stayed, but usually they opted to move into the main lobby. We had the chairs and speaker's stand set up and the songbooks distributed when the rest of the VS unit arrived. Then closing the door so not disturb other YMCA guests, we sang, prayed, read, and discussed our Sunday school lesson. We listened intently to Brother Clyde's challenging message.

The service was followed by a time of fellowship before we left to regroup around the huge table in our dining hall. Hospital talk flowed freely about the table as we enjoyed a delicious Sunday dinner provided by our domestic volunteers.

"Late last evening we admitted a nineteen-year-old motorcycle accident victim," Earl told us. "He has head trauma, but no skull fracture is visible," he explained, "and the X-rays were clear. The doctor said his brain was shaken up and probably bruised. He has double vision, which Dr. Capp thinks is due to brain swelling."

"Was he unconscious?" I asked.

"No, I was working in the ER when they brought him in. He was conscious, but pretty shook up," replied Earl. "Dr. Capp admitted him to 1-West, so you'll probably be working with him tomorrow."

In report the following morning, I learned from the out-going charge nurse that Mr. Hanson was doing well with his amputation. He would be taking physical therapy to learn how to use crutches and prepare for a prosthesis.

"Room 119," she continued, "is Mr. Eugene Masterson, nineteen years old, motorcycle accident victim, head injury, patient of Dr. Capp and Dr. Glosser. Dr. Glosser's diagnosis is severe concussion and mild brain swelling. Patient complains of headache and double vision. Dr. Glosser orders complete bed rest and vitals with pupils' reaction to light checked every two hours for possible intracranial bleeding or additional brain swelling. He wants to be notified immediately of any change."

I looked forward to having Eugene Masterson among my six patients for that day. He was just one year younger than I. After introducing myself, I brought him the needed articles for bathing. Soon the breakfast trays arrived, but he had very little appetite.

I took his vitals and asked him to close his eyes for a few seconds. "Okay, now open your eyes." I watched closely as his right pupil first appeared large then quickly constricted in reaction to the light I was holding. "Good, let's do that again," I said, and Eugene complied. His left pupil constricted beautifully as well.

"Why does everybody keep shining lights in my eyes?" he asked.

"With the type of head trauma you've experienced, there is the possibility of bleeding that could become life threatening. An early sign is the pressure buildup affecting the involuntary reaction of the pupils to light. So when you close your eyes for several seconds, your pupils open wide in the dark. When you open your eyes, I can see momentarily how large the pupils are. If everything is normal, they will immediately react to my light and become very small."

"So, is everything all right?"

"Your pupils are reacting normally," I assured him.

"And what happens if they don't?" he asked.

"Well, they might need to do surgery and drill through the skull to remove the accumulated blood which is causing the excessive pressure."

"And if they don't do that?"

"Well, a brain hemorrhage is very serious. It can even be fatal."

Eugene was sobered by our conversation, and I began making his bed with him in it. "Tell me about your accident," I requested. "What happened?"

"Well," he began. "I was just cruising down the road and enjoying my ride when a dump truck pulled right out in from of me. I probably would have been all right if he had kept going, but he must have seen me coming and stopped, blocking most of the road. I hit the brakes—maybe a bit too hard 'cause it scared me, and I started skidding. That slowed me down, so I wasn't going all that fast when I hit the truck. But you oughtta see my helmet. It really got busted up bad."

"And what about your motorcycle?" I asked.

"Oh, I think it's history."

"Eugene, you need to thank the Lord that you are alive. You could very easily have lost your life in that accident," I told him.

"I know," he agreed soberly.

For the next several days, Eugene's condition slowly improved except for his persistent double vision. We enjoyed discussions on many subjects and learned to know each other quite well.

When I walked into Eugene's room on Friday morning, I was shocked. There, blatantly pinned to the corkboard among several get well cards, was a full page photo of a scantily clad dancer! I needed to be in and out of Eugene's room all that day. That picture smote my conscience. What should I do? I didn't dare just remove it, since patients do have rights. Would he understand if I told him how much I detested working in that erotic atmosphere?

Finally, I could remain quiet no longer. I asked, "Eugene, why do you have that picture up there?"

"I like it," was his ready response. "Don't you?"

"No," I said. "You know I am a Christian and want to faithfully serve the Lord, but that photo is a hindrance to me. May I please take it down?"

"Ah, come on," he said. "There's nothing wrong with that. It's pretty!"

That evening, I read God's Word and prayed specifically for God to remove that vile image from my mind. The following day, I received another shock when the doctor openly admired the photo. I was also disappointed to overhear nurses laughingly discussing Eugene's *wall decorations.*

I continued waging a one-man war against Eugene's brazen display of pornography.

"Are you going to allow me to take that picture down now?" I asked as I brought Eugene his lunch tray.

"Why? It's not hurting anyone," he protested.

"But it is hurting me," I countered. "I'm trying to honor the Lord, and that photo hinders me from having pure thoughts. It's not right. May I take it down for you?"

"You're serious, aren't you?" he observed. "You really don't like it?"

"No, Eugene, I really do not like it. Please, may I take it down?"

He studied my face in silence, but finally said, "Oh, all right, I guess you can." I had it off the corkboard in seconds. As I handed it to Eugene, I said, "Thank you very much! I sincerely appreciate it."

"Oh, okay," he said without enthusiasm. "You're welcome."

I continued working with Eugene during the following week and was relieved that he didn't seem to resent my cleansing his room of the sensual photo. His double vision slowly improved to the point that he could be discharged. I bid him a fond farewell and prayed that someday his spiritual vision would clear also.

Mr. Andrew Sanders in Room 108 was suffering from abdominal cancer. He had survived his operation and was receiving radiation treatments several times a week. The radiation often left him weak and nauseous. His chart indicated that the surgeon was unable to remove all the tumors, and his future looked bleak. The skin of his abdomen appeared burnt from the radiation he received to shrink his tumors. And yet, Mr. Andrews possessed a calm endurance based on his faith in Jesus Christ, and I enjoyed working with him. Each day, he asked to be placed in a chair where he could look out the window and enjoy the new life of spring. From his chair, he could also see the activity in the hallway.

I was working in the ward when I heard a piercing scream from the charge nurse. I sprinted down the hall to help. I arrived in Room 108 to find Mr. Sanders lying on his side in the bed, retching. His incision had burst under the strain of vomiting, and about ten inches of small intestine protruded from the opening.

I quickly lowered the head of Mr. Sanders' bed, then rolled up his blue pajama top as a barrier to keep my friend from viewing his own intestine. The charge nurse took over with sterile saline and bandage material. Her voice was shaky, and I noticed her hands trembling as she worked. Once the errant intestine was covered with sterile, saline-moistened bandages and taped into place, she administered a sedative. A short time later, Mr. Sanders was wheeled away to surgery where his intestine was placed back into his abdomen and the incision closed once more.

The following day, Mr. Sanders asked, "Do you think it was because of my radiation treatments that my incision did not heal properly?"

"I think that may have had something to do with it," I agreed. "I believe radiation can slow the healing process." Our conversation turned to spiritual matters, and we shared together from the Scriptures.

I continued to minister to Mr. Sanders throughout the next few weeks, but I was shocked to find his bed and chair empty upon my arrival one afternoon. My friend had been called from Room 108 to the mansion prepared for him in heaven.

On Saturday evening, our close-knit group stood on a low, grassy knoll bordering the sidewalk in downtown Zanesville. Brother Clyde set up the speakers and microphone, hooked them to his car battery, and we began our street meeting.

We sang familiar hymns such as, "My Faith Looks Up to Thee," "Blessed Assurance, Jesus Is Mine," "Down at the Cross Where My Savior Died," and "There Is a Name I Love to Hear." A well-dressed pedestrian paused to listen, leaning against the postal box near the curb. Cars flowed past with occupants going about their business, but some slowed to hear the singing.

Clyde began preaching the call to repentance and obedience while pointing the listeners to the Lamb of God. The man by the postal box listened intently. Following several more songs, we closed the meeting, and I approached the man to introduce myself. He politely asked who we were and where we were from. He seemed surprised that we fellows were serving at Bethesda Hospital instead of the military, and he seemed intrigued by our belief that it was wrong to take human life, even in self-defense.

My new friend expressed appreciation for our work and began telling me about his own spiritual journey. "You know," he reflected, "I was so enthusiastic when I got saved that I witnessed wherever I went. My friend Grace worked at the post office, and whenever I had business there, I told her how God saved me, cleansed my sin and pride, and changed my life.

"One day, Grace leaned over the counter and said, 'Randal, you are always talking about being saved. Just what is this "being saved thing" all about?'

"I explained that the lust of the flesh, the lust of the eyes, and the pride of life are sins from which we must be saved. She wanted definitions for each of those categories, and I explained them as best I could. But as I began explaining the pride of life, I decided to use an object lesson. I reached up and flicked her large, dangling earring and said, 'That, Grace, could be an example of the pride of life!'

"Grace was silent for a moment, but then she reached down and fingered my big, expensive, gold wristwatch and asked, 'Randal, if my earrings are the pride of life, what's this?' Her words went straight to my heart; I was just as guilty as she was. I slipped that watch off my wrist and said, 'Grace, you will never see it there again!' And you know what? I have kept that promise! It's far too easy to see the specks in the eyes of others, but fail to see the beam in our own."

I had often left our street meetings thinking about the people I had met or witnessed to. But this man gave me more than usual to consider as I traveled back to the VS unit on Outlet Street.

The following week, I was introduced to Mr. Herald, a construction worker who had passed out on his job and was transported to the hospital by ambulance. He was admitted to Room 111, and Dr. Glosser examined him.

Dr. Glosser determined there might be an aneurysm, or bleeding within the brain. He ordered a lumbar puncture tray and asked me to assist him. I helped position the patient on his right side and pulled his knees up close to his head. This bent the lower spine sharply. Dr. Glosser injected Xylocaine, then gloved up for this sterile procedure.

With a long needle, he probed between two vertebrae and penetrated the spinal column. He screwed two long, calibrated glass tubes together and asked me to stabilize the upper portion while he attached the lower end to a valve and the needle. Then, opening a tiny valve, he observed the spinal fluid rising inside the sterile glass tubing while instructing the patient to apply pressure on his diaphragm. After allowing the patient to relax, he again read the level of the spinal fluid in the glass.

Next, he opened the valve and caught a sample of spinal fluid in a vial. Having obtained the needed sample, Dr. Glosser extracted his needle and placed a bandage over the puncture site. As I cleared away the tray, Dr. Glosser sat with the patient and explained what he had done. "You see this sample?" he asked. "Normally, it should be as clear as water. But as you can see, your spinal fluid has a rosy tint to it that indicates the presence of blood. Your spinal cord and brain are surrounded by the same fluid, so this rosy color tells me that you have had some bleeding on the brain. It could become life-threatening, so we must do what we can to stop that bleeding and allow the ruptured vessel to clot and heal. I am ordering you complete bed rest. I do not even want you to take those few steps to the restroom. We have urinals and bedpans here and plenty of good help. I want you to lie as still as possible for the next few days and see if we can't get the bleeding to stop and the healing to begin. Any questions?"

"Can't I even sit up to eat?" asked Mr. Herald.

"You can roll on your side to eat, but I do not want you sitting up and then lying back down. Those movements could trigger the bleeding, and we must avoid that at all costs. You see, a major hemorrhage can easily be fatal," he warned.

I cared for Mr. Herald for nearly two weeks. Dr. Glosser performed another lumbar puncture and was pleased when the second sample was noticeably clearer.

As I gave Mr. Herald his backrub to help him relax for the night, he commented, "I am so relieved that the bleeding has stopped and that my pressure headache is finally gone. I still feel weak, but I'm so much better!"

"I am glad for you too," I said. "That's not always the way it works out. I had a patient once who could hear a swishing sound in his ears every time his heart beat. He had it checked out, and his doctor finally told him he had an aneurysm, which is a ballooned-out, weakened section of artery in his brain. He was told he had a 50/50 chance of surviving the brain surgery necessary to repair it. Naturally, he wanted to know what would happen if he declined the surgery, and the doctor said the aneurysm would probably burst eventually and he would not survive it."

Mr. Herald said, "That would be a hard decision to make, wouldn't it?" I had to agree.

"Do you think I can be discharged soon and get back to work?"

"I have no idea. That's something you will have to discuss with your doctor."

After my weekend off, I returned to 1-West and walked into Room 111 to see how Mr. Herald was doing. I found his empty bed neatly made and his room cleaned. As I walked toward the nurses' station, I met Mrs. Stevens and asked, "When was Mr. Herald discharged?"

She paused, raising an eyebrow. Then she asked, "Haven't you heard? Saturday afternoon, we found him unconscious and rushed him into surgery. Evidently, he suffered severe bleeding from a ruptured aneurysm, and he passed away before they could even get him onto the operating table."

Throughout that day, I rehearsed our conversations of spiritual matters. Had Mr. Herald been ready to meet God? Should I have probed deeper into his relationship with the Lord? Had I known death was drawing so near, I surely would have spoken more directly about Jesus Christ and His power to save. But now, that opportunity was gone forever.

CHAPTER 8

The Dalton Family

Brother Clyde called a meeting with the VS fellows, and we met in the dining hall. After opening with prayer, he explained that we needed to make some changes for the good of the VS unit.

"We are placing a sign-out sheet on the wall of the dining hall," he began. "Except when going to work, any time you leave the premises, you need to write in the time you leave, where you're going, and what time we can expect you back. As unit leader, I am responsible for you, and when your parents call, I want to be able to tell them where you are and when they can call back. Please do not embarrass me by leaving without signing out. I don't want to have tell your parents that I don't know where you are. That wouldn't sound very responsible, would it? Any questions?"

"What if I just want to run down to the filling station for gas?" asked someone.

"I don't think you would have trouble spelling a message—down to the station to get gas—would you?" smiled Clyde. "Even if you are leaving for a short time, please use the sign-out sheet."

"Also, we are placing a sheet beside the phone. When you make a long-distance call, write in your name and the number you called. At the end of the month, we will bill you for the cost of your calls. Any questions?"

I raised my hand. "What if I don't make enough in a month to cover the cost of my calls?"

Clyde grinned. "Perhaps you need to do more writing and less calling to balance the budget."

"But I already have writer's cramp," I bantered good-naturedly.

One of the boys suggested, "Maybe you'll have to quit dating."

"Better yet, get married!" said someone else.

I said, "I'll vote for the second option!" There was a chorus of laughter, including Clyde.

He brought the meeting back to order. "Don't forget, you are also responsible to keep a record of the four hours per week you spend in VS unit maintenance. If you are looking for work, contact my wife or me. We keep a list handy.

"Now, on a more serious note," continued Clyde, "some of you are fun-loving and do quite a bit of teasing. That has its place. However, I believe some of you take things a bit too far at times. I just want to caution you to be more considerate of others. A bit of teasing now and then can lighten the atmosphere, but when it becomes routine, people can be hurt."

I felt my face burn with shame; everyone knew I was probably the biggest tease in the group. After hearing Clyde's gentle reminder, I resolved to be more considerate and to curtail my teasing impulses.

"There's something else I want to share with you," Clyde continued. "Most of you know Will Salmons. As the hospital plant manager, he is my boss in the maintenance department. Well, on Monday, he said he wanted to talk with me, so we sat together in the cafeteria.

"He has been watching you fellows working in your departments for a long time. He said he's not believer and not at all religious. He asked what I believe and why. I told him that I believe all men are sinners, born with a sinful nature. Then I explained that we can only be cleansed from our sins through repenting and asking for the blood of Jesus Christ to wash our sins away.

"He stopped me and said, 'Most religious people believe that. What else do *you* believe?' I explained that as followers of Jesus, we cannot kill another person. He wanted to know why, and I said that in the Bible, Jesus commanded us to love our enemies.

"Mr. Salmons interrupted again. 'I didn't ask you what the *Bible* says. I want to know what *you* believe! The Bible is not part of this discussion.' But I told him that if I cannot refer to the Bible, then there will be no discussion. Now, I said that respectfully, but I meant it! When an unbeliever tells me I cannot quote from God's Word to explain my beliefs, I won't stand for it. I believe we need to be courteous, but we do not have to throw out the Bible just because an unbeliever objects to it."

Wow, I thought, *Clyde sure has nerve!* And deep down, my respect for him had just increased.

It was a beautiful Saturday afternoon in July. I walked across the lush field to the hospital, clocked in, and listened to report. Things were normal and relatively quiet as I helped care for patients on 1-West. As I returned from my supper break, the ward secretary announced I would be going to 4-North to assist with electric shock treatments.

Upon arriving in 4-North, I found that the nurse had already administered the mild sedative, and three patients were waiting quietly in their beds. I knew there would be a flurry of activity as soon as Dr. Benning arrived. He seemed to rush purposefully from room to room, allowing little time for his patients to develop anxiety. Electrical shock treatments were fearful experiences. The patients were usually sore for several days from the muscle stress caused by the induced seizures.

I followed two nurses and Dr. Benning as he rolled the machine into the first room. All went smoothly as the electrodes were positioned. Then Dr. Benning said, "Jim, I'm going to give you your treatment now, okay?" Jim murmured around the padded tongue depressor held in place by the attending nurse. The machine shot a controlled jolt of electricity through Jim's brain. His body stiffened and went into tremors from head to foot. Dr. Benning quickly removed the electrodes and ordered me to watch Jim as his team moved efficiently into the next room.

However, instead of going into a full seizure and becoming unconscious, Jim had mild tremors from head to foot. Dazed, he suddenly fastened his eyes, wild with fear, upon me! He made a whimpering, incoherent sound. In his mind, I was the reason for his suffering. And like a horrible nightmare, Jim began slowly, deliberately pushing himself up in bed. His facial expression was terrifying, and his hands kept reaching, zombie-like, for my face. I caught his wrists and talked as soothingly as I could, but found my voice high-pitched with tension.

Jim's gaze was fixed on me as he continued clawing at me. All the while, I was desperately trying to force him to lie down. The stainless steel bed rails must have looked like prison bars to his befogged mind. He saw me as the person responsible for holding him there unjustly. He fought me with incredible strength. I glanced desperately toward the nurse's call button far out of reach in its wall bracket. "Lord, help me!" I cried, and with all my strength forced Jim back onto his bed.

Despite his terror, Jim could still reason. He began worming his way toward the foot of the bed where only a low footboard blocked his exit! Like a drunken, disoriented man he fought me with crazed determination. If he overpowered me and got out of bed in his current condition, he would certainly fall and injure himself on the concrete floor. I could not allow that to happen!

Suddenly he flung his leg over the bedrail and tried to climb out. Dropping his hands, I grasped his leg, and with great effort, forced it back into the bed. But in that moment, he sat up with his hands tensed, and like eagle's claws, they flew at my face. Just in time, I jerked out of harm's way and again grabbed for his wrists. His legs immediately came back over the rail in a frenzied effort to free himself from his horror. Afraid to release his hands, I held them fast and balanced on one foot while I pushed his legs back into the bed with my free leg. In the struggle, I lost my balance and nearly fell. This was terrible! Panic rose within me. At that moment, the welcome voice of another orderly sounded right behind me. "Johnny, you are wanted in ER stat!"

"Then you will have to take care of Jim!" I quavered. "He never lost consciousness, and he has been fighting me to get out of bed. Be careful, he will try to attack your face!"

My friend moved in and grasped Jim's struggling arms while I snatched the nurse's call button and fastened it to the bed rail. After rushing to the elevator, I found myself impatiently jabbing the DOWN button several times, but saw that it would be coming all the way from the basement. I dared not wait that long! Dashing to the stairwell, I ran down the three flights of stairs to the first floor, wondering what could have prompted the urgent call from the ER.

I was immediately sent to the treatment room where two nurses were struggling with a young man on a cot. He seemed to be semi-conscious. His face was twitching, his fists clenched, and his eyes rolled wildly. A nurse was attempting to tape his arm to a padded board while the other one struggled to restrain the patient. But her strength was no match for his involuntary spastic movements. I grabbed the arm and pinned it down while the nurse secured it with bandage tape. All the while, our patient exerted extreme effort to retract his arm. His tremors continued unabated as the lab technician made several attempts to find a vein. I tried frantically to hold that trembling arm as still as possible, countering his pushing and jerking.

At last the nurse inserted the needle into the vein, released the tourniquet, and drew the necessary blood for admissions, type, and crossmatch. "He's headed for emergency surgery," she announced, "and we have to get this IV running."

I grabbed the IV stand and rolled it into place, then moved to stabilize the patient's shoulders. As the lab nurse finalized the IV and regulated its input, the charge nurse explained, "This is Jerry Dalton. He's only fifteen years old and was injured in an explosion. He has sustained a right frontal depressed skull fracture." The lab technician stashed the vials, syringes, and tourniquet into her tray and headed for the lab. Personnel arrived from surgery to wheel Jerry's bed toward a waiting surgical team, headed by our neurosurgeon, Dr. Glosser.

The head nurse told me, "The patient was semi-conscious when he arrived by ambulance all the way from Woodsfield. He was thrashing about so wildly we couldn't control his movements. Thank you for coming! You can go on back to 1-West, and we'll do the cleanup."

"Fine," I said heading for the door, "but please call whenever you need me."

"Don't worry, we will!" she assured me.

I was interrupted by the charge nurse while replenishing fresh water, finishing back rubs, and tucking my patients in for the night. "Johnny," she announced, "we need to clear the beds from Room 107. Just park them in the crossover hall for now. We have a patient being admitted directly from surgery, and he will already be in a bed."

The personnel from surgery, dressed in their green scrubs, carefully maneuvered the surgery patient into our room. His head was swathed in bandages, an IV was running, and Dr. Glosser was in the nurses' station writing the orders for his patient. LPN Ruth Zimmerman was on duty, and I assisted her in carrying out Dr. Glosser's orders. "He has a tracheostomy," she said, pointing to the metal breathing tube that had been surgically inserted into his throat just above the collar bone. A urinary catheter directed urine into a plastic collection bag hooked low to the side of his bed.

Dr. Glosser entered and watched in silence as we finished getting things situated. He stood for a long moment at the bedside, gazing down at his patient. The doctor's face registered fatigue and tension. It had been a grueling surgery. "We removed a sizable skull fragment and relieved the pressure from the brain with burr holes. He is a very, very sick boy. I want someone to 'special' him tonight, taking vital signs every fifteen minutes around the clock. Measure and record urinary output at the end of each shift. Notify me immediately of any change. His family is in the surgical waiting room, and I will send them in as soon as I have briefed them." He walked out.

My mind was in a whirl as I went about my responsibilities. Would Jerry live, and if so, would he be able to walk, talk, or think normally?

Five minutes later, when I stepped into Jerry's room, LPN Ruth was counting the IV drops and adjusting the valve. She finished and then recorded his temperature. Suddenly, our unconscious patient retched slightly. Ruth moved swiftly to the head of the bed. Jerry retched again.

"Johnny, quick, help me roll him!" she exclaimed. I jumped to her side. Together, we rolled him just as he retched hard. Vomit shot halfway across the room. Another retch and another spout of stomach contents was hurled across the room. Thinking fast, Ruth grabbed the suction tube, flipped its control to maximum, and began suctioning Jerry's breathing tube to remove any vomit he might have inhaled into his trachea. Jerry's retching ceased, but he was breathing hard. It took several minutes for his respirations to return to normal.

"Look at this," Ruth said as she removed a bit of peanut stuck on the end of the suction tube. "He must have eaten peanuts, and they were being inhaled during his vomiting." As I began to clean up, Ruth explained, "Projectile vomiting often results from severe head trauma."

Jerry's parents arrived, and I led them to the sitting room at the far end of the wing, explaining that we had a few more things we needed to do. I promised to notify them just as soon as we were ready.

Our 3:00 to 11:00 supervisor arrived and reviewed Dr. Glosser's orders. She spoke reassuringly to Mr. and Mrs. Dalton. Then she explained to the 1-West staff that she needed a volunteer to work a double shift and give Jerry undivided attention throughout the night. This did not seem to fit into the schedule for most of our workers. I felt led to volunteer, so I asked Ruth to notify the VS unit that I would not be coming in until 7:30 a.m.

I invited the Daltons into Jerry's room and made them as comfortable as possible under the circumstances. They were grave, sober, and in shock from the events of the afternoon. I soon learned that Jerry was the oldest of their three children, and they had two younger daughters. The Dalton family operated a tire business in

Woodsfield and were very active members of the Church of Christ. I was blessed to discover how serious they were about their relationship with God. I prayed with them as we stood around Jerry's bed. Knowing that their only son was hanging between life and death added urgency to our prayers.

Concern filled my mind as I registered Jerry's vital signs every quarter hour. Would he live or die? He was only fifteen years old—would he ever live a normal life again? I felt deep compassion for his parents, who had been through so much. I brought them snacks, coffee, and water from our kitchenette and spare blankets and pillows from the linen closet. It was going to be a long night!

I glanced at the clock as I registered Jerry's 11:45 p.m. vitals. In another fifteen minutes it would be Sunday morning. Remembering that we 1-W workers had agreed to donate our Sunday labor, I excused myself and quickly clocked out.

The night dragged on, and I worked as quietly as possible, keeping a sharp eye on Jerry's IV and vital signs while his parents dozed fitfully in their chairs. At one point, Jerry's breathing rattled with mucus, and I suctioned his trach tube until his breathing returned to normal.

By 4 a.m., I felt numb, and the thought of a bed was alluring. Finally, the rays of the sun began pushing the night away. The arrival of the new day revived me somewhat until the morning shift arrived. Finally I was released to head for the White House and bed.

CHAPTER 9

Encouragements

I clocked in on Monday morning, wondering about our head trauma patient. I couldn't get Jerry or his family out of my mind. Report progressed to Room 107, and I listened carefully.

"Jerry Dalton, fifteen years old, depressed right frontal skull fracture, post-op patient of Dr. Glosser," intoned the night nurse. "On 3:00 to 11:00 shift, he developed an elevated temp of 102. Dr. Glosser ordered a white count and a hypothermal unit to be applied this morning. It is to be activated as needed." She paused for a moment before explaining, "Patients with head trauma or brain injury often lose the ability to regulate body temperature, and prolonged high temperature causes permanent neurological damage."

Following the morning routine of TPRs, bathing, breakfast, and bed changing for my patients, I went to assist in Room 107. I was introduced to a formidable looking stainless steel machine on rollers. Six-foot-tall, it had a confusing array of tubes, wires, dials, gauges, and two rubber blankets embedded with a pattern of tubing.

Mrs. Stevens explained, "This is the hypothermal machine Dr. Glosser ordered. I would like you to familiarize yourself with its operation. Let me know when you are ready, and we'll have one of the student nurses assist you in getting the rubber blanket under the patient." She left me to study the operator's manual.

The refrigeration unit chilled an alcohol solution and circulated it through connecting tubes to the rubber blanket which would be placed under Jerry. A probe monitored internal body temperature and a master dial was set to the desired temperature of the patient. In more severe situations, a second blanket could be placed over the patient, thereby doubling the cooling capacity. The instructions indicated that the vent at the top of the alcohol reservoir had to be closed for transportation but opened for operation.

During the following weeks, I checked this machine regularly. Among the turnover of nurses between shifts, there were several who just couldn't grasp the mechanics of this unit. Fortunately, my plumbing experience allowed me to understand how to operate it.

Mrs. Stevens assigned one of the orderlies to "special" Jerry whenever we were on duty. I looked forward to working with him, and although he was unconscious, I learned to give him daily passive exercises. This consisted of deep muscle massages to his extremities, as well as flexing all his joints. The goal was to keep Jerry's muscles from deteriorating so his limbs would still be usable if he ever regained consciousness. But even so, Jerry eventually developed atrophy, and I learned that these exercises needed to be taken just beyond the threshold of pain to regain muscle tone. After the routine of movements were completed, I held his wrist and straightened his fingers. While watching Jerry's face, I flexed his hand backward until his grimace told me I had reached a point where pain was registering. I then relaxed those muscles and repeated the process from eight to ten times before moving to the next limb.

I was deeply impressed by the commitment of Jerry's family. His father, Carl, remained at the bedside of their only son the entire day while his wife, Thelma, returned to their home, an hour and half away, to care for their daughters.

When Thelma Dalton returned to relieve her husband, they spent the evening together talking in Jerry's room or dining in the cafeteria. When it was time to leave, Thelma made herself comfortable on a cot in Jerry's room, and Carl drove home to their daughters and to his work the following day. Carl returned to his son's bedside the next evening, and his wife drove home to care for their daughters. This cycle continued for several months as they waited, watched, and prayed for their son to regain consciousness.

Along the way there were improvements. Jerry's eyes sometimes opened, and when people walked past him, he would occasionally follow them with spastic eye movements. We assumed Jerry could hear and understand conversation, so we talked to him while we worked.

I was running a bit late with an evening shift, and only a handful of people remained in the cafeteria as I filled my supper tray and sat alone at a table. I loved people and enjoyed conversation, but I also valued peaceful, relaxing moments. I thought about the coming weekend when I planned to visit Ruth and her family in Minerva. I would enjoy their church service and the change of atmosphere. But I would have to drive back to Zanesville on Sunday evening because I was working the Monday morning shift.

Turning my thoughts to 1-West and noting that my supper break was nearly over, I scooped up my tray slid it into the rack for dirty dishes. As I turned to leave, a voice behind me said, "I saw what you did." I quickly examined my tray in the rack, but couldn't see any cause for the nurse's comment.

"Excuse me?" I asked. I wasn't sure what I had done wrong, but I was certainly willing to correct it if I could.

"I saw what you did," she repeated. "You prayed before you ate. I always say grace at home, but I have been reluctant to do it here in front of others. Your example made me ashamed of my fear, but it has also given me courage. I am going to begin praying here at the hospital as well."

I hardly knew what to say. "W–well," I stammered. "I'm glad if that has been an encouragement to you. Thank you!" I smiled at her and hurried to 1-West and the patients waiting for my care. I was blessed to observe later that this nurse did indeed keep her resolve.

Back on the floor, I saw visitors in Jerry's room. I entered to check on Jerry and was introduced to Mr. and Mrs. Stout and their eighteen-year-old son Richard, who had come to encourage the Daltons.

Richard was a head trauma survivor, and he wanted to tell his story of what it was like to be comatose. He had been unconscious for six weeks with no responses whatsoever. Then in minute increments, his brain began registering bits of his surroundings. But he was still helpless to communicate. Richard eventually regained his ability to chew and swallow food that was placed into his mouth, but his speech was gone, and the nerve path between his brain and his limbs was disconnected. He had been trapped inside his own body with no way to communicate.

The Daltons had many questions for Richard and his parents, and they were greatly encouraged by this visit. Richard's mother explained that as their son's brain was healing, they learned to recognize his likes and dislikes by close observation. They noticed he was often restless or agitated when attended by a particular caregiver. His agitation had been a mystery to them. "Richard," she encouraged, "tell the Daltons why you did not like that worker."

"Well," he began in a raspy monotone, "for two months, I was sustained only by IVs and had nothing by mouth. I was longing for real food, but had no way of asking for it. Finally, they began offering me soft foods. My parents were often present when my food tray was brought in. I was famished, and that food smelled so good. I was unable to move my arms, so Mother often fed me. I remember when this nurse's aide offered, 'Why don't you go to the cafeteria, and I will feed Richard.' My parents thought that was kind of her. I heard and understood what was being said.

"When my parents left, this aide raised my bed so that I was in a sitting position, and she began to feed me. It was slow going, because I had to focus intensely on the motions of chewing and swallowing. I was hungry, and the food tasted so good, but I was struggling to eat. This aide decided to help herself to my food, and ate over half of it. That made me angry, but I was helpless to protest or even tell anyone about it.

"This happened day after day. Eventually, she was eating most of my food herself, leaving me very hungry and frustrated. I came to detest that aide for her dishonesty while everyone thought she was so dedicated in caring for me."

As Richard shared his story, every syllable was the same pitch and volume. His brain injury had left him with no inflection or expression. He walked with a faltering gait due to nerve damage sustained in his accident. Even now, nearly a year after his release from the hospital, Richard was still suffering from a deep bedsore.

Despite his disabilities and all he had suffered, Richard was glad to be alive. His story brought great hope to Carl and Thelma Dalton.

On another evening shift, I was sent to assist in the ER. Nineteen-year-old Larry Andrews lay on his ER cot, quivering with pain in spite of an injection of pain medication. His left leg was unnaturally bent about eight inches above the ankle. Larry was a football player who wound up on the bottom of a pile of bodies following a tackle. His X-rays showed both bones of his lower leg completely broken. Dr. Lance was on his way to set the bones and protect the break with a cast. I began by preparing the casting materials.

However, when Dr. Lance examined the X-rays and the patient's swollen leg, he formed a different plan of action. He summoned an anesthetist and had an IV started for Larry. He was going to put the patient to sleep to set the broken bones. Dr. Lance explained as I looked over his shoulder at the X-ray, "These jagged bone ends have slipped past each other, see here?" He traced them with his pen. "We will need to set them end to end for proper healing. This swelling has caused the muscle to retract, pushing the broken bones past one another. Our job is to stretch these muscles to full length and set the broken bone ends together again. I'm going to need your help."

Dr. Lance fashioned a stirrup-like arrangement from heavy bandage material as the anesthetist added meds to the IV, and Larry was soon unconscious. Under Dr. Lance's direction, I helped position Larry so his knee bent at a right angle and hung vertically off the edge of his cot.

"Now, Miller," directed Dr. Lance as he fastened his harness about Larry's foot, "I want you to place your foot in this loop below the patient's foot, and slowly exert increasing downward pressure. Stretch that leg out completely, and I'll see what I can do.

"Bill," he asked the anesthetist, "how's he doing?"

"Fine," the other responded with a thumbs-up gesture. "Heartrate 80, respiration 12, blood pressure 130 over 75."

Dr. Lance said, "More pressure, Miller." I pushed down hard, but it still wasn't enough. "More," he commanded. I was finally balancing on the makeshift stirrup with my full body weight stretching Larry's leg.

"Here," said Dr. Lance, "grab the cot and push down in addition to your own weight." I did, and the doctor maneuvered the break back and forth. I heard the bones grating together—we were almost there. "Push a little harder!" Dr. Lance ordered. Then, without warning, the stirrup snapped, and I fell backwards, barely catching myself. Larry's poor leg, suddenly relieved of all the stretching, snapped up and flopped against the undercarriage of the cot.

"We're going to have to do something different," commented Dr. Lance. "Bill, what about a muscle relaxant?"

"We can try," came the anesthetist's reply, but he didn't sound overly confident.

Dr. Lance fashioned another stirrup while the anesthetist slowly introduced the muscle relaxing medication intravenously. The doctors chatted as they waited for the medication to take effect. When all was ready, Dr. Lance instructed me to stand in the stirrup once again. I was surprised at the ease with which Larry's leg now stretched out, and with a bit of rotation, the leg was set.

"Dr. Lance," I asked, "what made that difference?"

"Have you ever heard of curare?" he asked. I hadn't, and he explained, "It's a bean pod that grows in the jungles of Central and South America. For generations, hunters have used a potent extract from that bean to poison the arrows which they used to kill large animals. It is not actually a poison, but a powerful muscle relaxant," he explained. "A derivative of curare is where we obtain our muscle relaxant for situations like this one."

Following another X-ray and the application of a full leg cast, Larry was admitted to 1-West. I stopped in to see him the following day and asked how he was feeling.

He responded, "Well, I am pretty good, I guess, but I certainly have a sore leg!"

"I'm sure it will feel better soon," I assured him. I felt it best to say nothing of the actions which had undoubtedly contributed to that soreness.

CHAPTER 10

Worship and Work

I found personal devotional time essential in maintaining a dedicated walk with the Lord. At times, when schedules permitted, several White House boys shared informally.

On Wednesday evenings, those not working gathered in the dining hall for Bible study and prayer meeting. This was a much-needed time of focus on the Word of God. The young men spoke on Biblical topics or specific texts, and we enjoyed lively discussions. We shared prayer requests for personal needs and for patients. We then formed smaller groups and knelt for prayer. These times strengthened my spiritual life and added to the closeness of our unit. Maintaining steady Bible input sharpened not only our spiritual understanding, but also our daily walk with the Lord.

The day after a prayer meeting, one of my patients was Mr. Shatler. He was sitting in his chair, so I took the opportunity to change the linens on his bed. "So, Mr. Shatler," I said as I prepared to leave with the used bedding. "How are you getting along?"

"Well," he replied, "things aren't going so well. I'm diabetic, and that has affected the circulation in my feet."

"Oh, and what can be done about that?" I asked.

"We're not sure at the moment, but let me show you." With that, he removed the slipper from his right foot, and to my shock, I saw his big toe was nearly black – the color of a ripe olive!

"You see," he continued, "I have developed gangrene, and they are talking of removing my toe."

"Oh, I am sorry to hear that. Isn't there anything else that can be done?"

"Not really. If the gangrene progresses, it would eventually mean that I lose my entire foot." Two days later, Mr. Shatler went to surgery and his toe was amputated. Two days post-op, he was released.

Three months afterward, I was sent to 3-East to administer a urinary catheter for a patient, and found that Mr. Shatler was a roommate of the patient. Mr. Shatler was soaking his foot in a basin of medicated water, and I said, "It's good to see you again, but what brings you back to our hospital?"

"Well," he said, "we've been having trouble getting this thing to heal." He lifted his foot from the water for me to see. The raw, gaping wound gave me the shivers! It appeared that after three months, the healing process had not even begun. Seeing that gave me new sympathy for those suffering from diabetes.

Back on 1-West, as I was charting my afternoon TPRs, Dr. Lance entered the nurses' station and said, "Miller, come with me." He marched off toward Room 120, and I followed, wondering what he was going to tell me today. I loved the personal interest he took in me, and the way he shared his knowledge and experience. He had taught me so much, and I admired him. We entered the room from which one of his patients had just been discharged. Pointing to the head of the bed, he snapped, "You know better than to install a trapeze bar like that!" It was dangling loosely, and he angrily grabbed it and wrenched it from the headboard. "I don't ever want to see another one installed like that, do you hear?"

In shock, I answered meekly, "Yes, sir." Although I had not even installed this trapeze bar, I saw no point in telling him that. I knew from experience what was wrong. Whoever installed it had failed to loosen the bolts and readjust the center beam to fit our beds.

"You are going to have to learn to install these properly!" the doctor flung over his shoulder as he headed for the door. "See to it!" was his parting shot. I felt stung and disappointed by Dr. Lance's outburst, but set about immediately to make the needed adjustments. His painful accusation played over and over in my mind.

Mr. Black was a college professor who had suffered a stroke several years earlier. Although his mind and speech were unaffected, the stroke left him with partial paralysis of the right side. Recent tests revealed a cancerous tumor growing in his right lung. The medical-surgical floor was full, so Mr. Black was admitted to 1-West. He was an intelligent man and deeply interested in why we orderlies were working in the hospital. This had sparked serious discussions and I was able to share my testimony of nonresistance.

Dr. Wise, our lung specialist, performed the operation to remove Mr. Black's tumor and a third of his right lung. On Mr. Black's second day post-op, I entered his room to bring him fresh water. He had just lighted a cigarette, and sitting on the edge of his bed, he took a deep drag and blew a cloud of smoke toward the ceiling. I said nothing, but went about my duties while he watched me. He took another drag before glancing at the cigarette in his hand. He shook his head as if in disbelief and said, "A man has to be crazy to do this. As near death as I was, you'd think I would never smoke another cigarette, but here I am, smoking again."

However, even this realization did not deter Mr. Black from continuing his life-threatening addiction. He was later discharged and went his way, accompanied by his addiction and its continuing threat upon his life.

Dr. Lance's wife had been admitted as a patient in our private deluxe room. She was rundown, both physically and emotionally. Dr. Lance stopped in several times a day to see her. I learned from the student nurses and aides that Mrs. Lance also smoked. I was disappointed that a doctor who was committed to enhancing health and saving lives had a wife who was a habitual smoker.

Occasionally, I had been asked to take cigarettes to a patient, or in the case of a person with emotional problems, I had to stay with them while they smoked. But my conscience began to bother me. The scripture from 1 Timothy 5:22 spoke to my heart. "Neither be partaker of other men's sins: keep thyself pure." I was unsure of how to process this, but I prayed for wisdom.

My next test came when a lady in Room 109 asked me to please buy her cigarettes. I responded as graciously as I could, "You know, I do not believe in smoking, and I do not want to assist someone who is smoking."

The lady looked at me in surprise, tilted her head to one side, and said, "Oh, I see."

Later, as I brought the supper trays into the room, the lady in the other bed said, "We've been talking about you. We admire you for your stand against smoking. It is right that you want to live out your beliefs. My husband called, and I told him about you. When he comes to visit, I want you to meet him." I noticed the other lady was nodding in silent agreement. I left, not exactly patting myself on the back, but feeling pleased at the way things had turned out.

During visiting hours the following evening, I was called into Room 109 and introduced to the husband who had come to visit his wife. He immediately began asking questions about my religious beliefs and was soon grilling me. He was a Seventh Day Adventist who seemed to uphold the Old Testament above the New Testament. He finally ushered me into a vacant room where he began explaining his beliefs to me more forcefully.

I took a Gideon Bible from the nightstand and opened it to Hebrews, the book of better things, and read several verses showing that the blood of Jesus Christ, not the sacrifice of animals, is the remedy for our sins. The merits of Jesus Christ and not the keeping of the ceremonial law are what justify a person. He closed our conversation with, "You are much younger than me, and you needn't think there is anything you can tell me!" His attitude disappointed me, yet I felt I had done the right thing by explaining the Gospel and not merely keeping silent.

We never knew what to expect while working in the emergency room. One patient had been coon hunting at night. His dogs treed a raccoon, but he was having a hard time spotting it among the limbs of the tall tree. He stood there, shining his headlamp until he saw the gleaming eyes of the coon. He kept his focus riveted on his prey while reaching for the .22 pistol stuck in his belt. Something caught as he was trying to extract it, and *BANG!* The pistol fired, sending the bullet into his thigh. The purplish-blue, swollen entrance wound was just inches below where his leg joined his torso, but there was no exit wound. Dr. Yang ordered pain medication and an X-ray of the upper leg. Next, he ran through the normal list of admission questions while waiting for the X-rays. "Is there any cancer in your family? Diabetes? Any heart attacks, shortness of breath? Any history of liver problems? Do you smoke? Any thyroid problems? Are you on any prescribed medications?"

Just then the X-rays arrived, and Dr. Yang stuck them on the viewer to find the bullet. Depending where it was located, surgery might be required the next morning. The X-ray gave a very clear picture of the upper leg. But look as he might, there was absolutely no sign of that bullet. Dr. Yang examined the leg all over again, and then sent the patient back for an X-ray of the lower leg.

As we waited for the latest X-rays, Dr. Yang began pacing the hallway impatiently. Soon he stepped into the ER kitchenette and drew a pack of cigarettes from his pocket. He lit one and began smoking to calm his frayed nerves. I had often heard him ask patients if they smoked, and then warn them of the health hazards. I concluded he must be one of those doctors who could more readily prescribe the right thing for his patients than do it himself.

The second set of X-rays clearly showed the bullet had passed over the knee joint and under the kneecap. It was now embedded in the large tendon connecting the kneecap to the lower leg. Dr. Yang ordered an ER surgical tray, and I set it up for him. After studying the X-rays carefully, he shaved the area and cleansed the site with an antiseptic solution. He injected Xylocaine, gloved up, and began the surgery. The bullet was lying against the bone, and the pain was almost more than the patient could bear as Dr. Yang's scalpel sliced through layers of tissue. He carefully spread the fibrous strands of the large tendon without cutting them. Somewhere below there was a bullet.

When Dr. Yang could finally see the bullet, he tried to extract it with the surgical forceps, but they kept slipping off the bullet's rounded surface. Each attempt was causing our patient excruciating pain. He squeezed his leg with trembling hands as the procedure continued. At last, Dr. Yang succeeded with forceps that had a small, sharp spur which gripped the lead bullet. He began closing the wound. The patient received a tetanus shot and a prescription for an antibiotic, and was released to go home, a limping but wiser hunter.

An elderly woman had fallen and injured her shoulder, and Dr. Lance was called. He ordered an X-ray and said he would arrive shortly. The patient had just returned from X-ray as he walked into ER. "Here, Miller," he said with his closed hand extended in my direction. I instinctively reached out, and he dropped some money into my hand. "Run down to the vending machine in the basement," he instructed, "and get a pack of Salem cigarettes for my wife."

I froze, hand outstretched, the money in my open palm. "Uh, Dr. Lance," I said, "I do not believe in smoking, and I would rather not aid someone else in doing so." A look of longing momentarily passed over the doctor's face as we stood there. Then softly he said, "I would pay any amount of money if I could get my wife to stop smoking."

At that moment, Nurse Janette reached between us, scooped the money from my hand, and said, "Dr. Lance, your patient is in Room 3. I'll get the cigarettes for your wife."

After examining the X-rays, Dr. Lance determined the patient's left shoulder was dislocated rather than broken. He helped her lie on the ER cot and asked me to bring a large towel. He placed it around the patient's upper torso, just under the armpits. He took her left hand and began to use gentle, firm traction, increasing the tension as he slowly moved her hand toward her head, occasionally twisting it from side to side. All the while, he instructed me to exert more pressure on the towel in the opposite direction. "More, more!" he said as he pulled harder. Suddenly there was a subtle *plop,* and the patient breathed a sigh of relief. The dislocated shoulder had returned to its rightful position. However, Dr. Lance placed the arm in a sling and asked the patient not to use it for several days.

Dr. Lance thanked me, picked up the cigarettes from the nurse's desk, and wished us a good night as he headed for home.

A week passed, and I was again assigned to the ER for the evening. Dr. Lance was called, but this time to examine the tightly swollen ankle of a young basketball player. After the X-rays revealed no broken bones but a severely sprained ankle, Dr. Lance began taping it with wide bandage tape. I assisted as needed.

"Say, Miller," Dr. Lance said as though he had just remembered something. "I hung my jacket in the hall, and I have something in the right-hand pocket. Would you mind getting that for me?" I felt a bit uneasy about digging in a doctor's jacket pocket, but I followed his instructions and found a plastic envelope. I brought it back to Dr. Lance just as he put the finishing touches to the injured ankle.

"I brought that for you," he said, nodding toward the envelope. "You know what it is?"

My eyes opened wide. It was a dainty pair of the gold-plated bandage scissors which he presented to each graduate of the Bethesda School of Nursing! I'm sure the shocked surprise showed on my face as I profusely thanked Dr. Lance several times over. But I didn't miss the kind twinkle in his eye as he said with feeling, "You are welcome!" Clearly, his earlier anger toward me had been long forgotten.

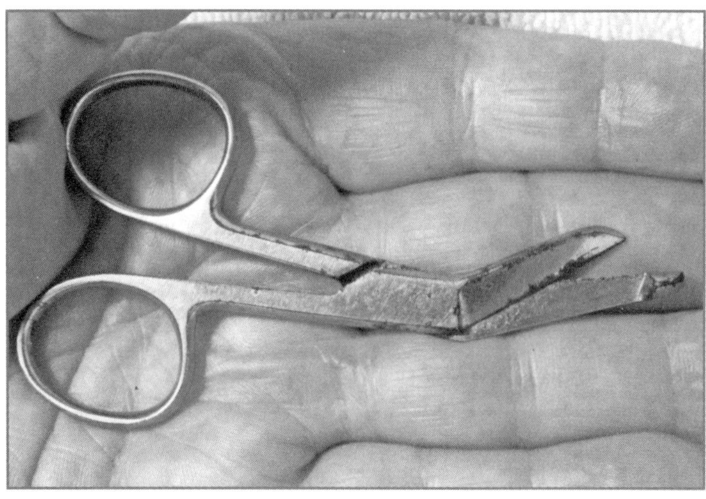

The gold plating on Dr. Lance's gift has worn thin, but the memory of his kindness remains undiminished.

CHAPTER 11

Trauma

The 3:00 to 11:00 shift on 1-West was unusually busy. There had been two dismissals with rooms to strip and clean, one post-op patient to monitor, and several admissions. I joined the team with the charge nurse and two aides. We were nearly running through the halls in our attempt to keep up with all the demands.

Glancing toward the lobby, I saw a figure walking toward 1-West. There was something about him that seemed vaguely familiar, but I dismissed it as a quirk of memory or simply resemblance to someone I might have known in the past. I turned into Jerry Dalton's room to check on him.

Jerry's IV needle had slipped out of the vein and had temporarily been discontinued. We were waiting on the lab technician to come restart it. Due to several months of intravenous feedings, it was becoming increasingly difficult to find a suitable vein. Jerry was fidgety, as though something was bothering him, but we had no way of knowing what that was. I had suctioned his trach tube, fluffed up his pillow, and repositioned him farther up in his bed, but nothing had helped.

Jerry's temperature was back to normal, and he no longer needed the hypothermal unit. His urine output was a bit lower than usual, but that was to be expected with his reduced fluid intake due to the disconnected IV. I asked his mother whether she had any idea why Jerry was agitated. She replied that his restlessness had begun that morning. It was puzzling.

I exited Jerry's room just as the man I had noticed minutes earlier came abreast of me. To my surprise, he stuck out his hand and said, "Good evening, Johnny."

"I can't believe my eyes!" I blurted. "Ernest Hanson!"

"Yes," he said. "It's me, and on two legs!" He chuckled at my surprise.

I grasped his hand, genuinely delighted to see him. "I have thought about you often during the past few months," I told him. "I wondered how you were dealing with your amputation and whether you had received a prosthesis. I can hardly believe your progress. Why, you walk with almost no limp at all!"

"Johnny," he said earnestly, "my only regret is that we did not amputate sooner. I am getting along so well that I'm planning to go back to work next month."

"But how are you going to climb ladders?" I asked.

"Don't worry, my ladder-climbing days are over. I'll be doing my cutting and welding with both feet firmly on the ground. How are things going for you?" he asked. "Are you still dating that wonderful girl of yours?"

"Oh, yes, we are continuing our relationship, and I'm planning to visit her family soon."

"I'm glad for you, and I'm so glad I got to see you again," Ernest said. "Thank you for all you did for me while I was lying in the hospital wondering if I even had a future."

"Thank you for stopping by. And give my regards to your wife."

We clasped hands in parting as he said, "Take care."

I stood there watching Mr. Hanson walk back toward the lobby. He had overcome the loss of his leg and was determined to make the best of it. We had been drawn together because I had helped him bear his burden in some small way and thus fulfill the law of Christ.

These pleasant thoughts were interrupted by a reminder to pick up the rest of the empty supper trays. I had barely completed this task before the kitchen personnel arrived to retrieve them. As I began delivering fresh ice water to the patients, the ward secretary called, "Johnny, we are getting a new patient admitted directly from ER. He's going into Room 117. Would you please clear the way for him? It's a head trauma case."

I acknowledged her message and hurried to comply. In Room 117, the bedside table needed to be moved, the covers turned down, the bed moved to one side, and the visitor's chair placed in the hall. When all was ready, the ER personnel arrived with the new patient, and I helped get him settled.

I addressed the patient as I repositioned the bed and brought his bedside stand within reach. "Ronny, how are you feeling?"

"Not so good," he replied. "I've got a splitting headache. Man, does it hurt!"

"Have they given you anything for pain?"

"Yeah, they gave me some pills, but they aren't doing much good," he responded slowly.

"Tell me what happened," I requested.

"Well," he began, "I was standing on top of a stepladder at work, reaching for a shelf, and the ladder just kicked out from under me. I guess I hit the cement pretty hard when I fell."

"Are you seeing double, or is your vision clear?" I asked.

"Oh, I can see okay. It's just that I've got this terrible headache."

"I see. Look, Ronny, here is a urinal, and I need a urine sample to complete your admission. I need to leave for a few minutes. See if you can get that sample for me, and I'll be right back. Okay?"

"Okay," he responded.

Leaving the urinal within easy reach, I shared my progress with the ward secretary, gave two belated back rubs, and then returned to see Ronny Wagner. I checked his urinal and found it just as I had left it—empty. Ronny was asleep. I woke him and asked again for the needed urine sample. "I must have this to complete your admission," I explained.

"Oh, all right!" he said groggily.

"I'll be back in a few minutes to collect it," I said, pulling the curtain around his bed for added privacy.

I returned to find Ronny fast asleep, and still no sample. "Ronny," I called, but there was no response. "Ronny!" I shook him. He opened his eyes. "Ronny, we cannot finalize your admission until we have obtained this urine sample. You understand?" He nodded.

When I returned several minutes later, Ronny had soaked his bed, but the urinal was dry. I was irked as I got fresh linens to change his bed. "Wake up, Ronny. You have to roll over so I can change your bed!" I said rather forcefully. There was no response, so I shook him. Still no response. Suddenly, it occurred to me that Ronny might be unconscious rather than asleep. With my thumbs, I gently raised his eyelids. His right pupil was dilated, but then constricted normally in response to the light. However, his left pupil remained large and unresponsive. Furthermore, it was staring unseeingly to the far left, out of alignment with his right eye.

I was shocked and rushed to find the charge nurse. "Come quickly!" I urged. "Our new patient is unconscious, and one eye doesn't respond to light!" We rushed together into Room 117, and a quick examination was enough to convince her. She dashed to the nurses' station to call Dr. Glosser. As I changed Ronny's linen, emergency surgery was scheduled to try saving his life. Ronny's mother arrived and stood at the foot of her son's bed as I finished. I tried to convey the gravity of the situation as gently as possible. "Ronny is in a precarious condition," I explained, but refrained from telling her that Ronny's tightly curled hand indicated compromised brain activity.

She responded, "I prayed to the good Lord, and I know he's gonna be all right."

I watched as personnel rolled the cart down the hall to surgery where burr holes would be drilled through Ronny's skull to relieve the pressure from his life-threatening, intracranial bleeding. His mother followed as far as the surgical waiting room.

Ronny didn't come back to 1-West. Only nineteen years old, he died of injuries sustained in falling from a six-foot stepladder. The experience spoke deeply to my heart. Ronny's short life was ended. Had he been ready to stand before the Judge of all the earth?

Several days passed, and my schedule changed to morning shifts. I learned in report that Jerry's situation was becoming worse. He had a bladder spasm, wetting his bed in spite of having a urinary catheter. Something was very wrong! Head nurse Mrs. Stevens asked me to remove Jerry's old catheter and install a new one, speculating that irritation might have caused the spasm. I performed the task even though all appeared normal. An open catheter should offer no resistance to the flow of urine, and I knew it should handle even a spastic emptying of the bladder through the tubing and into the receptacle on the side of the bed.

Taking a scalpel blade from the cart in the treatment room, I carefully slit the catheter tube lengthwise and showed the results to Mrs. Stevens. We were both surprised and relieved at what we discovered. Evidently, Jerry's metabolism was unable to completely process the contents of his IVs. His kidneys were producing fine, sand-like crystals which had built up in his catheter. No doubt these obstructions grew as more and more mineral adhered to the granules until they produced enough backpressure to trigger a spasm.

Jerry settled comfortably into our routine of exercises, and we began experimenting with his progression of consciousness. Even in his comatose condition, I could tell when he was asleep or awake. When I turned on the light at the head of Jerry's bed, he occasionally blinked. So, along with the exercise of his limbs, why not exercise his eyes and his perception? Several times each day, I repeatedly switched Jerry's light off and on, and half the time, he blinked. Eventually his blinking progressed to 75 percent of the time. We all waited anxiously for the day when Jerry would become fully alert.

I was working in ER when Bill came in. He had suffered multiple bruises in an auto accident. Bill was rather shaken up and a bit disoriented. He was only twenty years old, but sported a huge frame with enough muscle to tip the scales at a solid 300 pounds. Of course, all his friends called him Tiny. The doctor ordered multiple X-rays, and even though there were no broken bones, the attending physician was concerned about a deep gash to Tiny's right temple. He also appeared to have suffered a concussion. The moderate amount of blood in his urine indicated possible internal injuries, and he was admitted to 1-West for observation. Tiny was ordered on complete bed rest and had an IV to provide nourishment without taxing his digestive tract until we were sure everything was back to normal.

However, two days later, while I was working on 1-West, Tiny still showed symptoms of his concussion. He was withdrawn and only responded when spoken to. I was supposed to check his vital signs every four hours as well as test his pupils' reaction to light.

We were getting along well, and things were relatively quiet, so I took the opportunity to sort out returned traction equipment in the cast room. I had barely begun when I heard the hysterical, high-pitched voice of Nurse Oakland screaming my name. I couldn't imagine what was wrong, but I took off at a dead run up the hall in the direction of the shouts. As I drew even with the nurses' station, I heard another piercing scream of "In here!" from Room 110.

I dashed in to find Tiny's bed empty and the IV stand lying on the floor with Nurse Oakland desperately trying to set it up again. However, the IV tubing was stretched taut from the floor upward until it disappeared through the crack in the bathroom door. Tiny's blood was flowing backward through the tubing toward the IV bag lying on the floor. I quickly lifted the bag of IV fluid from the stand and raised it as high as I could reach. Immediately, the blood began flowing back into Tiny's veins on the other side of the door where it belonged. Nurse Oakland thanked me for coming to her rescue and righted the stand. I assured her I would get Tiny back into his bed and report to her.

She left, and I waited. Soon Tiny emerged. He glanced in my direction as he climbed back into bed and said casually, "I had to go to the potty." I had to smile at his innocent remark and his oblivion to the stir he had caused by not asking for assistance. I explained that the doctor had ordered complete bed rest, so he was not allowed to walk about until the doctor released him to do so. "We do not want you to become dizzy and fall or injure yourself," I told him. "The next time you need to use the toilet, please push this call button and I'll come help you. Okay?"

"Okay," he agreed amiably.

Meanwhile, Jerry was running into more and more difficulties. They had to stop giving him intravenous fluids because of the deterioration of his veins. A huge needle was inserted deep into each thigh muscle, and he was now absorbing life-sustaining liquids intramuscularly. But as the weeks passed, his legs swelled alarmingly. Jerry's heels were developing blisters, due in part to the added weight of the edema buildup pressing on his heels. His blood flow also diminished through his deteriorating veins. The doctor ordered soft foam heel covers for Jerry's feet and a special tubular pillow to support his calves and relieve the pressure on his heels.

I now had to omit Jerry's legs from the regular exercises due to the needles and tubing attached to his thighs. After massaging his muscles and flexing his arms, fingers, and hands, I began exercising his eyes and perception. Pressing my hands together and moving them rapidly toward his face, I split them apart at the last second, missing his face by a mere inch. Jerry blinked. I did it again and again, and Jerry blinked almost every time. He was making progress even though the infusion was taking its toll. I showed his father when he came to stay with Jerry that evening, and he was pleased with this latest development.

CHAPTER 12

Improved Methods

We enjoyed many visitors who came to see the Zanesville VS Unit, one of the first of its kind. My family visited, eager to see how this VS unit functioned and how I was faring. Pastors frequently visited and preached for us. Youth from other states and even Canada heard of our program and came to see it for themselves. We experienced much spiritual encouragement.

The men whose vision had spawned this spiritual haven also visited frequently. Because of their efforts, young people could pay the debt owed to their church and country while simultaneously serving God by serving others. We were dedicated to ministry for hurting souls, but God was also using this experience to mold us more perfectly into Christ's image.

Back on duty, I listened to report on 1-West. There was a new admission in Room 106, Martha Blackstone, a thirty-nine-year-old patient of Dr. Glosser with severe headaches and dizziness. In Room 107, Jerry continued receiving intramuscular infusions while suffering heavy edema buildup. Room 119 had a repeat patient of Dr. Yang's:

Ernest Rogers, forty-three years old, diagnosed with malignant brain lesions. His symptoms included loss of motor control and mini seizures. He had been hospitalized six months earlier.

I went to work with a will, conscious of the many who were suffering all around me. Not only were the patients hurting, but their loved ones were deeply affected as well. I introduced myself to Ernest Rogers and tried to put him at ease. He sat for hours in a chair facing the open door, watching the constant flow of hospital activity. One eyelid drooped slightly, and he experienced occasional tremors in his right arm which he attempted to conceal by clasping his hands together. But it was obvious those lesions were having their effect. His spastic movements gradually intensified and became more frequent.

In Room 107, I discussed Jerry's situation with his father as I began the exercises. "Carl, I want you to know that our VS unit has been praying for Jerry and for your family."

"Johnny, you don't know how much that means to us," he said. "This has been the hardest thing I have ever faced. I have never prayed so hard for anything as I have for Jerry's healing. Every day, I think this might be the day that Jerry will wake up. But nothing seems to change." He was close to tears.

I worked in silence, trying to imagine what Carl was feeling.

"You know, Johnny, there's something I don't understand," he continued. "You and Earl both seem to be such dedicated young men. Your Christian testimony is as good as—well no, I may as well be honest. I believe you have a better testimony than many of us. But I just can't see why you are not members of the Church of Christ."

I watched Jerry's face as I increased the pressure on his extended hand and fingers, and then answered thoughtfully. "Actually, Carl, I do consider myself a member of the church of Christ in the Biblical sense. In every nation, he who fears God and work righteousness is accepted by Him."

"What do you mean by that?" he asked.

"Well, when a person has come to the place in his life that he sees he is a sinner and needs salvation—he confesses, repents, and turns away from his sinful life. God has promised to wash away his sins. He is born again by the Spirit of God. That is what makes him a member of the body of Christ."

"But, Johnny, we all sin," he objected. "I sin every day!"

"Carl, you don't need to," I replied. "Do you believe that Jesus Christ has enough power to keep you from sinning for five minutes?"

"Well, yes, I'm sure He does."

"What about one hour? Does he have enough power to keep you from sinning for one hour?"

"I suppose so."

"What about six or even twelve hours?" I asked. "Does Christ have power to keep us from sinning for an entire day? He does, and you know He does. His power is available, but if we expect to keep on sinning, we probably will do just that."

"You have a point," Carl admitted, "but think about this: even a little anger, a bit of pride, or a wrong thought—that's sin, and we all do them."

"You know, John wrote about that in 1 John 2:1. 'My little children, these things I write unto you, that ye sin not.' Carl, I firmly believe it is God's will that we do not sin. That is why Jesus came. It was to get us out of the sinning business, so we can become His true followers. John continues, 'And if any man sin, we have an advocate with the Father, Jesus Christ the righteous.' So, the way I see it, we become born again by the Spirit of God and turn from our sin to Christ. We are then members of His body and the spiritual bride of Christ. Our goal then is to live in victory. If we stumble, we repent and ask to be forgiven. We get back up, determined to follow Christ faithfully. Isn't that right?"

I moved around to the other side of the bed and started massaging Jerry's other arm.

"So how do you think a person follows Christ?" was Carl's next question.

"God's Word reveals how we are to live, and I believe the Holy Spirit gives us power to live above sin as we faithfully follow His Word."

"Like what, for instance?"

"Okay, Jesus plainly commands His followers to put away the sword and to show love even our enemies. He commands us to pray for those who persecute us. In obeying Jesus, I dare not take any part of the military that is killing fellow human beings. I just *cannot* do that as a follower of Jesus. That's why I'm working here in this hospital assisting to save lives rather than being in the military fighting to take lives. To me, that is one part of following Christ. Do the young fellows in your church enlist in the armed forces?" I asked.

"Well, some of them are being drafted," Carl conceded.

"But they could opt for alternative service like Earl and I have done, couldn't they?"

"I guess they could, but if everyone refused to fight, who would defend our country?"

"Do we trust God or not?" I countered.

"I can admire that as an ideal," said Carl thoughtfully, "but I don't see how it could work in a practical sense."

"But isn't the Word of God practical?" I asked.

"Yes, I know that it has to be."

The intercom crackled, and the ward secretary interrupted. "Johnny, are you there?"

"Yes, I'm right here."

"The food trays are up," she announced.

"I'll be right there," I responded.

"Carl, I have to pass out the trays, but let me say this. We must follow Christ whether the government agrees and regardless of any opposition we might face. Jesus said if we are not willing to bear our cross, we cannot be His disciples."

Carl was quiet for a moment. Then he thoughtfully responded, "I'll have to think about these things. They are different from what I have been taught."

After passing out the trays, I returned to Room 107 to complete Jerry's exercises. Carl had gone to the cafeteria, and I began to do Jerry's blink therapy. I was amazed at his alertness as he blinked eight out of ten times in response to my hand movements in front of his face. And then the thought hit me: *Suppose Jerry can swallow?* Would it be possible to feed him by mouth instead of infusing liquids through those troublesome needles in his thighs? If so, that would rid Jerry of all that edema and swelling!

"Johnny, can you see what is needed in Room 119?" My musings were interrupted by the ward secretary. I entered to find Ernest's wife standing beside him, rubbing his neck lovingly while he clung desperately to his right arm. It was being flung about violently, and Ernest had no control over its movements. His face was twitching spasmodically as well, and his wife was crying softly at seeing her husband so helpless.

"Ernest, if you would like to lie down, I can help you," I offered. He shook his head jerkily, indicating he wanted to remain in his chair. I brought in fresh water and opened the drapery, allowing the evening sun to shine into the room. I was deeply affected by the plight of Ernest's wife as she watched her husband sliding deeper into the canyon of cancer with nothing she could do to prevent his descent.

I continued checking on other patients, but I felt troubled. I knew I could do nothing to help Ernest improve, but I couldn't shake the thought that perhaps we could be doing more for Jerry. I recalled the visitor who had shared his story of having been unconscious for six weeks. He had learned to take food by mouth even before regaining full consciousness. Should I try the plan I was forming?

Circling back to Jerry's room, I found him still alone. I knew what I would do. Turning the vacuum to maximum, I pinched the suction tube shut and inserted it into Jerry's trach. All I would have to do was release that tube to immediately suck up anything that Jerry might inhale. With that in place, I cautiously dipped a drinking straw into a glass of water, held my thumb over its upper end, and released a few drops of water into Jerry's mouth. Nothing happened. I repeated the process until Jerry's mouth slowly began to fill.

When the first straw was empty and Jerry still hadn't tried to swallow, I loaded the second and dribbled in a bit more. Jerry became uncomfortable as his injured brain tried to process what he should do with this new development. His face twitched, showing his discomfort and frustration. Would he choke? I certainly hoped not as I waited with my hand clutching the suction tube.

"Come on, Jerry, swallow," I pleaded softly. His shoulders began to fidget restlessly. *Should I be doing this?* I wondered. *What if . . .* And then it happened! Jerry's Adam's apple bobbed. I was elated. He had swallowed! My hand trembled with excitement as I refilled the straw and repeated the process. This time, Jerry swallowed much more quickly. He could take liquids by mouth!

I could hardly wait until Carl returned. Thelma joined her husband for several hours that evening. Together, they watched with excitement as I demonstrated the progress their son had made.

We reported to the charge nurse that Jerry was taking small amounts of liquid by mouth. She insisted on seeing for herself, and we gladly demonstrated. She duly recorded Jerry's newly acquired ability in his chart for Dr. Glosser to see. The doctor ordered a blended liquid diet to feed Jerry by mouth, and we were able to remove all his IV bags, infusions tubes, and needles.

Following a week of brain scans and tests, doctors determined Martha Blackstone was suffering from a brain tumor. Dr. Glosser, the only neurosurgeon in Zanesville, began preparing his patient for surgery. He pointed out that if nothing was done, the growing tumor would eventually take her life. On the other hand, removing the mass could cause brain damage that would result in memory loss or physical disabilities.

Martha was a quiet, sensitive, middle-aged lady, and this decision weighed heavily upon her. What should she do? She had few visitors and only a small support group. Finally, however, she committed to moving ahead with the surgery. It was a lengthy procedure that required removal of a sizable patch of her skull, cutting through the membrane to expose the brain, and removing the tumor with as little disturbance as possible.

Dr. Glosser successfully removed the tumor, but Martha was kept heavily sedated for several days after her surgery. The doctor was rather pleased with his accomplishment in removing a benign tumor the size of a tennis ball. He spoke of this operation with obvious pride and ordered the hypothermal unit to regulate Miss Blackstone's temperature until her recovery was proceeding as expected.

"Good afternoon, Miss Blackstone," I said as I entered her room. "I'm here to check on this machine again. Have you been all right?" She looked at me with confusion, as though I were vaguely familiar but she couldn't quite place me. She pursed her lips in an effort to speak, but I couldn't understand anything.

"That's fine," I told her. "You rest, and I will check back soon, okay?" She nodded that she understood and closed her eyes as though relieved that she wasn't expected to respond.

I went to Room 120 next, where I met one of Dr. Capp's patients, Mr.

Greg. He suffered from severe back strain and was on bed rest with pelvic traction. Even in traction, he was in constant pain. I saw that the forty-five pounds of traction had shifted him toward the foot of the bed. I needed to help him back into a more comfortable position. Mr. Greg was over six feet tall and husky, but I grasped his shoulders as he hoisted himself up by the trapeze bar, and together we were successful.

"Mr. Greg," I asked, "how long have you had this back pain?"

"Oh," he responded, "I've had it off and on for years, but it's become almost unbearable lately. Several times when I was walking, my right leg just died as I went to take a step, and I fell flat on my face. I can't take too much of that! I don't exactly like doctors," he continued, "but if you need 'em, then you'd better have a good one."

"Do you like Dr. Capp?" I asked.

"I'm told he is as good as they come."

"Does Dr. Capp think this traction will heal your back?"

"Well, he said this was the first step. If it doesn't work, we'll have to think about surgery," Mr. Greg said.

"I know he is a good doctor, and you can trust his judgment," I told him. "I hope for your sake that this will allow your back to heal. I'll make my rounds about bedtime and will give you a back rub then, okay?"

"Sure thing," he said. "I could use a good back rub after lying in bed all day!"

A week later, I learned that Mr. Greg was scheduled for surgery to repair his herniated discs the following Tuesday. We discussed his upcoming procedure, and I asked if he would allow me to be present during his surgery.

"Sure," he responded. "I won't mind at all."

I asked Dr. Capp's permission, and he gave his approval as well. I had seen numerous minor surgeries in ER, but this would be the first major one I would witness.

CHAPTER 13

Major Surgery

On Tuesday, I completed my normal shift by 3 p.m. and reported to surgery by 4:00. The charge nurse instructed me to scrub for five minutes with a stiff brush and strong disinfectant soap. Next, she gave me a green gown to wear over my clothing. While the gown was clean, it was not considered sterile. Therefore, I was not to touch anything in the sterile surgical suite. The surgeons and surgical nurses would be dressed in blue surgical gowns, indicating that they were wearing sterile clothing and gloves and would adhere strictly to sterile procedure.

Mr. Greg was rolled in on a gurney with his IV hooked up and running. Overhead disc lights bathed the surgical table in brilliant white light.

The anesthetist approached the patient and asked, "How are you feeling, Mr. Greg?"

"Not too bad," he responded slowly, already a bit woozy from his pre-op medication.

"Good! Now I'm going to be putting some medicine into your IV to help you go to sleep so we can get started fixing your back, okay?" He was injecting the sodium pentothal even as he spoke. "Now, I want you to count from one to ten for me. Can you do that?" he asked as he slowly advanced the plunger.

Mr. Greg nodded and began, "One, two, thr . . ." His head slumped to one side, and his arm slid off his chest and dangled from the side of the cart. Mr. Greg was out!

The anesthetist tilted the patient's head back and opened the mouth wide. With a laryngoscope, he opened the airway and inserted a breathing tube into Mr. Greg's trachea. When it was properly positioned, he inflated the little rubber balloon to keep it in place during the operation. The patient could now breathe only through this tube.

The attending nurses carefully placed Mr. Greg face down on the surgery table with his bare skin touching a thin metal plate which was lathered with conductive cream. A ground wire was attached to this plate. The nurses lowered the bottom half of the operating table until Mr. Greg's legs were in a kneeling position. His breathing tube was connected to the anesthetist's machine to monitor his breathing and regulate his level of unconsciousness with proper amounts of anesthesia during the operation.

Medical partners Dr. Capp and Dr. Magill walked in after having scrubbed. Introductions were made as the attending nurses assisted them in getting gowned, gloved, and masked. Mr. Greg's back had been shaved and swabbed in antiseptic. A large, sterile, adhesive patch was securely applied to his back. Over his torso, a nurse placed a large sterile drape with an opening that precisely exposed the operation site. This provided a sterile field from which the surgeons could safely work.

Dr. Magill stepped into position and held out his hand for a scalpel. He deftly drew it across the plastic. To my surprise, it appeared the scalpel was so sharp that the plastic and the skin below it could hardly wait to be touched before willingly parting. He followed this first incision with progressively deeper cuts until the back muscles were exposed. As blood pooled in the cavity, it was suctioned out. Dr. Capp quickly moved close to fill the gaping wound with thick, absorbent pads. Each contained a blue stripe that was visible to X-rays in case any pads were ever left inside a patient.

Dr. Magill's hand shot forth again, and the alert attendants immediately gave him half a dozen hemostats for clamping blood vessels. With a sponge in one hand and a hemostat in the other, he dabbed and searched for the severed bleeders. Upon locating one, he tightened a hemostat over its end and clamped it off. He searched for another and repeated the process over and over.

As he worked, he said, "Say, Michael, wasn't that a hot game Zanesville played against Dover on Friday night?"

Our anesthetist exclaimed, "Was it ever! Did you see McLaughlin sink that shot from halfway across the court? It's uncanny the way that boy can play."

"Yes, and the way he dodged that block and still made the shot was absolutely phenomenal!" They discussed basketball, team members, and plays as they worked almost mechanically on the unconscious patient lying before them.

Finally, Dr. Magill had clamped off a dozen or more bleeders with hemostats cluttering the operative site. He then flipped them expertly out of the way, still clamped tightly to their bleeders, and laid them on the sterile plastic. A nurse handed him an electric, pistol-shaped tool with a thin barrel. He touched its point to the first hemostat and activated the electric foot switch. There was a sizzling sound, and a thread of smoke curled out of the open wound as he cauterized the bleeder. "You think McLaughlin will ever go pro?" he wondered as he zapped another hemostat.

"My guess is that he will," offered the anesthetist.

"I agree," said Dr. Magill as he activated, sizzled, and released the last of the hemostats.

Having staunched the major blood flow, they were now ready to proceed with the operation.

A metal spreader came next. Its flat, curled fingers were especially designed to grip the cut edges of the operative site. These meshed with geared connectors that could be turned by a wrench. Dr. Capp expertly cranked the spreader, stretching the opening larger and larger. He reached up to grasp the sterile shield on the overhead light and readjusted its beam to shine directly into the incision. Then, seeing my fascination, he explained, "Stretched tissue heals much more quickly than cut tissue."

"Oh, I see."

Dr. Magill worked his way deeper and deeper until the spine itself came into view. He asked for special pliers equipped with turtle-like jaws and began nipping the upper fins from each of the three exposed vertebrae that had been detached from the connected muscle.

"Miller, over here," commanded Dr. Capp, and I quickly moved to his side of the operating table. Looking over his shoulder, I watched as he poised a tool over a bit of exposed tissue protruding from a vertebra.

"That's the nerve," he said. "Now watch his right leg." He nudged the nerve gently, and Mr. Greg's right leg twitched. He touched the nerve again, and although Mr. Greg was deeply unconscious, his leg responded with another involuntary twitch.

"See, here is the problem," explained Dr. Capp. I leaned closer to see into the depth of the opening, but at that moment I felt a tap on my shoulder. Looking up, I saw an attending nurse shaking her finger rather severely in warning to me! She had been carefully observing and noticed that the front of my green gown had brushed against the back of Dr. Capp's blue gown. I quickly straightened, realizing I had violated surgical protocol since my nonsterile green gown had brushed against his sterile blue gown.

"With movement," Dr. Capp continued, "this herniated disc slips out of the joint and applies pressure against this nerve, causing Mr. Greg extreme pain and loss of control."

Dr. Magill continued nipping away bone from the third vertebra as Dr. Capp carefully maneuvered his instrument below the joint between two vertebrae. With intense concentration and deliberate movements, he slowly squeezed the levers of the tool, closing its jaws over a torn portion of the disc. Moving ever so gently, he extracted half of the torn, degenerated disc. Immediately, the attending nurse extended a tissue basin into which he dropped the fragment. He repeated the process until he had cleaned out all the fragmented discs from the two affected joints.

I continued to watch, utterly fascinated. By this time, Dr. Magill had finished nipping the raised portions from three vertebrae. The wound was filled with sponges and the tension on the spreader partially released.

Dr. Magill then opened a large donor site over the left pelvis, stopped the bleeders, and positioned a handheld retractor. He began working on the pelvic bone with a small surgical hammer and chisel, shaving off the exterior surface of the bone.

"Did you ever notice how the hip muscle developed through man's evolution as he learned to walk upright?" asked Dr. Magill.

The anesthetist responded, "It is truly amazing. I recall seeing that as I did some dissecting in med school."

Dr. Magill continued tapping his chisel, and the curl of bone rising above it reminded me of a carpenter working with wood. "Ever wonder what man was like before he was fully evolved?" he continued.

"That would be interesting to discover, wouldn't it?" The discussion on evolution continued to flow between Dr. Magill and the anesthetist as they worked.

I was shocked by their conversation! I could hardly believe that men as educated and skilled as these would embrace the idea that man evolved from a lower animal. Couldn't they see that the very body upon which they were operating was not only intricately designed but also created in the image and likeness of God?

After chiseling away a sizable area of bone surface, Dr. Magill began working deeper into the interior of the porous pelvic bone. This was the material he needed; without taking his eyes from his work, he handed the tools to the surgical nurse. She received them and immediately placed into his hand a small sharp stainless-steel gouge. With this he harvested the softer bone material from the pelvis until about a half-cup had been placed in a tissue basin.

The doctors applied a bone wax preparation to the gouged-out area of the pelvis to impede bleeding and speed the healing process. They packed sponges into the opening and removed the retractor. This incision would be closed later.

Next, they reopened the initial surgical site, removed the blood-soaked sponges, and scraped the vertebrae until the bone surface began to ooze. At this point, the harvested material from the pelvis was packed tightly about the three prepared vertebrae. "That," said Dr. Capp, "will solidify in a short time, fusing the three vertebrae completely together. Of course, the patient will lose a bit of mobility, but this will relieve the nerve pressure that was causing the severe pain and loss of motor control. He will heal up and be just fine."

A circulating nurse gave the used sponge count as 143. This was tallied with the unused ones, and the total came to the exact figure laid out for this operation. Thus, Dr. Capp was assured there were no sponges left inside his patient to potentially cause an abscess within a few weeks.

The surgeons used chromic suture for the underlying tissue as they began closing the operative sites. This material was designed to dissolve with time, so it would not need to be removed. They placed a drain deep within the main site and extended it well beyond the surface. There, a vacuum receptacle would remove the internal drainage and relieve the surrounding tissue of the need to absorb it, thus speeding the healing process.

As closure began, the anesthetist began reducing the amount of anesthesia to allow Mr. Greg to begin regaining consciousness. He would have to remain in the recovery room for nearly two more hours before being returned to 1-West.

I was very grateful to Dr. Capp and Dr. Magill and thanked them for allowing me this experience. It gave me a greater respect for their skill and deeper compassion for my hurting patients. But it also jarred me to realize that these doctors attributed the marvels of the human body to chance evolution.

As I entered Mr. Greg's room the following day, I asked, "How are you feeling?" He groaned and shook his head. "Man," he exclaimed, "I feel like I've been run over by a dump truck! And my hip hurts as much as my back. What did they do to my hip?"

"Hey," I said, "look on the bright side. Your traction is gone, and your operation is behind you. From here on, things will start getting better. What did Dr. Capp tell you?"

"All he said was that the operation went well and he was pleased with the outcome. He also said that with help, I can get on my feet tomorrow."

The following day, I was ordered to assist Mr. Greg as he was going to stand for the first time since his spinal fusion. As I placed slippers on his feet in preparation, he said, "Boy, I don't know how we are going to do this!"

"That's exactly why I am here," I assured him. "This will be a breeze. Just follow instructions, and we'll do this together. I'm going to roll you onto your left side. Ready?"

"I guess."

"Allow me to do the work. I want to roll your shoulders and hips together so your back doesn't twist. Understand?"

"Sure."

"Here we go, slow and easy. Tell me if you're hurting, and I'll stop."

"It's not too bad," he grimaced.

"There now, are you comfortable on your side?"

"Yeah."

"Good, now I'm going to pull your knees up into a bunny position. How's that?"

"It's okay, I guess," said Mr. Greg.

"I'm going to let you get used to that, and then I'll pull you to the edge of the bed. As I lower your feet toward the floor, I'm going to lift you up sideways so your back remains straight at all times. We're going slow and easy. You ready?"

"I reckon I'm as ready as I'm gonna get," he said as he smiled up at me. I could tell my explanations were easing his anxieties and he was starting to trust me.

"Okay," I said. "Here we go." Slipping my left hand around his knees and my right hand about his neck, I eased him to the edge of the bed. I lowered his legs slowly to the floor even as I lifted him sideways until he was sitting on the bed.

"Uh, I feel a bit lightheaded!" exclaimed Mr. Greg.

"That's perfectly normal," I reassured him. "If you take several deep breaths, it will clear up. Try it," I encouraged, and I breathed deeply to show him. Mr. Greg did as I instructed and was soon smiling. All was well.

"Now, when you think you are ready, we will work together to get you standing on your own two feet. By the way, did Dr. Capp indicate when he might release you?"

"He mentioned I'd have several days of physical therapy before being released."

"That is wise. He may want you to start out with a walker just to be on the safe side. Well, shall we stand up?"

"I suppose so, but . . ."

"But what?" I asked.

"Well I'm pretty big and, well, you're kind of small."

I chuckled. "I know, but you are going to be doing the work. I'm only going to guide you. Now, I want you to place your arms about my neck. That's good. Now, bend your hips but not your back, and lean on me as I back away from the bed. Perfect! Start putting your weight on your feet. More . . . keep your arms locked about my neck. Now straighten your legs. And there you are. You're standing! Better take several deep breaths just to keep from getting lightheaded."

He stood before me, smiling but still a bit shaky. I grasped his shoulders to steady him for several minutes before suggesting that might be enough for the first time. I eased Mr. Greg back onto the edge of the bed. He wanted to sit there for a bit before lying back in his bed.

"Mr. Greg, you really did a fantastic job," I told him. "In a day or two, you'll be walking on your own."

"You think?" he asked hopefully.

"I'm certain you will."

CHAPTER 14

Real Emergencies

One week, we gathered in our rented room at the YMCA each evening for special services. All VS unit members who were not on duty were expected to attend, and we were mightily blessed in doing so. Ministers Andrew Stutzman and Aden Gingerich shared in a week of teaching focused on the Christian ordinances.

On Monday evening, the speaker explained water baptism as an initiatory rite into the visible body of believers, just as Spirit baptism brings a repentant believer into the spiritual body of Christ. Numerous Scriptures showed that water baptism represented cleansing by the blood of Christ and a public testimony of one's desire to faithfully follow Christ.

We also heard teaching on communion that explained the breaking of bread as symbolizing the body of Jesus Christ which was broken for our redemption. The speakers emphasized our unity in Jesus Christ, partly to prepare our hearts for the coming weekend, when we planned to remember the suffering and death of our Lord.

They also spoke of washing one another's feet according to

Christ's example and instruction. In obeying Him, we express our willingness to become one another's servants and to allow others to examine our walk of life.

Brother Aden's compassionate reasoning from the Scriptures helped solidify our faith and practice of Biblical commands, while Brother Andrew's direct expositions anchored that faith in irrefutable Bible truths. These brethren labored each evening to teach us the value of the Christian woman's covered head, the meaning and practice of the Christian greeting of the holy kiss, the ordinance of a godly marriage, and anointing with oil and prayer for healing.

On Sunday, these brethren led us in a communion service in which we rejoiced in the sacrifice of Jesus Christ and reconfirmed our commitment to Him. It was a special time of fellowship and spiritual uplift, and we were thankful for the pastors' willingness to serve us.

A patient of Dr. Wise came into ER with a bloodied cloth wrapped about his hand. We ushered him into an available room and carefully unwrapped the makeshift bandage. Where the rounded tip of his middle finger should have been, there was only a flat spot, dripping blood.

He had been mowing his lawn when the push mower began making an unusual noise. Thinking something was tangled in the blade, our patient reached down, grabbed the frame of his running lawn mower, and lifted it to investigate the problem. He curled his finger a bit too far inside the mower's frame, and the blade neatly cut the flesh from his fingertip.

By the time Dr. Wise arrived, we had scrubbed the injured hand and applied an absorbent bandage, but we were not able to staunch the flow of blood. Dr. Wise, however, placed a tourniquet on the finger and injected it with a heavy dose of Xylocaine. After making sure the bone had not been injured and was still covered with a thin layer of flesh, he injected the inside of the man's wrist as well. Opening the pack of suture material, Dr. Wise unwound it from the sterile card which held it. He loosened the tourniquet momentarily and allowed just a little blood to flow to the injured tip. Laying the sterile card to the fingertip, he then retightened the tourniquet and stopped the blood once again. With a scissors, he cut a pattern around the blood spot on the card. Laying this pattern on the numbed area of the man's wrist, he neatly cut the skin around it with his surgical scalpel. I was in awe at what I was witnessing and at the explanation Dr. Wise gave as he worked.

"You see," he said, "the skin on the inside of the wrist is quite elastic and makes an excellent skin graft. It can be stretched back into place when closing the donor site. Miller, could you steady his finger?"

I reached under the sterile drape and held the base of the finger as Dr. Wise carefully placed the freshly cut skin graft onto the raw fingertip. With my free hand, I repositioned the light so its most intense beam fell directly on the spot where Dr. Wise was working. He commented, "I appreciate the way you notice where the brightest light is needed. Thank you!"

"You have my father to thank for that," I explained.

"Oh, is he a doctor?"

"No," I chuckled, "he's an auto mechanic. As a boy, I used to crawl under cars with him and hold the light while he made repairs. When I daydreamed and allowed the beam to wander off the work area, he would tell me, 'Johnny, shine the light where I am working.' I often think of that when I'm working with you doctors in ER."

"Your father did a good job of teaching you," Dr. Wise observed.

By this time, he was completing the fifth suture to hold the graft securely in its place. Next, he concentrated on closing the donor site and demonstrated how easily the skin of the wrist could be stretched across the bare spot.

We were surprised, however, when he removed the drape and loosened the tourniquet from the finger. As we watched, the blood flow bulged under the skin graft like a tiny balloon. Dr. Wise made a small slit in the grafted skin to relieve the pressure and explained as it deflated, "The cells of the skin graft must be in direct contact with the cells of the finger in order for the graft to take. Otherwise the skin would die." He supplied a snug, absorbent bandage with a protective finger guard and released his patient with orders to see him in his office in three days. I loved the way Dr. Wise freely shared his knowledge with anyone who was interested, which I certainly was.

As the afternoon progressed, we had the usual flow of patients in and out, but nothing spectacular until nearly 5 p.m. About ten miles outside of Zanesville, a tractor on a hillside rolled over and severely injured its middle-aged driver, David Emery. A telephone call notified our emergency department, and the ambulance, with siren wailing, soon screeched to a stop at our door. The attendants sprang out and opened the back door. With swift, sure movements they rolled the patient into ER and released him into our care.

David Emery was the father of a respected nurse who worked on the third floor of the hospital. She had just arrived home from working her shift when she was told to rush back to the hospital because her father had been gravely injured.

One look was enough to convince me this was an urgent case. The patient suffered a disfigured forearm, and his left leg had an unnatural bend midway between the knee and ankle. I was sure both were broken. Mr. Emery's color was a sickly grey, and he appeared to be going into shock from his pain and injuries.

We hurriedly transferred him onto our bed and checked his blood pressure. It was very low, 90 over 50. I was ordered to watch the patient and keep tabs on his blood pressure while the nurse rushed to make the necessary phone calls. Dr. White was called, and he barked into the phone, "I'm on my way. Alert surgery. We may need them!"

I took Mr. Emery's blood pressure every five minutes, and it continued dropping. I prayed that Dr. White would arrive in time. The next time I took his blood pressure, it was 60 over 30. This patient was going to die if he didn't get help fast! Five minutes later, it showed 40 over 0!

Mr. Emery opened his eyes at this point, and said with a look of stark finality, "I'm going!"

I raised my voice in alarm and said, "No you're not! Take a couple of deep breaths for me. Listen, Dr. White is due to arrive any minute. You hang in there! Don't give up!"

Mr. Emery took several deep breaths as a car screeched to a stop outside. A door slammed, and Dr. White dashed through the hallway, ripping off his dinner jacket and flinging it in one direction while his tie flew the other way.

"Where?" he shouted. The nurse rushed ahead of him into our room, where he grabbed the patient's wrist and felt for the feeble pulse. His practiced eye took in the ashen color, the beads of sweat, the cold, clammy skin, the drooping eyelids, and the slow, distant responses of the patient.

To the nurse, he said, "Prepare me a normal saline IV." As she hurried to comply, he snapped, "Miller, get me a cut-down tray, gloves, a scalpel, and a number 23 blade, quickly!"

I ran to the cupboard, retrieved the items, and set them on the stand in front of him. In that short time, Dr. White had removed the patient's right shoe and stocking and rolled up the pant leg. Opening the tray, he pulled on his gloves and hurriedly injected Xylocaine just above the ankle. He swabbed the ankle and immediately made a vertical cut without even giving the anesthesia time to numb the area. He located the vein and threaded the line into it. The nurse was ready, and in mere moments the saline was running—not dripping—rapidly into his veins!

"Call the lab," he ordered. "We'll need an emergency blood type and cross-match, and let surgery know we are coming in!"

While listening to the abdomen with a stethoscope, Dr. White said, "Miller, get me a paracentesis tray!" I brought it, and he began working with the special needle designed to remove blood or fluid from the abdomen.

"Miller, get air splints on his arm and leg!" the doctor ordered.

"Yes, sir," I responded as I headed to the supply room.

The lab technician arrived and drew blood. Dr. White said, "Have multiple units readied for surgery, and please hurry!"

Mr. Emery's daughter arrived in time to speak a few words to her father as she squeezed his hand. Moments later, the green-suited men from surgery arrived and wheeled Mr. Emery away. Following the cleanup and paperwork, things returned to normal ER pace. I hung Dr. White's jacket and tie in the hallway, wondering how things were progressing in surgery.

Later, I would learn that Dr. White and his partner, Dr. Irving, said almost nothing during the surgery. Each seemed to know what the other was thinking as they worked in silent desperation, doing all they could to save Mr. Emery's life.

Blunt trauma force had burst the liver, and the internal bleeding was profuse. At first, the VS unit member working in surgery was compressing bags of blood by hand. Finally, they began putting the bags into blood pressure cuffs and compressing them to force blood into the patient as fast as possible.

Dr. Irving scooped double handfuls of clotted blood out of the abdominal cavity even as suction was attempting to draw away the incoming blood. Finally, Dr. White could clearly see the lacerated liver, and he began the tedious job of suturing those life-threatening lacerations with woven silver thread. With the skill of a practiced surgeon, he worked quickly and efficiently, being careful not to tear the soft liver tissue. Those silver sutures would remain in Mr. Emery's body for the rest of his life.

Finally, the internal repairs were completed and the physicians began closure. Mr. Emery stayed in recovery for part of the night before being admitted to the Intensive Care Unit. His first twenty-four hours would be the most critical.

An exhausted surgeon stopped in ER to retrieve his jacket and tie before heading home for some much-needed rest. He brought with him a liver needle with several inches of braided silver attached for our examination. He explained that the fine silver threads were actually braided together to create a broader surface area, thus reducing the potential for tearing the soft liver. He explained that the body also tolerates silver better than many other materials.

The following day, I was back on 1-West working with Jerry. He was fidgety and uncomfortable. I conferred with the charge nurse, and she suggested I make sure his catheter was free of obstructions. I did, and all was well. I checked his urine output, and it was normal. What else could it be? Rushing in and out of his room while attending numerous other responsibilities, I had that niggling sense that all was not well. But I just couldn't put my finger on what the problem might be.

I had a bit more time near the end of my shift, so I stood at the foot of his bed to observe him. Something was clearly bothering Jerry. He was twitching and wriggling in discomfort. I moved closer and watched more intently—and then I heard it! Jerry's inhalations were normal, but his exhalations were raspy and constricted. Something was amiss.

I suctioned his trach tube, but there was no mucus to speak of. I was puzzled. Then I felt led to grasp the flange of his metal trach tube and gently lift it as far as the neck strap allowed. Jerry's breathing immediately sounded free and normal. When I released the tube, his exhalations became raspy and constricted once again.

I retrieved a sticky foam pad from the bandage cart and took it into Jerry's room. From this material, I was able to cut shims to raise the metal trach tube a three-eighth inch out of Jerry's throat. He breathed normally, and his fidgeting ceased. I surmised that the tip of his metal trach tube had rubbed a raised irritation on his trachea. It was probably drawn aside by his inhalations, but was partially obstructing the tube when he exhaled.

I explained all this to the charge nurse and showed her my remedy, but I was surprised by her reaction. She said, "You should never have applied those shims without Dr. Glosser's explicit orders!"

Following her into the nurses' station, I listened as she phoned Dr. Glosser. She explained Jerry's breathing difficulties but withheld the fact that we had already solved the problem. When she asked him what we should do, Dr. Glosser considered for a bit and then suggested we place shims under the trach tube flange to raise it and allow Jerry to breathe normally. With a smile of satisfaction, the nurse hung up and recorded on the chart that we had followed the doctor's orders.

Four days later, I was assigned to work in ICU. At report, the first patient on the list was Mr. Emery, and I listened with particular interest.

"Mr. Emery, age fifty-three, patient of Doctors White and Irving, fourth day post-op emergency surgery. Repair of lacerated liver sustained by tractor accident. Fractured left tibia and fibula to be reduced and cast by Dr. Lance when he has gained more strength. The same with left radius and ulna."

We paused as a young man in military uniform was ushered past the office where we were seated. The outgoing charge nurse explained, "This visitor is Mr. Emery's son who was granted leave and flown home from Vietnam, where he is serving in the U.S. Army. He came to see his father at the family's request, not knowing if Mr. Emery would live or die. His coming was kept secret from Mr. Emery. He will be surprised!"

She continued with report, picking up where she had left off. "Dr. White has ordered around-the-clock blood pressure—"

Froomp! A sound like a sack of potatoes hitting the floor stopped her short. Jumping to her feet and tossing the patient record book onto her chair, the nurse dashed out of the office and into Mr. Emery's cubicle, where she stopped short. The soldier son was sprawled on the floor, passed out cold. The combination of jet lag from flying halfway around the world and the sight of his father so near death had been too much for his constitution.

With smelling salts and a little assistance from a cold, wet cloth, we soon had him sitting in a chair with a glass of water to refresh himself. The charge nurse concluded report, and the shift change went forward without a hitch.

CHAPTER 15

Suicidal and OB Patients

My continuing work with Jerry drew me close to his family, and we gained mutual respect for each other's religious beliefs. However, we also discussed our differences. Carl was firmly convinced that the Church of Christ, of which he was a member, was the only legitimate church. Yet he admired the faithfulness he witnessed in the VS personnel who cared for his son.

As I tidied Jerry's bed and exercised his limbs, we discussed tithing. I voiced my belief of the importance of giving to the Lord's work before spending for personal needs. I used the pattern in 1 Corinthians 16:2—upon *the first day* of the week we are to give as the Lord has prospered us. This naturally led into related subjects, and I asked, "How do the members of your church observe the Lord's Day?"

Carl responded, "Well, they attend church, sing, pray, and listen to the Word of God being preached."

"They don't work on Sunday, do they?" I wondered.

"Well, of course, there are those who have jobs in factories and are required to work on Sunday, but there's nothing they can do about that."

"Wait a minute," I objected. "What do you mean, there is nothing they can do about that? Couldn't they find jobs where they would have Sunday free as a day of rest and worship?"

"Well," Carl defended, "a factory just doesn't give you that choice."

"But they *could* find jobs where there would be no conflict with observing the Lord's Day. Don't they have a conscience against making Sunday just another workday?"

Flicking my hands in front of his son's face and monitoring his level of consciousness, I waited for Carl's response. I was thrilled to note that Jerry blinked every time.

Following a thoughtful pause, Carl said, "Wait a minute, Johnny. You work on Sunday. In fact, Jerry came in on a Saturday evening, and you pulled a double shift and worked on into Sunday, didn't you?"

"Yes, Carl, I did. Sick people need care even on the Lord's Day, but that night when Jerry needed someone to "special" him, I clocked out."

"You mean you watched my son during the Sunday morning shift *after* you clocked out?" he asked in surprise.

"That's right, I am not comfortable doing unnecessary labor on the Lord's Day. Not only that, but we VS workers feel so privileged to not be forced to serve in the military service that we *gladly* donate our time in caring for the sick on Sundays."

A smile of understanding spread slowly across Carl's face, and he shook his head. "That's amazing!" was all he said.

As I started for the clothes chute with a load of dirty linens, the ward secretary told me, "Someone called from ER, and they want you there."

"Okay, I'll head right over."

I gave a mock salute to the nurse, Mrs. Truby, upon my arrival in ER. “Orderly Miller reporting for duty. How may I help you?”

She smiled faintly and motioned me to follow her. In the secluded corner of the ER nurses’ station, her expression became serious, and she lowered her voice. Instantly, my frivolity evaporated.

She explained, “We have a patient by the name of Roger Benson, twenty-five years old, in Room 1. His condition is almost certainly due to attempted suicide.”

This was new to me. I had never worked with a patient who had tried to take his own life.

“It appears he shot himself through the mouth,” Mrs. Truby continued, “but miraculously survived somehow. We have already done X-rays, and the doctor is coming. In the meantime, we nurses would feel better if you took care of Roger.”

“Okay, but what do you want me to do?” I asked.

“You will need to clean him up,” she explained. “There is quite a bit of blood from the exit wound in the back of his neck. Get a hospital gown on him and procure a routine urine specimen for admission. And it would be good if you could talk with him and let him know he is going to be admitted.”

“All right.” I sighed. “I may as well get started.”

“Keep your call button handy in case you need help.” She waved a dismissal, and I walked apprehensively toward Room 1 with a prayer in my heart. I entered the room acting far more normal than I felt.

“Good evening, Mr. Benson,” I said. “I’m the orderly who is going to help you get cleaned up and ready to see the doctor. Let’s raise the head of your bed, okay?” With that accomplished, I moved to the head of the bed and surveyed the back of the patient’s neck. Most of the blood was dried, and I could see it had come from a small bullet hole two inches below the base of his skull.

I took a sterile basin from the cupboard, carefully unwrapped it, and filled it with sterile water. Adding a disinfectant soap, I used sterile pads to gently wash the dried blood away from Roger's neck wound. As I began at the exit wound and spiraled outward to avoid further contamination, I said, "Let me know if I hurt you. Some of this blood is dried on rather hard. What time did this happen?" I hoped I sounded relaxed.

"Oh, about two hours ago," he said without offering further information.

I noticed that when he needed to raise his head and shoulders as I scrubbed, he tugged on the bed rail with his left hand to help sit up. His right hand did not move at all, and I wondered if it might have been injured somehow. After all the blood was cleaned up and he was settled, I investigated his right arm a bit more. Maneuvering to the right side of his bed, I held out the urinal, explaining that I needed a urine sample for the lab. There was a momentary hesitation, but his right arm never moved. Instead, Roger reached across his body with his left hand and took the urinal from my grasp. I continued filling out the ER registration form. Later, I asked Mr. Benson to squeeze my hands as I clasped both of his. His left hand responded normally, but his right hand felt completely dead. Apparently, it had sustained severe nerve damage.

Taking a portable light, I asked Mr. Benson to open his mouth so I could inspect his throat. The small-caliber bullet hole was very noticeable. It had passed through his tonsil and narrowly avoided hitting the spine and causing complete paralysis. The bullet must have severed the nerve to his right arm, rendering it completely paralyzed. What a price this poor man had to pay! If only he had known the Lord and had a purpose to live.

"Just how did this happen?" I asked, carrying the basin to the sink. I listened intently as I rinsed the basin and disposed of the soiled pads.

"Uh," he began. "I mean, you know, my girlfriend was mad, and we argued. She pointed the rifle at me, and I opened my mouth to holler for her to stop, and she . . . she just shot."

"Well, you do understand that with such a serious injury, a patient is usually admitted for observation?" I asked.

"Oh," he responded. "I see."

Although his story sounded plausible, I doubted that Roger was telling me the truth. The doctor finally came, and following a lengthy private consultation, Mr. Benson was admitted to 4–North where the psychiatrist would try to help him work through his difficulties.

There were no other patients in ER, and Mrs. Truby said, "It's late, and things are quiet now. I need a break. The cafeteria is closed, so I'm going to get a bite at the snack shop. Do you want anything?"

"No," I replied. "I had supper."

When the nurse noticed my anxious look, she quickly added, "You'll be all right. I won't be gone long."

I knew she was not supposed to leave ER with only an orderly present. I had limited training and was far from qualified to be alone in the emergency room. What would I do if a patient with major injuries came in?

As she headed for the door, the nurse tossed over her shoulder, "It's late. I doubt anyone will be coming, but if they do, just take down their information. I'll be back soon." The door to the main floor clicked shut behind her.

I emptied trash cans, put in fresh plastic liners, and washed up several instruments. Then, while I changed linens on a cart, the electric lock on the ER entrance door buzzed. A closed-circuit camera allowed our operator to monitor the entrance door after regular hours and admit doctors or patients by remotely unlocking the door.

I hoped the buzzer simply indicated the arrival of a doctor making late rounds, and I hoped he wouldn't ask for the nurse. Moving into the hallway to see if my assumption was correct, I saw a man and a woman slowly making their way into ER. The man had his arm around the lady, and she appeared to have trouble walking.

"Come right this way," I instructed, motioning for them to enter the closest examining room. However, at that moment, the poor lady doubled over in pain. She clung to her husband, unable to take another step for a few moments. The spasm seemed to ease, and she took several more steps before being incapacitated by another jolt of pain. I helped her into the examining room and set out a small stepstool to help her climb onto the cot. I positioned a pillow under her head, raised the side rail, grabbed a clip board, and began asking questions.

"May I have your name, please?"

"She is my wife, Abigail Jenkins," the man interjected. "She's having a miscarriage, and she's bleeding!"

I hid the chill that shot up my spine. I had not the slightest idea what I was supposed to do!

"Who is your doctor?" I asked, stifling my rising panic.

"Dr. Morris," Mrs. Jenkins groaned as another spasm racked her body. I quickly recorded the information and headed for the phone. This was too much. I lifted the receiver to page Nurse Truby, then stopped, uncertain what to say. If I told the operator to page Mrs. Truby and request her to return to the ER, every worker in the hospital would know she had left her station. She would be furious with me for exposing her absence!

I replaced the receiver without dialing and hurried back toward the patient's room. Another deep, agonizing groan pushed me into action. I spun back to the phone, and this time, I dialed the operator. I listened impatiently as it rang three times.

"Operator. How may I help you?" At that moment, I heard the click of a door latch and glanced at the door to see Nurse Truby striding into ER!

"Operator!" repeated the voice on the phone. I gently replaced the receiver without uttering a word, and then frantically motioned for Nurse Truby to hurry. I pointed into the examining room and hissed, "Miscarriage!" as she whizzed past.

"Good evening," she calmly greeted the patient as she entered the examining room. Releasing the brakes on the ER cot, she pushed it toward the door. "We will transfer you directly to OB." Motioning to Mr. Jenkins, she said, "Follow us, please."

Ten minutes later, Mrs. Truby returned with the empty cot to be scrubbed and fitted with fresh linens. She kindly informed me that when ER received a pregnant patient, our only responsibility was to take them immediately to OB. "They don't even stop here," she explained.

"I–I'm so sorry," I sputtered in embarrassment. "I didn't know!"

"Hey," she said, "it's not your fault. No one had informed you, but you will know if it ever happens again. OB patients go straight to OB without stopping in ER."

"Good," I said. "Now I know."

Earl and I alternated from afternoon to day shifts in ER every two weeks. Although this transition was a bit hard on the body clock, it gave us a broader spectrum of experience and exposed us to the doctors' individual preferences. For example, Dr. White used Zephyrin chloride as an antiseptic when cleansing wounds, while Dr. Donalds said, "Don't put that on my ER tray. You can grow bugs in that stuff! Give me hydrogen peroxide!" Dr. Lance always asked for Johnson & Johnson casting material because he said its plastic reinforcements made it more water resistant. But Dr. Capp preferred the plain, old-fashioned plaster.

Two weeks had passed, and I was on evening shift working with Nurse Truby once more. Early in the evening, Stanley Thompson was brought in by ambulance. He had been knocked from a high catwalk in a factory when a crane operator made a mismove. The patient had fallen twenty feet and landed on a pile of crushed limestone. He sustained a large laceration to his scalp, but avoided broken bones. He was, however, complaining of shortness of breath and lower right chest pain. Our lung specialist, Dr. Wise, ordered a chest X-ray from the portable machine that could be rolled into the examining room.

Dr. Wise continued examining Mr. Thompson as we waited for the X-rays to be developed. He called, "Miller, step this way a minute."

I moved to the doctor's side. Guiding my hand, Dr. Wise placed it on the bare chest of the patient, saying, "I want you to feel this. Do you recognize the bubbly feel of his skin?"

It felt like miniature bubble wrap. "I feel it, but what causes it?" I asked.

"This is an indication that our patient has suffered a pneumothorax," he explained. "The lung has been compressed so severely that air has been forced through the wall of the lung and is trying to find its way out of the chest cavity. These little bubbles you feel are tiny pockets of air working their way outward through the chest wall and even through the skin.

"Mr. Thompson," he continued, turning to the patient, "we will have to admit you. Once you are stabilized, we may have to do something further to remove this air. But for the moment, we are much more concerned about your overall condition. You have suffered a powerful blow to the chest, and I am most concerned about that."

The X-rays arrived, and Dr. Wise placed them on the viewing monitor. "Look at this!" he exclaimed, tracing a horizontal line across the lower third of the lung area. "That is blood accumulating in the bottom of his chest cavity. The patient will have to be carefully monitored, and we will have to remove this blood to keep the lung from collapsing further."

The patient was admitted to 1-West, Room 121, and ER quieted down. By 9:30 p.m., Nurse Truby felt she needed a break and said she was running down to the snack shop for something to eat. "I won't be gone long," she said as she headed for the door. Remembering the earlier episode, I hated the thought of being left alone in ER. I busied myself with routine cleanup while twenty uneventful minutes dragged by with no sign of Mrs. Truby.

The quiet peace of ER was shattered by the rasping buzz of the entrance lock being activated. I glanced down the hall to see the all-too-familiar scene of an anxious husband supporting a plump little wife. But even with his assistance, she was having a hard time making headway. Every few steps, a wave of pain doubled her over. *Oh my,* I thought, *she must be transported straight to OB, and that will mean ER is completely deserted. If a doctor walks in and finds ER empty, Mrs. Truby will be in big trouble. I'll rush this patient to OB and be back in record time. Hopefully, no one else will come!*

"Stay right there!" I ordered. "I'm coming." Grabbing a wheelchair, I positioned it right in front of the patient, locked its wheels, and eased her into it. "Follow me," I barked to her husband as I started down the long corridor toward the elevator at a rapid pace. Her husband was having a hard time keeping up, but I thought he could catch up while we waited for the elevator. My thoughts were interrupted as my patient looked up at me quizzically and asked,

"Honey, where are you taking me?"

"To OB," I said, confident that this time I was doing the right thing.

"But," she sputtered indignantly, "I'm not pregnant!"

"Oh, excuse me!" I said, deeply mortified. Making a U-turn, I hurried back the way I had come and placed her in the examining room. I hid my blushing face behind a clipboard and began asking the questions I should have asked in the first place. I tried to use as much time as possible to allow Mrs. Truby to return to her station.

"Who is your doctor?" I asked. "Name and address? Describe your symptoms. At what time did you first notice this pain? Is it localized? Would you describe it as a sharp pain or a dull ache? Has the pain moved from where it first began, or is it still in the same place?" I was racking my brain to think of more professional-sounding questions when Nurse Truby finally returned from her break. She made the appropriate phone calls, and the lady was admitted to 3-East.

A week later, while weaving through a crowded area near the elevators, a patient in a passing wheelchair reached out and stopped me. "Say," she asked, "weren't you on duty the night I came in?" It was the lady I had tried to take to OB!

"Yes," I sheepishly admitted. "I was."

"Well, I need to show you something," she said, digging into the depths of a large purse as the crowd surged around us. She extracted a glass medicine vial, its open end plugged with a cotton ball securely taped into place.

"Look at this!" she exclaimed. "How could something so little cause such terrible pain?"

Down in the bottom of the vial was a tiny white crystal about twice the size of a large grain of sand.

"They didn't have to do surgery," she beamed. "I passed this kidney stone all by myself!"

"Wow!" I exclaimed. "It looks kind of like a tiny glass star with sharp points sticking out in every direction. No wonder it hurt!"

"I thought you would be interested," she smiled. "I'm glad I got to see you before I was discharged. And now I am on my way home," she announced, placing her kidney stone back into her purse for safekeeping. The volunteer who was transporting the patient smiled at me as I wished the patient well, and they continued on their way. It was obvious she had forgiven me for almost taking her to OB for the birth of her kidney stone, and now I had to extend the same grace to myself.

CHAPTER 16

Crisis!

I had just completed registering my afternoon TPRs when Dr. Wise stepped into the nurses' station. "Miller," he asked, "would you have a free moment?"

"Sure," I responded, and followed him into Room 121 where Mr. Thompson was the patient. "We performed surgery this morning on Mr. Thompson," Dr. Wise explained. "I inserted a tube into his lower chest. As you can see, the tube connects to a suction machine that applies gentle but constant suction. Notice how the fluid in the tube fluctuates with Mr. Thompson's breathing. The vacuum is slowly pulling the fluid from his chest cavity and into this receptacle. It will take several days to rid his chest of all the fluid buildup. Now, I believe you have some experience as a plumber," he continued with a smile, "so I would expect you understand the flow of liquids, kinked tubing, and air traps that could hinder this necessary evacuation, right?"

"Yes," I responded, "that is true."

"I would like to make you responsible to check in on Mr. Thompson several times per shift, just to be sure all is in working order. Could you do that for me? You see," he continued, "I stopped in earlier and found kinked tubing hidden under a fold of bed clothing. It had stopped the drainage." He turned to his patient. "We cannot afford that, can we, Mr. Thompson?"

"That's right, Doc." Mr. Thompson coughed. "I need to heal so I can get out of here."

"We are going to do everything we can to get that lung fully inflated, and a critical part of that is the removal of fluid and air from the chest cavity. Has your cough improved at all?" the doctor asked.

"Yes, it only bothers me now when I talk." Here Mr. Thompson coughed again. "Or when I take an extra deep breath."

"Good. I'll check on you tomorrow and see how you are progressing."

I kept close tabs on Mr. Thompson and found the fluid level in the suction receptacle was slowly but steadily increasing. I also learned that by neatly coiling the excess tubing and securing it to the foot of his bed, the straight descent into the suction machine was aided by gravity. This was a decided improvement.

Two days later, the drain tube was removed and Mr. Thompson's chest opening closed. The following day, Dr. Wise asked me to bring Mr. Thompson to the ER for a minor surgical procedure. The operative site was prepared with an antiseptic scrub and a shave. A little injection of Xylocaine numbed the tissue, and Dr. Wise was poised to begin.

I adjusted the light, and Dr. Wise made a small incision just below the collarbone between the first and second ribs. As he worked, he explained, "The linings of our bodies, such as our skin or abdominal or chest linings, are the most sensitive to pain."

He slowly worked long-nosed surgical pliers deep into the incision, reminding me that stretched tissue heals much faster than cut tissue. He pushed deeper into the tissue and opened the pliers, stretching and spreading. This formed a deep channel. Suddenly, there was the hissing sound of escaping air, and a satisfied smile spread over the doctor's face.

"Now we are making progress," he said. "This air was trapped and forming a bubble between the lung and the ribcage. The moist surfaces of the lung and ribcage bind them to each other, rather like two pieces of glass with several drops of water between them. However, a pocket of air between the lung and ribcage breaks that surface cohesion, and the lung simply collapses."

As he spoke, he placed a short, perforated tube through the channel and a short way into the ribcage. He then stitched it securely in place. With a bit of gauze and tape, Dr. Wise completed his operation and clamped off the tube. He asked us to move the patient back into his room on 1-West.

Dr. Wise met us there an hour later and set up a unique system to extract the unwanted air from Mr. Thompson's chest. He attached the tubing from the chest to a metal tube that extended one inch below the surface of the water in a receptacle which was vented to the atmosphere. Each time Mr. Thompson exhaled, a slight positive pressure was exerted on his chest tube, forcing a tiny bubble through the tubing, up through the water, and into the vented receptacle. When Mr. Thompson inhaled, the slight negative pressure was not enough to draw water up the tubing, thus forming an efficient one-way air valve. In four days, Mr. Thompson's lung was fully expanded, his tube extracted, and he was dismissed to go home.

Back in ER the following week, I was working the 3:00 to 11:00 shift with Nurse Janet. At 8:30, she received a call asking her to slip over to 1-West for a few minutes. She soon returned with the shocking news that Jerry Dalton was not doing well. He had become increasingly fidgety and nervous, and his temperature was elevated.

Someone from the Daltons' church had volunteered to stay with Jerry for the night so Carl and Thelma could spend the evening with their two daughters.

"It's strange," commented Nurse Janet, "but do you think that even in Jerry's unconscious state, he might realize that his parents are not present?"

"All I know is that over the past month, his level of consciousness certainly has progressed. Have they called Dr. Glosser?" I asked.

"That's the problem," the nurse explained. "The staff have called everywhere they can think of, but they cannot locate Dr. Glosser! Not only that, but they've called the contact numbers for the Dalton family, and no one knows where Jerry's parents are. The reason they called me to 1-West was because I've worked with Jerry and they wanted my advice."

"I've 'specialed' Jerry for nearly four months," I said, "and he has never had an elevated temp since his initial recovery from brain surgery. What is his temperature?"

"It was 103, but it has been steadily climbing."

"How's he acting?" I asked.

"He is very agitated and restless," she responded. "He's constantly twisting and turning as if he's in pain. I don't know what to tell them."

"Why don't they put the hypothermia unit on him to keep his temperature from going dangerously high?" I asked. "Wouldn't that eliminate the danger of further brain damage?"

"Yes," she responded, "they would like to, but they cannot find the doctor to obtain the order."

"Order?" I protested. "Dr. Glosser has a *standing order* that any of his head trauma patients can have the hypothermia unit applied whenever needed! That's standard procedure with him. I know, because I have seen the order."

"Okay, but they haven't been able to find that order," she explained.

"Let me go over," I begged. "I know there's an order for Jerry to have that unit as needed!"

"You're sure about that?"

"I certainly am! May I go?"

"No, you stay here," she told me. "I'm going over again to see if we can find that order."

I busied myself scrubbing used ER utensils to be sterilized later. As I worked, I prayed, "Oh God, help them find Dr. Glosser. Help them find the order. Help them find Jerry's parents!"

Nurse Janet returned. "Jerry's temp is now 104, and he has gone into seizures!" she exclaimed. "I went through every last page in his huge file, and there is no order there from Dr. Glosser for the hypothermia unit. It just is not there!"

"Please let me go over," I pleaded. "I've seen that order, and I know it is there. Don't you remember Jerry was on the machine to stabilize his temperature right after his surgery? That would never have happened without a specific order!"

"That's right, I do remember!" Nurse Janet exclaimed. "I'm going back over to see what I can do."

Once again, I was stuck in ER, but with all my heart I wanted to be with Jerry on 1-West. Until clockout time at 11 p.m., emergency care handled a case of flu, a broken wrist, and a patient with mild symptoms of heart disease. I stood at the clock with my timecard in hand, and the moment our shift was ended, I clocked out and dashed for 1-West.

As I rushed through the door into Room 107, the charge nurse and the night supervisor were bending over Jerry. He was flushed, and his face and head were jerking about uncontrollably. His arms and legs were in constant spastic movement. His entire body was convulsing heavily, and his breathing was erratic and raspy. They had placed an ice bag on each leg to try reducing his fever. But despite their best efforts, his temperature had risen to 106 and remained there for quite some time. I was appalled! The nursing supervisor walked past me, shaking her head, and I followed.

"Please ma'am!" I begged. "The hypothermia unit is sitting idle in Room 106. That patient hasn't used it for the past month. Just let me roll it into Jerry's room and get him situated with it. We will bring his temperature down in a matter of minutes."

She looked at me sadly and exclaimed, "I *cannot* let you do that without an order!"

"But," I persisted, "I'm just an orderly. What are they going to do—fire me?"

She raised her voice. "No, you cannot do it!" Then her tone softened, and she continued, more to herself than to me. "We can't locate the doctor. We've called the police to try and find Jerry's parents. There is no order here!"

"But ma'am," I interjected, "there is an order, as with all of Dr. Glosser's head trauma patients. I have seen it."

"You've seen it?"

"Yes, I read it in Jerry's chart with my very own eyes. I *know* it is there!"

"I've looked all through his chart," she said, "but I will do it again."

I followed as she strode into the nurses' station and spun the huge Rolodex file to "D" and pulled out Jerry Dalton's thick file. I watched, hoping against hope as she painstakingly flipped page after page from the beginning to the very end as the minutes ticked

Jerry's missing file was finally found in the large Rolodex.

slowly by. She found no order on the hypothermia unit for Jerry. Pausing, she flipped back to the first page and stared at it for a long moment, then asked, "When was Jerry admitted?"

"Near the beginning of July," I said.

"That's strange," she said, pointing to Jerry's file. "The very first page is dated August 24."

"But that can't be right," I insisted. "I cared for him post-op the very evening he came in, and that was around the fourth of July."

"Hmm," said the supervisor as she thoughtfully spun the Rolodex file again. Suddenly, her hand shot out, and she pulled an unmarked file from the slot marked "Miscellaneous." Her head bent forward in concentration as she opened it and began flipping pages. She stopped, and her shoulders sagged as she said, "Here's the order! Put that unit on Jerry!"

In a flash, I was into Room 106, retrieving the heavy, liquid-filled rubber blankets and lugging them into Jerry's room. Our nursing supervisor helped roll Jerry's convulsing body to one side while placing the blanket under him. They covered him with the second one as I rolled the machine into place.

Inserting the temperature probe and hooking up the tubing, I fired up the machine. But in my excitement, I momentarily forgot to open its vent. With that corrected, the machine began the daunting task of cooling the volume of room temperature alcohol in the blankets, tubing, and reservoir. However, within several minutes it had begun to make progress, and within fifteen minutes Jerry's internal body temperature, although still high, had dropped three degrees. His convulsions also diminished, and we rejoiced that his crisis had peaked and things were looking better.

"So, just where did you find the order for the unit?" wondered the charge nurse.

"Jerry has been here so long," explained the night supervisor, "that not all of his papers fit in his main file. There is a miscellaneous file where I found the order, written shortly after his admission."

"Jerry should have had this hours ago," commented the charge nurse, and we all agreed.

It was midnight, and I was thinking of heading home when Jerry's parents came in, looking haggard and worried. They had stopped to eat at a restaurant to celebrate their first time in months to just be together. After leaving the restaurant, they were nearly home when the police stopped them. They were shocked to receive the urgent message to return immediately to the hospital. They arrived just in time to see the last of their son's seizures as they stood anxiously at Jerry's bedside. The supervisor took them aside and explained, "We do not understand what caused Jerry's spiked temperature and seizures. But it is possible that he sensed neither of you were with him, and his agitation could have triggered this crisis."

In the wee hours of the morning, Thelma took their friend back to her home in Woodsfield while Carl stayed with their son.

During the following two months, Jerry's condition stabilized, and I continued working with him and interacting with the Dalton family. I gave Jerry all the physical exercise I could. I also tried repeatedly to get him to blink when I snapped on the light or flicked my hands toward his face, but to no avail. From that fateful night of high temperatures and seizures, Jerry's level of consciousness seemed frozen without further progress. It was heartbreaking to watch this dedicated father standing at the bedside of his only son day after day and week after week. I could see hope beginning to fade from Carl's face and from his heart.

Six months after he had been admitted, Jerry Dalton was transported back to his parents' home. Every day and throughout the night, they came to Jerry's bedside and turned him over to prevent pressure sores and pneumonia. They took turns feeding him and caring for his every need. Months later, when I visited the Daltons, they were still giving their son the best of loving care.

Carl showed me around the tire shop where Jerry had been injured. At a machine designed to grind old tread from used tires in preparation for recapping, he paused. Staring at a piece of scrap metal in his hand, Carl's face grew sad. A lump rose in my throat and tears stung my eyes as he slowly explained, "I had told Jerry never to use scrap metal to lock this aluminum hub onto a tire." He pointed to the grooved shaft and the hardened steel clip made to hold it in place. "But one act of disobedience was all it took."

He sighed and shook his head mournfully. I knew his heart was asking, "Why, God, why?" But then he continued, "I know Jerry didn't grasp the danger. But twenty pounds of pressure when multiplied by the square inches in that hub's surface is tremendous! When this soft metal sheared off, the hub blasted off this machine like a rocket. It struck him with such force that it crushed part of his skull and knocked him over backward." Pointing above us,

Carl asked, "Did you see the hole where the hub shot through the ceiling and into the attic?"

At times, human suffering is best answered with caring silence and presence. This was one of those times, and I silently shared Carl's grief.

CHAPTER 17

Problem Solving

The new, modern hospital in which we worked enjoyed a country atmosphere on its large tract of land at Zanesville's northern boundary. The old, vacant brick building, which had housed the original hospital for many years, now stood forlornly on a high hill overlooking Interstate 70.

Several of our 1-W brothers were grounds men for Bethesda Hospital, landscaping, planting shrubbery, and mowing during the summer. Snow removal and general maintenance occupied their time during the winter.

On a sweltering August day, I was assigned to work with maintenance instead of patient care. A drain was needed in the large courtyard, which was bordered on two sides by the four-story wings. The cafeteria and boiler operations sealed off the other two sides.

We needed to dig a ditch diagonally across the courtyard to a storm drain located at the center. Armed with determination and a shovel, I began. However, I quickly discovered that in digging hardpan clay, I needed to jump and come down with both feet on the shovel to make any headway. To make matters worse, the sun beat down in the enclosed courtyard, with no cooling breeze. I had well over 200 feet of ditch to dig, and it needed to be properly sloped to receive the pipe which the maintenance department planned to place there. After two hours of torturous labor, I noticed that from more than half of the fifty large picture windows, patients were intently observing my labors from their air-conditioned rooms.

Although my shovel remained faithful, following several hours of this intense labor, my determination began to wane. My soft hospital muscles were crying for mercy. I was overheated and miserable when a Scripture popped into my thoughts. *And whatsoever ye do in word or deed, do all in the name of the Lord Jesus . . .* Colossians 3:17. Invigorating energy surged into my tired muscles. I was no longer digging for the Bethesda Hospital; I was digging this ditch for the Lord Jesus. A wave of thankfulness washed over me, giving me renewed determination and endurance.

The night nurse was giving report to my incoming shift. "In Room 103," she said, "we have Mr. Simpson, a forty-six-year-old patient of Dr. Glosser. He was diagnosed in ER with multiple frontal skull fractures and admitted to us last evening for observation. Mr. Simpson must be a man of unusual strength, because he sustained skull fractures without losing consciousness. He went into emergency surgery at 12:30 a.m. for removal of skull fragments and closure of the dura to stop intracranial drainage. He will be on the hypothermia unit as needed until he recovers sufficiently to regulate his own body temperature."

Over the next several days, I obtained further details about Mr. Simpson's accident. A brick mason by trade, Mr. Simpson was driving his pickup home from work when an oncoming quarry truck lost a rock about the size of a softball. It bounced on the pavement, glanced off his hood, and smashed through his windshield, striking him full on the forehead. The ER staff had closed the wound on his forehead and taken X-rays. His vital signs were within normal range, and Mr. Simpson was speaking coherently when he was admitted to 1-West.

An hour and a half after Mr. Simpson's admission to 1-West, the inhalation therapist, James Wesson, gave a decongestant treatment to Mr. Simpson's roommate. While his patient was taking the breathing treatment from the portable machine, James glanced at Mr. Simpson, who was sitting up in bed. Shocked at seeing heavy seepage leaking from the bandaged forehead, James rushed to notify the night nurse, who investigated and found it to be intracranial seepage. She immediately called Dr. Glosser, who performed emergency surgery in the middle of the night. The doctor removed a three-square-inch patch of shattered skull from Mr. Simpson's forehead and sutured shut the dura, the lining of his brain.

I was assigned to oversee the hypothermia unit for Mr. Simpson while student nurses were assigned to monitor his condition. One of the first post-op discoveries was that Mr. Simpson had gone completely blind through his ordeal. In addition to his blindness, he had cerebral fluid draining through his nasal passage.

Dr. Glosser ordered complete bed rest, stating that if they could not stop this new drainage, he would have to perform another brain surgery. Lying still would reduce pressure fluctuation and hopefully allow healing to stop Mr. Simpson's drainage altogether. "The danger here," Dr. Glosser explained, "is that any opening that allows drainage can also permit pathogens to enter the patient's brain, and that can be fatal!"

I maintained a close watch on Mr. Simpson's temperature and was eventually assigned to care for him each day I worked on

1-West. He had been ordered complete bed rest. Student nurses or volunteers fed him since he could not see to eat.

Entering his room one morning, I said, "Good morning, Mr. Simpson, this is Johnny. How are you feeling this morning?"

"Not bad," was his response, "but it sure is cold in here! Why don't they turn up the heat?"

"You think it's cold?"

"It sure is! I been hanging on to this blanket all night, and it ain't enough. Can't you tell 'em to just turn that heat up a little? Tell 'em I asked."

I had to smile in spite of myself, for as he spoke, he grabbed the refrigerated rubber blanket of the hypothermia unit and pulled it up over his shoulder, not realizing this was the very thing chilling his body. He was barrel-chested and had the strong, muscular arms of a man used to heavy labor.

Instead of his usual rounded forehead, Mr. Simpson had a sizable hollow which pulsed with every heartbeat. As I spoke with him, he squinted his eyes and blinked rapidly as if willing his blind eyes to see once more. However, when no one was present, he lay there staring at nothing without blinking his unseeing eyes. This caused the tears which lubricated his eyes to evaporate, leaving a crust on his eyes. This had to be dissolved and carefully cleaned from his eyes every day with a 1 percent boric acid solution.

One evening as I retrieved the sterile swabs and the boric acid from the treatment room, an idea flashed into my mind. What if I shone a light directly into Mr. Simpson's eyes? Perhaps he could see that as a tiny glimmer of light. I took an otoscope with me, anxious to try the experiment.

"Mr. Simpson," I greeted him, "it's time for me to clean your eyes again, okay?"

"Sure, Johnny," he responded. "I was wonderin' when you was

coming. What you been doing all day?"

"Well," I responded, "they sent me up to 2-East to help a man who had an operation this morning, but has been unable to pass water since his operation."

"Really? How come?"

"General anesthesia often upsets the central nervous system to the point that a post-op patient cannot void. Usually though, normal functions are restored within the first eight hours. Now I'm going to drop a little solution in your right eye and clean it for you, okay?"

"Yeah, go ahead," he said. "Wow, that stuff's cold." He blinked, rolling his eyes back and forth as the crusty matter began to dissolve. Ever so gently, I wiped the residue out of his eye with boric acid-soaked swabs, and then repeated the process on his left eye.

"That feels better," he declared.

"It always does, doesn't it? Now, Mr. Simpson," I continued, "tonight I want to shine a light into your eye. I want you to concentrate and tell me if you see anything at all. Are you ready?"

"Yep," he responded.

"Okay. I am holding a light in front of your right eye, and I want you to tell me what you see."

He was silent. "Do you see anything at all?" I encouraged.

"Nope. Nothing," was the disheartening reply. The left eye was equally disappointing.

"Okay, we will try again tomorrow night," I said. "In fact, I'm going to do this each time I clean your eyes, and maybe you'll see it one of these days."

"All right," he said as I gathered up the used swabs.

"Good night, Mr. Simpson," I said cheerily. "Sleep tight. I'll be in to see you tomorrow."

"Sure thing," he responded. "I ain't goin' nowhere."

One evening, we were extremely busy with several admissions

late in the shift, and I nearly forgot to give Mr. Simpson his much-needed eye care. I rushed into the treatment room, glanced at the labels, selected the necessary items, and hurried to his room. "Mr. Simpson, I'm here again to clean your eyes," I announced.

"Sure thing," he drawled. "I was waitin' for ya."

"Are you ready?" I asked.

"As ready as I'm gonna get," he responded. With that, I held his eyelid open and allowed several drops of solution to dribble into his right eye.

He winced and said, "Wow, Johnny, that stings!"

"I know it stings a little," I said.

"No," he insisted forcefully. "This really burns!"

I double-checked the handwritten label taped to the dispenser and was horrified to see it was Zephyrin chloride!

"I'll be right back!" I exclaimed as I dashed out the door and ran down the hall. I was back in moments with an identical bottle from the med cart. This one had "1% Boric Acid" scrawled on it. I apologized profusely as I repeatedly rinsed out his eye with the soothing solution rather than the irritating antiseptic solution I had mistakenly applied earlier. I had been so confident I had the correct solution that I had failed to double-check before applying it. It was a lesson I would carry with me for many years!

Two weeks later, as I was finishing Mr. Simpson's eye care, I shined the light of the otoscope into his right eye again and asked, "Can you see anything there, Mr. Simpson?"

"No . . ." he began, but then said, "wait a minute! I thought I saw a little glow for a bit."

"Close your eyes and rest them, and we will try that again," I said. He closed his eyes obediently and swallowed nervously.

"Are you ready?" I asked. He didn't respond, but opened his eyes. I moved the light again until it was shining directly into his right eye, and a smile spread over his face.

"I see a tiny glow, like a light a lo-o-ong way off," he rejoiced.

I moved the light away and asked, "Do you see it now?"

"Nope," he said rather dejectedly. "It's gone."

"You sure?" I asked, silently moving the light back over his eye.

"Yeah, there it is again!" he said excitedly.

"Okay," I suggested. "Let's try it on your left eye. What do you see?" I asked, shining the beam directly into his eye. "Anything?"

"Nope," he responded. "Nothin' at all." After several more unsuccessful tries with his left eye, we again tried his right eye, and Mr. Simpson could see a faint glow!

That night, I went to bed with a glow in my own heart, praying that Mr. Simpson would indeed recover his sight. How blessed I was to be working with suffering people, and to extend to them compassion and empathy. *Thank you, Lord, for leading me to Zanesville!* I thought.

Around that time, Nurse Towner began working on 1-West, but only on day shift. She was forty-four years old and had a pleasant personality. Her daughter was a nurse who worked on one of the other floors. I made my rounds near the end of my day shift and had just delivered fresh water to the last of my patients. I was standing in the doorway of Room 110 talking with my patient about our VS unit.

"So how did you choose to come all the way up here from Virginia?" he wanted to know.

"Well, I am a Christian and a conscientious objector to war, and I'm working here instead of being in the military. This work allows me to pay the debt I owe my country—without taking human life. I am also part of a church-sponsored voluntary service unit which gives spiritual oversight to us while working away from our home communities."

"That's great. I'm glad for you," was his response.

At that moment, I felt an arm slide across my shoulders. Wondering who this could possibly be, I turned my head just in time to hear Mrs. Towner say, "Isn't he just the most darling young man?" I was shocked when she pulled me toward her! "We think the world of him!" she cooed.

I blushed with embarrassment, but I was also speechless with anger at Mrs. Towner's indiscretion. I am sure my discomfort was obvious to both the patient and Mrs. Towner. When she released me after several awkward seconds, I vowed this would never happen again!

The following week, I kept a wary lookout for Mrs. Towner, and all went well. That is, until Friday, when the nurses' station was full of both the incoming and outgoing nurses. I was registering my TPRs at the end of the shift when an arm came down on the desk on either side of me. I glanced at the glass surrounding the nurses' station and saw the reflection of Mrs. Towner leaning inappropriately close to me. I was trapped, and again, I was incensed! What was wrong with this nurse? Had she no sense of decency?

The hierarchy in the hospital was well established. The top people were the doctors, with the brain surgeon at the very top, then general surgeons, followed by the non-surgical doctors. Below them was the administrative head of nursing. On down the line were the supervisors, the head nurses, charge nurses, student nurses, and finally the aides and orderlies. As an orderly at the bottom of the totem pole, I was baffled about how to extricate myself without disrespecting Mrs. Towner's position as a nurse. I quickly completed my last entry in the registry, swiveled my chair about, and rose, forcing her to move out of my way without any obvious rudeness on my part. But inwardly, I felt the injustice of her imprudence.

I was most watchful during the next week, and then I had the day off. I was still awake, just beginning my personal devotions, when my roommate, Earl Nisly, returned from his 3 to 11 p.m. shift. I invited him to join me to share our devotional time together. We read a Scripture and discussed its purpose. Then we began discussing our work. Earl mentioned he felt uncomfortable when certain people were working his shift.

"Earl, are you having trouble with Mrs. Towner?" I asked bluntly.

He looked away for a moment before asking, "Has she been bothering you too?"

We discovered that we had both endured her inappropriate advances, and we discussed how we could properly deal with it.

"She is old enough to be our mother!" I exclaimed in disgust. "You know, we must be extra careful whenever we are speaking to a patient. I've learned to always walk fully into the room and not stand talking with my back toward the doorway. And that's not all. I've also learned I cannot relax my vigilance when registering TPRs. I make a habit of glancing at the reflection of the glass surrounding the nurses' station every few seconds, and if she enters, I pick up the pad with one hand, place the registry on my lap with the other, and swivel to face her as I finish writing. Even though it is more difficult to write with the registry on your lap, at least it's safe!"

"I never thought of that," said Earl. "That's a good idea."

That night as we prayed together, we included our problems with Mrs. Towner in our petitions, asking God to increase our alertness and His protection.

The following week was uneventful as we were very alert to any inappropriate overtures. Earl and I switched shifts again. He worked day shift, and I came on in the afternoon. I stood in the doorway of the nurses' station one afternoon, chatting as he registered his TPRs. He was telling me about Mr. Simpson wanting to get up and use the restroom rather than the bedpan. He had become quite insistent, but had to be told by the head nurse that his doctor had ordered him to stay flat in bed so his head injury could heal. Earl said, "We had to put a Posey™ belt on him, locking him in bed with a key. He's a pretty opinionated individual." With that, Earl turned back to his registry.

"Earl!" I hissed, but he didn't hear me. Mrs. Towner had entered the opposite side of the nurses' station and was sauntering in Earl's direction. In a moment Earl found himself hemmed in by the desk in front, with Mrs. Towner grasping the desk on either side of him. Earl's actions were smooth, calculated, and determined. He swiveled his chair until it was at a right angle to the desk, and then as effortlessly as though he had practiced this maneuver many times, he slid out of the chair, ducked under Mrs. Towner's arm, and walked away.

The surprised nurse was left standing there blinking at the empty chair in her embrace! The entire episode only lasted ten seconds, but Earl's actions sent an unmistakable message to everyone who saw it. We never learned whether the head nurse had a chat with Mrs. Towner about her impropriety, or whether it was Earl's actions that clinched the lesson. But we rejoiced that neither of us ever had any more problems with Mrs. Towner.

CHAPTER 18

Helping Hands

Fifty-two-year-old Bruce McHenry was admitted to Room 121 with a life-threatening coronary blockage. He was ordered on absolute bed rest and was not even allowed to feed himself. This was to eliminate all exertion to his heart for thirty days, giving the coronary artery time to grow a new branch around the blockage.

As I fed him his meals every day, we learned to know each other well. We compared spiritual values, and naturally, we discussed my working in the hospital instead of performing military service. Bruce was a thoughtful, mild-mannered farmer from twelve miles outside of Zanesville. His wife was struggling to keep up with the farming as her husband lay incapacitated in the hospital, but she did her best.

Bruce shared his worries with me. "Dr. Shirky told me that even after I'm discharged, I can't do normal manual labor for several more months, and I just don't know what I'm going to do."

"Don't you have children who could help you?" I wondered.

"No," he responded. "It's just the two of us. What is bothering me most is that my final cutting of hay is almost ready, and I have no idea how I'll get it into my haymow."

The following day, I sat at lunch in the dining hall of our VS unit, discussing Bruce's dilemma. "Say, fellows," I began, "how many of you would be willing to help put up hay for this farmer who is recuperating from a heart attack?"

"When?" several chorused together with obvious interest.

"In a week or two, but it will depend a little on the weather," I explained. "He's being discharged next week, and the doctor says he can do light work like driving a tractor, but there is no way he can pitch heavy hay bales."

"I'd be willing," said Earl.

"Me too," said Lee.

"Count me in," said another. "It will feel good to get out of the hospital and stretch a bit."

Armed with their enthusiasm and commitment, I went to work that evening to see what could be arranged. "Bruce," I said, "several young fellows in my voluntary service unit grew up on farms. When I explained your heart condition and that you need help to put up your hay, they immediately offered to help. So here is our phone number. If you could call us a day in advance, I think several of us will be able to come help any time. But if you could arrange it on a Saturday, almost all of us would have the day off and come help."

"Well, I hardly know what to say," said Bruce. "I mean, I never expected anything like this. But yes, I will gladly receive your help."

"This is not for pay," I explained. "This will simply be our gift to you."

He seemed deeply impressed as he said with feeling, "Thank you!"

Twenty minutes before my shift ended, the charge nurse said, "Johnny, we just received a call from 3-East, and they are asking for an orderly to apply a urinary catheter. Since it's so near the end of our shift, we could leave it for the night orderly if you prefer. It would probably run you past quitting time," she explained.

"Oh, I don't mind," I said. "I'll be glad to do it." Knowing she would probably be gone before I returned, I bid her good night and headed for the elevator.

"Where is your patient who needs a catheterization?" I asked as I entered the third floor nurses' station.

The nurse in charge gave a sigh and explained, "It's Mr. Palmer, a patient of Dr. Donalds in Room 304. I ordered the tray, and it is waiting for you in the treatment room." She looked tired as she turned to finish her charting.

I carefully added the catheter, Zephyrin chloride, and sterile pads before closing the tray with its protective covering and laying the packaged sterile gloves on top. I was heading out when the charge nurse stopped me and said, "This is the third time Mr. Palmer has needed catheterization since his operation twenty-four hours ago.

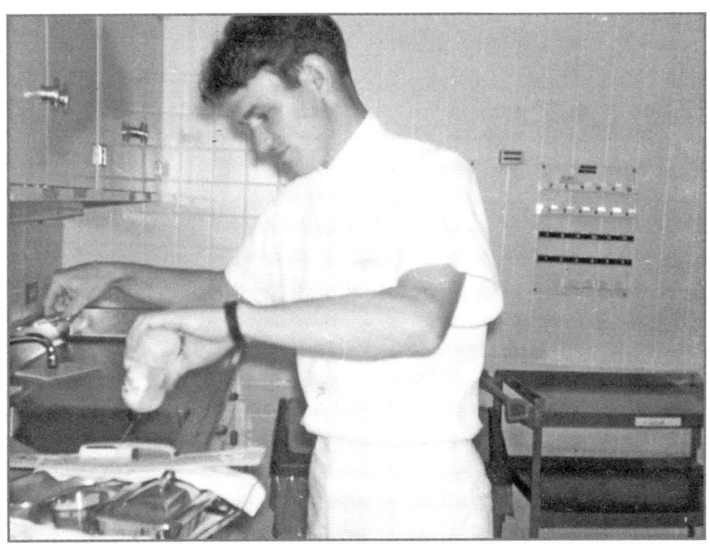

Johnny carefully prepares a sterile catheter tray.

He is not only sore from the resulting irritation, but he's a real bundle of nerves! We hardly know what to do with him. I suggest you make no sudden moves and keep the call button handy." She raised a knowing eyebrow and gave me a warning nod.

I seldom had trouble with my patients, but her serious warning unnerved me. As I paused outside Room 304 and took a deep breath, a sudden inspiration seized me. Carefully balancing the tray on the palm of my hand and raising it above my shoulder, I entered the patient's room just like a waiter in an upscale restaurant. Mr. Palmer gave a start at my entrance. With a flourish, I lowered the tray from my shoulder and gave it a delicate twirl. I slid it neatly onto his bedside table as though I had just delivered a plate of filet mignon. During this show, I exclaimed, "I heard you are having water problems. I'm the plumber, and I've come to fix them!" Mr. Palmer laughed out loud.

Before opening the tray, I asked, "So, what type of operation did you have?"

"Gallbladder," he explained.

"That can certainly make a person feel miserable," I empathized.

"It sure did me in!" He shook his head.

"Did you ever have a urinary catheter before?" I asked innocently, wanting him to talk.

"I'll say I did! Twice, and was it ever painful!" He shivered with revulsion at the memory.

"That's too bad," I said, "but I will do my utmost to keep from hurting you further. Let me explain." I opened the tray, donned my sterile gloves, and took each item from the tray as I explained their uses to him. Next, I explained that the muscle we needed to pass through with the catheter was constricted by tense nerves. "When we get to that point," I explained, "I'm going to ask you to take a couple of really deep breaths to relax that muscle and keep from causing unnecessary pain." Even as I explained, I was working. Several moments later, I asked, "Can you give me several nice deep breaths?" The receptacle began to fill.

"When did you say you had your gallbladder surgery?" I asked.

"It was yesterday afternoon," he replied.

"How did you detect that you were having gallbladder problems?"

"I thought I had a bad case of indigestion at first, but it continued getting worse. Then two days ago, I had a severe attack and came to the emergency room. Dr. Donalds was on call and he diagnosed it as gallstones. He said a large one had completely blocked the duct."

"Did he do your surgery?"

"Yes. Would you say he is a good doctor?"

"I think very highly of him," I said as the last of the bladder contents emptied into the receptacle and I very gently removed the catheter.

Watching me strip off my gloves by turning them inside out to prevent the spread of bacteria, Mr. Palmer asked incredulously, "You're not done already, are you?"

"I certainly am," I assured him with a smile.

"But–but, I never even felt a thing!" he sputtered.

"You weren't supposed to. I told you that relaxing that muscle with deep breathing does the trick, didn't I? Look, as soon as you can, go into the bathroom where you can relax. Let a trickle of water run into the sink. That sound has a soothing effect. It's relaxing." I smiled. "Do that, and I don't think you will have any further need of *plumbers*."

Mr. Palmer smiled and reached out to shake my hand, saying, "You have done me a great favor. Thank you so much! Good night."

After disposing of the used tray, I washed up and headed for home, late but satisfied.

We received word from Bruce that he had mowed and baled most of his hay and would deeply appreciate if we could come on Saturday afternoon. Five of us who had Saturday off left at 2:00 and followed Bruce's direction to his farm. He was glad to see us, and I was surprised to see the same man who had been our patient for a month now seated on his Farmall tractor, driving us to his bale-dotted hayfield.

We went to work with a will to see if we could toss the bales on faster than our man could stack them. As we drove back to the farm and started up the hill toward the barn, Bruce had to shift to a lower gear. Suddenly, the load shifted, and the bales began to tumble off the back of the wagon. The two fellows riding on top of the bales had an extra thrilling ride as they tumbled off with the bales, but no one was hurt. We all helped reload the hay more carefully before continuing to the barn.

A motorized elevator carried the bales into the haymow to be stacked. My job was to grab the bales after they dropped ten feet from the top of the elevator and throw them to the stackers. I was slinging bales as fast as I could. My hands were soon rubbed raw by the rough fibers of the baler twine, and my throat burned with thirst. I could not give up; to do so would tell everybody I was weak. However, the elevator was gaining on me as the fellows on the wagon below were racing to see who could stack more bales on the elevator. I could not keep up and was soon stumbling over jumbled bales. I reached for a fresh bale, straightening my aching back when – *wham!* Another bale falling from the top of the elevator landed squarely on the top of my head. I felt disoriented for a moment, and pain shot into my neck. It scared me. Still, I could move my head, and my limbs worked. I continued throwing bales, although more cautiously, but I gave up trying to match the speed of those farm boys.

When the last load of hay was stacked securely into his barn, Bruce treated us to cold watermelon and graciously thanked us for our help. For several weeks, I had a stiff neck which could only be relieved by pushing my chin from side to side with my hand. My neck discomfort would continue for many years.

I was assigned to work in ER for the following week, which was a break from the routine of 1-West. Sometimes several accident victims arrived at once, and we didn't even have time to eat. But there were other periods when we had no patients for hours at a time.

During one of these quiet periods, inhalation therapist James Wesson dropped by and engaged in conversation with the ER staff. He and the nurse on duty began playing around with a Ouija board. They asked it questions and tried to clear their minds to allow some unseen force to move the pointer under their hands to letters spelling out the answer.

"Some people think this is tapping into evil powers, but it's just a game like Monopoly," said James. "It's fun. Come on, Johnny, try it."

However, recalling a warning from one of my schoolteachers, I declined and walked away. I busied myself straightening cast materials on the shelves and sweeping the rooms.

My eighth-grade teacher, Lester Hershberger, had been a man of deep spiritual insight. He had warned our class, "If you are ever invited to play with the Ouija board, don't even consider it! Many people have opened themselves up to demonic powers by playing with this device, and Satan eventually took control of their lives. Stay as far away from it as you can. The Ouija board has no place in the hands of a Christian." His words rang in my conscience that night and protected me from participating with evil.

My ER coworkers tried several times that week to get me involved, but I steadfastly refused. I had been forearmed by a thoughtful teacher whose influence helped guide me.

Late on Saturday evening, the buzzer on the ER door sounded, and Mr. Wright came in with his hand wrapped in a towel. He had been using a circular hand saw at an awkward angle above his head, and when the cut was completed, he dropped the saw quickly to relieve his tired muscles. He had instinctively raised his left hand to help his tired right arm lower the saw, but the guard was stuck open, allowing the coasting blade to slice deeply across the back of his left hand.

Mr. and Mrs. Wright were personal friends of Dr. Peters, one of our two female doctors, and we called her to attend to Mr. Wright. While we waited, we cleaned the wound and set up the suture tray.

Dr. Peters arrived within twenty minutes and greeted our patient like an old friend. They caught up on family news as Dr. Peters cleansed and anesthetized the wound. She then began a thorough examination. One tendon had been nicked, and two had been severed completely. I stood by to assist, not wanting to miss anything. Dr. Peters saw my interest and carefully explained what needed to be done to repair the damage.

"Tendons," she said, "consist of very strong fibers, but the tissue between the individual fibers is too soft to hold suture. We will be using a fine, dissolvable suture material to draw the cut ends of these tendons together. However, we will need to begin a little distance from the cut and bring the suture through the severed ends to be joined. We will push back a little distance before bringing the suture to the surface of the tendon."

As she spoke, she was gazing at an open channel where the upper end of the severed tendon had disappeared into the forearm. As Mr. Wright concentrated on the doctor's explanation, I saw the elusive tendon slowly creeping back into view. Dr. Peters continued her explanation. "We will then move across the top of the tendon . . ." She moved to grasp the tendon with a tissue forceps, but when Mr. Wright saw the movement, he instinctively tensed, and the tendon disappeared up his arm once more.

"Okay," smiled Dr. Peters, "this will never do. We will be here all night." She turned to Mr. Wright and said, "Turn your head away, and I do believe we will have better luck."

"As I was saying," she began again, "we will cross over the exterior of the tendon before re-inserting the suture back into the tendon and out through its cut end. All this has to be loosely done so there is still room to work the needle between the two ends." Without giving any verbal indication that might cause Mr. Wright to react reflexively, Dr. Peters continued speaking smoothly as she deftly grasped the errant tendon and forcibly tugged it into sight. She clamped it into place and continued, "Once we have brought the suture back into the end where we began, we must again cross over and securely tie the two ends together so the severed tendon ends are pressed together to heal."

I saw the second tendon just barely peeping out at us, but not enough to grasp. Dr. Peters was the picture of patience as she continued explaining, "It will take some time for the tendons to heal enough for physical therapy to begin." At this point, she captured the other tendon and continued, "But it should heal with no permanent effects."

After securing the second tendon, Dr. Peters spent the next half hour performing all that she had described. With both tendons sutured securely together, she said, "Mr. Wright, I want you to raise and lower you ring finger for me. Can you do that?" I watched, fascinated, as the sutured tendon slid back and forth through the open wound, raising and lowering the ring finger at Mr. Wright's command.

"Good," she said, "and can you do the same with your middle finger?" Mr. Wright complied with the same successful results, and Dr. Peters chuckled, "That proves he doesn't have his wires crossed!"

She closed and bandaged the wound, administered a tetanus shot, an antibiotic, and a prescription for pain, and sent Mr. Wright and his wife on their way. I ended my shift in awe of Dr. Peters and of the God who created the wonderful human body.

CHAPTER 19

Pain of Death

It was a quiet afternoon in ER, with only a few minor injuries to treat. Then an elderly lady who had stumbled and fallen was admitted. Her heart rate and blood pressure were normal for a person of her age. Her reflexes were good, but she was complaining of intense pain in her wrist. We sent her for X-rays, and they showed a nasty break of the ulna near the wrist joint. Dr. Capp examined the wrist and the X-rays. The broken fragment of bone no longer made contact with the break.

"See," said Dr. Capp as he studied the X-ray for the fourth time. "I must bring this broken joint piece back into contact with the ulna. If they are not firmly in contact, this fragment will die, permanently impairing the wrist. Bring me a Kirschner wire and drill," he ordered. The nurse left to bring those items. "Miller," he continued, "I'll need the finger cuffs, the bucket with the yoke handle, and a pair of gloves."

Having worked with Dr. Capp before, I knew about his bucket with its broad, soft handle which he filled with water to the proper traction weight. But I had no clue what he meant by finger cuffs. I located his specialized bucket and placed it at his disposal alongside his gloves. I intercepted the nurse as she returned and asked, "Just what are finger cuffs?" She smiled knowingly and silently led me to a drawer in Room 2 where she showed me a package marked, "Dr. Capp's Finger Cuffs."

I brought the package to Dr. Capp, who opened it, exposing five strange-looking wire mesh webbings which he pushed onto the patient's fingers and thumb. Each finger mesh was woven in a loose diamond pattern and had a wire connecting the tips to a common ring. When pulled, the meshes naturally tightened about the fingers, making it impossible for the fingers to be withdrawn by pulling. But the mesh expanded when pushed upward from the bottom, thus releasing its grip.

I helped Dr. Capp place the yoke-handled bucket over the patient's arm as she lay on the ER cot. He then fastened the ring of the finger cuffs to a cord from an IV stand and partially filled the bucket with water, exerting the precise amount of traction he wanted on the broken wrist.

The nurse had set up the tray with the sterile Kirschner wire and drill. Dr. Capp injected Xylocaine into the injured wrist and donned his sterile gloves. Steadying the drill with his left hand, he proceeded to turn the drill with his right hand, spinning the Kirschner wire into the ulna just below the break. Although the arrowhead-shaped tip was quite sharp, it crept to the edge of the rounded ulna and slipped past. Dr. Capp tried a second time, but again it slipped off. Bracing the butt of the drill against his chest and carefully cranking with his right hand, he steadied the broken wrist with his left hand as he exerted pressure. Maintaining that pressure against his chest, he began to crank when, suddenly, the point of the Kirschner wire slipped from the bone. It punched completely through the back side of the wrist, penetrated Dr. Capp's sterile glove, and buried itself deep into his index finger! I will not record his cursing, but I well remember his action. He jerked his bleeding finger free of the impaling wire, retracted the wire right back into the patient's wrist, and jabbed it forcefully against the bone. Then with steely determination, he proceeded to drill it right through the ulna.

When he finished, the patient had almost an inch of steel wire protruding from the front and back of her wrist. This wire was then imbedded in the cast to stabilize the ulna, while the cast held the patient's wrist bent sharply away from her thumb. The final X-ray showed a complete closure of the break that would ensure proper healing. The patient was dismissed, and Dr. Capp left for his home. No one mentioned the error we had just witnessed; after all, he was the doctor.

A short time later, we were alerted by the wail of a siren and saw the flashing lights of an ambulance turning off Maple Avenue and heading toward the ER entrance. I rushed down the hall and held the door open. The driver and attendant burst out and ran to the back of the ambulance. They jerked open the door to reveal another attendant desperately administering CPR to the man lying on a cot. He continued even as the cot was being moved out, and then he ran along beside them as they rushed into ER. I followed, wondering how I could help.

The nurse was taking down the information from the driver and calling a doctor. The attendant, who was about my age, never stopped his efforts. His dedication to saving the patient's life truly amazed me. The patient's stomach contents hampered the attendant's efforts, but that never fazed him. In desperation, he simply wiped it aside with his hand and continued his mouth-to-mouth resuscitation. A nurse ran to assist him and checked for a heartbeat, but found none. Recalling that a sharp blow would sometimes shock a stalled heart into beating again, she balled up her dainty little fist and slammed it down in the center of the patient's chest. Instead of the usual firm resistance from the sternum and ribcage, her fist encountered a mushy mess, and she recoiled in horror. Probing a bit more, she discovered this patient had a crushed sternum and broken ribs.

Just then, Dr. Yang arrived and took command. First, he examined the eyes to check for any reaction to light. Next, he asked for the blood pressure. And finally, he asked the young man who had continued with CPR all this time to cease for a moment. The man was drenched with sweat and panting from exertion.

Dr. Yang placed his stethoscope over the patient's heart, and, bowing his head with eyes closed in concentration, listened intently for a heartbeat. Moving the stethoscope to a new spot, he listened again and then again. We looked on in hushed silence. No one moved.

Dr. Yang slowly straightened and removed his stethoscope from his ears, but he never took his gaze from the face of the patient. Then he spoke those two hope-shattering words: "He's gone." I heard a collective sigh and realized we had all been unconsciously holding our breaths. Glancing at the young ambulance attendant, I saw his shoulders sag in defeat. He appeared absolutely drained.

The nurse returned with the necessary forms and said, "Johnny, there are people in the waiting room. Would you see to them?" I closed the door behind me and took my station at the front desk. After several minutes, a thin lady with wet, stringy hair and a raspy voice appeared at my window. "May I help you?" I asked.

"How's my husband?" she cried. "I want to see my husband!

Where do you have him?"

I knew now was not the time for her to see her husband's corpse. She was not prepared emotionally, and his body, covered with the contents of his stomach, was in no shape to be seen by her.

I explained, "You will have to wait because the doctor is with your husband at present. Just have a seat until the doctor completes his examination." She turned away, sobbing, and took her seat among family members and friends.

Ten minutes passed, and the nurse came to make a phone call. Upon seeing the family seated nearby, she opted to make her call from the central ER phone out of earshot.

The frantic wife of the deceased man approached me again. "May I help you?" I asked politely.

"Mister, just tell me he's not dead!" she wailed. "Please, oh please, tell me that my husband is not dead." Her whole frame was wracked with convulsive sobs, and tears had washed clean streaks through her makeup. She was disheveled, but my heart went out to her. She apparently had no hope. What could I tell her?

The ambulance attendant had explained that this family was having a high time drinking with friends on their houseboat. Darkness had fallen, but they had failed to turn on their running lights. A speedboat had rammed into them with such force that it bashed its way completely inside the houseboat.

"Ma'am," I said as kindly as I knew how, "you will have to speak with the doctor."

She turned from me with a heart-wrenching wail. "He can't be dead. He can't be!"

I swallowed the lump rising in my throat as my heart whispered, *But he* is *dead.*

The body was moved to an ER cart so the ambulance crew could remove their cot. The driver and older attendant walked respectfully past the waiting family with their now-empty cart, trailed by the young attendant. This had been his very first ambulance run as a volunteer.

Dr. Yang left the body behind the closed door of Room 1 where the nurse was washing and making the body more presentable. He invited the family into Room 2 for a consultation. After fifteen minutes, the family was shown into Room 1 where the body of their loved one lay still in death. The death certificate was filled out and signed, the family left with the heartbroken widow, and the mortician was called to receive the body.

My shift had ended. I headed for the White House, a quiet and sobered young man who had just witnessed firsthand the raw pain of death without hope in Christ.

Mrs. Vann called the orderlies in for a meeting. “The hospital administration has decided to give you fellows further training in CPR,” she announced. “We are planning that you, along with those working in inhalation therapy, will become our first responders for patients suffering cardiac arrest. What do you think about this?”

“It sounds interesting to me,” I agreed.

Another responded, “I’d like to learn all that I can.”

Others expressed their agreement and their eagerness to learn.

“This will be an in-service training,” Mrs. Vann explained. “We will be pulling you from the floors during your regular working hours. If you are all willing, we will get started next week. We won’t be able to pull everyone at once, so I will arrange the schedules with your head nurses and they will notify you. Any questions?”

“Once we have been trained in CPR, how or when will we know to use it?” asked Tim Good, who was working in inhalation therapy.

“I’m glad you asked,” said Mrs. Vann. “We are going to establish a special code and activate it when an emergency occurs. It will be announced over our public-address system with the location of the emergency. When you receive that code, get to that location as fast as possible. When a heart has stopped beating, every second is crucial!"

"What about our other obligations?" I wondered.

"The emergency code will take temporary priority over all other responsibilities. We will want you there STAT! After a doctor arrives, stay and help until you are dismissed to return to your normal duties."

This was exciting, and we were eager to learn all we could. Over the next two weeks, we were called into special, intense training sessions where we practiced pulmonary and cardiac resuscitation on realistic mannequins. Our rhythms and pressures were timed, measured, and corrected until we could feel and automatically adjust the proper speed of heart massage and the optimum volume and rate of mouth-to-mouth breathing.

Near the end of our training, we were informed that "Code Blue" with the location would be our call to action. Additionally, a crash cart was stationed in the treatment room on every floor. These were equipped with bags and masks for the breathing, mouth-to-mouth shields, tongue blades to clear the airway, blood pressure cuffs, and stethoscopes. Our new duty was to respond to the emergency code by rushing to the location with the crash cart. Although thrilled with this addition to my training, I sincerely hoped I would never be called to the daunting task of trying to save someone's life with my untried skills.

Back on 1-West, Mr. Simpson was making notable progress. He could now see and recognize people with his right eye, and he was gaining some blurry vision in the left one. I was so pleased by the news that I stopped in to see him.

"Hello there, Mr. Simpson," I said. "I heard you're getting along really well."

"Jake!" he cried with obvious delight. "Man, is it ever good to see you again!"

Wondering why he was calling me Jake, I decided to play along and said, "Yes, I was thinking about you and had a few minutes to spare, so I thought I'd stop by."

"Jake, how's that big job coming?" he asked.

Now I was stuck because I had no idea what job he was talking about, but his next comment gave me my cue.

"Did they get that big manhole finished?"

"Yep, they sure did," I responded. "They really missed you, though. It took them longer because you weren't there to help."

A smile of satisfaction spread over Mr. Simpson's face, and I concluded that either he was a very good actor or extremely befuddled.

"Okay, Mr. Simpson, I'm going to have to run. See you another time," I concluded.

"Okay, Jake." He poked his hand across the bed rail to shake hands, squinted his left eye, and said, "Hey man, thanks for comin'. Tell the boys I said hi."

"When I see them, I'll tell them," I promised as I started for the door.

The following day, I was working on 1-West, and Mr. Simpson was among my assignments. I was loosening his Posey™ belt and having him roll to one side so I could change his linens when he said, "Johnny, guess who came to see me yesterday."

"I wouldn't know," I said, only half listening. But his next words certainly arrested my attention!

"My old friend Jake stopped in to see me."

"He did? And what did he have to say?" I asked.

"Why, he told me about the big job they was workin' on, and how they got the big manhole done even if I wasn't there."

"Really?" I responded in surprise. He certainly recalled our conversation from the day before.

"Yep, and Jake said they was missin' me," he continued with satisfaction. "He's gonna tell the boys hi for me too."

"Well, isn't it wonderful to have friends like that?" I asked.

"Sure is!" he agreed.

Mr. Simpson puzzled me. Sometimes he made perfect sense, and at other times, his capacity for rational thought was distinctly lacking. Physically, he was improving. His eyesight was steadily returning, and his brain had healed enough to regulate his body temperature without the hypothermia unit. But he still had to be flat in bed to keep cerebral fluid from draining through his nasal passage. This was Dr. Glosser's gravest concern.

CHAPTER 20

Staying the Course

I had become comfortable with my work. The medical terminology and procedures were no longer foreign to me. Unit life became an enjoyable norm, and I loved our church services.

The gorgeous colors of the autumn leaves alerted us to another Ohio winter lurking just around the corner. Ruth and I had grown in our love and were engaged to be married in the spring. She would join me in sharing this 1-W voluntary service experience.

The ward secretary's voice crackled over the intercom. "Johnny, can you quickly check on Room 103? The student nurse reports a problem there."

I made it to Mr. Simpson's room in record time and found him sitting upright in bed, trying to figure out how to escape his belt.

"Hey, Mr. Simpson," I greeted him. "Just where are you going?"

"I am going to the bathroom," he announced emphatically.

"Here, let me get you a bedpan," I hurried to suggest. "Remember that Dr. Glosser has ordered you to remain in your bed."

"I told you I'm going to the bathroom!" he reiterated forcefully.

Thanksgiving 1966, with our first unit leaders, Clyde and Miriam Wagler.

"Well, you can't!" I said. "See how your catheter is connected to this tubing and routed through the Posey™ belt? Lie back down, and I'll bring you the bedpan you've been using."

He squinted at the connection with his good eye and said, "That ain't no problem." With that, he reached for the joint connecting the catheter to the tubing, and with one deft move, wrenched it apart.

As he squirmed backwards, pulling his legs through the belt, I placed my hands on his shoulders and said in a commanding voice, "Mr. Simpson, your doctor has ordered you to stay flat in bed so your injury can heal." At the same time, I pushed firmly to get him to lie back down. Instantly, he balled up his fist, drew it back, and took aim at my face, saying, "I am going to the bathroom!"

I suddenly realized that despite the doctor's orders, it would be better for him to go safely to the bathroom than to sustain a fall trying to climb out over the bedrail, which he was about to do. I lowered his rail, keeping a safe distance from his fist. He gave me a look that clearly told me to stay out of the way. His fist had already convinced me that was in my best interest.

After five minutes, Mr. Simpson emerged from the bathroom and climbed back into bed as meek as a lamb. I reconnected his catheter, locked his Posey™ belt, raised his bedrail, and headed for the nurses' station to report the most recent developments in Room 103.

On my day off, I was asked to meet with Mr. Will Salmons, plant manager of the hospital who was responsible for all the mechanical operations of this huge complex. He was from Georgia and spoke with a heavy southern accent. We met over a cup of coffee in the cafeteria to discuss what he had on his mind.

"You were a plumber before you came to work here in the hospital, correct?" he began.

"Well, I wasn't actually a licensed plumber, but I was working for Byler Plumbing Company as an apprentice," I told him.

"Would you like to make some extra money on your days off?" he inquired.

I smiled, thinking that might be a good idea. "What do you have in mind?" I asked.

"Well," Mr. Salmons drawled, "we're changing our assembly line in the food preparation area, and we have to move our coffee urn to a new location. It's heated by steam, and we are going to have to re-plumb the steam pipes and set it up at the end of the line, just before the food trays are completed and loaded into the carts. Let me show you," he said, rising.

I drained my cup of coffee and followed him into the huge hospital kitchen filled with enormous mixers and ovens.

"Here's the present location," he said, patting the ten-gallon coffee urn. "And here is where it needs to be." He indicated a wide area at the end of a heavy, stainless steel counter. "And let me show you where the shutoff valve for the steam is located." He led me to a huge mechanical room with a dizzying array of water, steam, and oxygen pipes and valves. Lifting a chained tag marked "Kitchen – Steam," he said, "This one shuts it off. You're going to have to make the change after 10 in the evenin' and before 5 in the mornin'. Do you think you can do that?" he asked.

"Oh, I believe we can get it done before the kitchen crew arrives in the morning," I assured him.

I burned some midnight oil on that coffee urn project. I became groggy with fatigue and wondered if the little extra money was worth it. It wasn't until the wee hours of the morning that I completed the job and returned all the tools to maintenance.

A week passed, and Mr. Salmons wanted to meet with me again. As we sat together, he outlined his plan. "Mr. Miller, I've got a proposition that I think you're going to like. You have a real aptitude for mechanical things, and you learn easily. I know you aren't making much money on your current arrangement. If you'll switch from the medical department to our maintenance department, I'll make you an apprentice fireman on our boilers. We run our boilers year-round, and by law, someone has to attend them 24/7. A boiler fireman makes a very handsome salary, you know. By the time your two years are completed, you would be ready to take your state exams, and you would be set for life. What do you say?"

"Honestly, I hardly know what to say," I responded. "This is a completely new idea." My first thought was, *Absolutely not*. I had been in the boiler room and had seen the firemen lounging in their chairs, watching a few gauges, and jotting periodic notations in their journals. I knew that was not a life for me! However, Will Salmons sounded so convinced that I could not reject his offer out of hand.

"Can you give me some time to think about this?" I asked.

"Sure," he responded graciously. "Just let me know, okay?"

"Thanks," I said. "I'll get back with you on this." But I was already 90 percent sure what my answer was going to be.

Returning from lunch three days later, I fell into step with Mrs. Vann and was shocked when she said, "I hear you are going to be leaving us."

"Me, leaving?" I asked. "What do you mean?"

"I was told you are going to leave us and join the maintenance department."

"Who told you that?" I asked.

"Mr. Salmons has been saying it."

"But I haven't been saying it, have I?"

"Well, I really don't know."

"It's true Mr. Salmons offered me a position, and I told him I would think about it, but that is all I've done."

"Mr. Miller, don't you let that Will Salmons talk you into leaving us," she warned. "Do not listen to him. We need you!"

I smiled reassuringly as we parted at the entrance of 1-West and said, "Don't worry."

Sitting with Mr. Salmons a little later, I explained, "Growing up in a Mennonite community and being a conscientious objector to war, I always knew that someday I would engage in 1-W service. My heart's desire has been that my two years of service to my country would be something meaningful and worthwhile. And although I appreciate your offer, after thinking it over and praying about it, I feel my time here will be better spent in patient care."

"But," he countered, "with a much bigger salary after your two years are complete, you could give a lot more to your church and help many more people. Think about that."

"Yes, that is possible," I acknowledged. "However, I feel led to continue as I am."

"Well, if that is how you feel, I guess it's your choice," he said reluctantly. "But you can't say that I didn't offer, and I hope you won't be sorry."

We agreed that I would still be available for occasional small maintenance jobs during off hours, but that I would continue as an orderly with the medical staff. We shook hands and parted as friends.

There were times in our work when the line between Christian nonresistance and the use of force was somewhat blurred for us. How should a follower of Jesus Christ respond to a belligerent or mentally ill patient? What if he was endangering others or even himself?

One afternoon, a call came asking that four orderlies hurry to 4-North to deal with a psychiatric patient. When we arrived, we learned that Thomas, a fifteen-year-old patient, was out of control and needed to be restrained.

We calmly entered the patient's room and found Thomas to be nearly six feet tall and very muscular. He was wary of us and kept edging away as we tried to talk to him.

"Why don't you just comply with what they're asking?" asked Mose Stoltzfus, who worked on 4-North and understood the circumstances.

"Hey man, that nurse has no right to tell me what to do, and I'm leaving. She can't keep me here!" Thomas raged.

"You are aware that you are under doctor's care and are committed to this psychiatric ward?" someone asked as we kept inching in his direction and away from the door.

"You touch me and I'll get even with you!" he threatened.

"Look," I said, "we really don't want to take you down by force, but you cannot go on like this."

"Where do you live?" he demanded. "I dare you to give me your address. I've got friends, and we will find you!"

Mose responded by quoting Scripture. "The angel of the Lord encampeth round about them that fear him, and—"

"Bring him on," interjected Thomas. "Bring him on!"

By this time, he had backed himself into the corner and was becoming reckless and desperate. My heart pounded in my ears. My mouth felt dry as the tension mounted. I hated this kind of confrontation.

Again, we tried to reason with him and get him to calm down. But Thomas was breathing hard, and a steely look crept into his blue eyes. He sneered, "You think you're so smart and you're gonna get me, but I'm taking some of you with me!"

Quick as lightning, and without warning, his long arm struck out at Mose! Just as quickly, Mose grabbed the arm before Thomas could retract it. Suddenly, Thomas was being held down by four orderlies.

He looked up at us rather pitifully and said, "I guess I did the wrong thing that time."

Thomas was forced to take his medication, and things began to settle down. The nurse felt if one of the orderlies was on duty, the situation would stay under control. But she explained to Thomas that reinforcements were readily available. That knowledge had a calming effect, and he became more willing to comply with orders from the doctor or hospital staff.

In Room 102, twenty-eight-year-old Edward Wine in Bed 1 had been told he would be dismissed in the morning providing there was no sign of infection. This was his fourth day since his arthrotomy and he had gotten along surprisingly well. His doctor, pleased with his progress and mobility, had discharged him. Edward called his wife to tell her the good news, and she responded that she would pick him up at 11 a.m.

Mr. Richards, who was in Bed 2, suffered from lumbar back strain and was undergoing pelvic traction. He envied his roommate, but he knew it would be some time before he would be up and moving about. The two men chatted as Edward gathered his belongings and placed them into his bag so there would be no delay when his wife arrived. He had gingerly tugged his trousers over his sore knee and buttoned his shirt when his hands suddenly jerked up and he collapsed backwards onto his bed.

"Edward!" called Mr. Richards. "Are you all right?" Realizing he couldn't get out of his traction, Mr. Richards grabbed his call button and rang for the nurse. The intercom crackled, and the voice of the ward secretary resounded in Room 102. "May I help you?"

"Hey, we need a nurse in here quickly!" he said. "Mr. Wine just fainted or something, and he fell across his bed!"

"We'll have someone come right away," the secretary assured him.

"We need immediate help for an emergency in Room 102!" blared from the intercom in every room on 1-West.

Dr. Donalds had just finished examining his patient in Room 101 and was already in the hall with the charge nurse when the plea for help came through. Quickening his pace, he hurried the few steps into Room 102. He grabbed Mr. Wine's wrist and searched for a pulse. Thinking quickly, he reached for his stethoscope and listened to his chest. Mr. Wine was in cardiac arrest, and he was not breathing!

Dr. Donalds flung off his coat and immediately began external cardiac massage, then breathed into Mr. Wine's open mouth while holding the nose shut to force his breath into the patient's lungs. The nurse grabbed the room phone and dialed zero. She spoke firmly and distinctly into the receiver. "Announce Code Blue for Room 102."

She had barely replaced the receiver when the hospital's PA system announced, "Code Blue, Code Blue! Code Blue for Room 102, Room 102!"

In less than a minute, the crash cart came careening through the door of 102, pushed by James Wesson, who had been giving an inhalation treatment at the end of the hall. Snatching the bag and mask from the cart, James immediately took over the pulmonary resuscitation, freeing Dr. Donalds to concentrate on the heart compressions. They worked desperately. It seemed that this young man should have a long life before him. Because of the short time between Mr. Wine's collapse and the onset of treatment, this was a textbook case, and it was hopeful his life could be saved.

Ten minutes into the resuscitation, a rosy pink began to color Mr. Wine's face. Moments later, he took the first breath on his own. James compressed his bag several more times before removing the mask, and the patient responded with several breaths on his own. Dr. Donalds paused and felt a weak, intermittent pulse. James Wesson watched the patient intently. Then a loud groan escaped Mr. Wine's lips, and he ceased breathing. Dr. Donalds could no longer detect a heartbeat, and they immediately returned to their former rhythm, working with renewed vigor.

Despite their expertise, Mr. Wine's face slowly lost its color and became ashen grey. Frantically, the two men worked like a well--coordinated machine. James counted Dr. Donald's compressions and synchronized the bag compressions and releases to match every fourth heart compression. On and on they labored. They would not concede defeat; this man had to live! But after forty-five minutes of intense struggle, Dr. Donalds was forced to admit that Mr. Edward Wine had departed this life, and there was nothing he could do about it. He sat down in the nurses' station, utterly spent, and began filling out the death certificate.

Mrs. Wine left her home, joyfully anticipating a reunion. But she arrived at the hospital to discover that her husband, with whom she had spoken just two hours earlier, had died, and she was now a widow.

We were all deeply affected by this death, and I was reminded that it is God, not man, who created life. It is God who holds our lives in His hands.

CHAPTER 21

Gordon Denny

"Mr. Miller," said Mrs. Stevens as we met in the hallway while I was delivering supper trays. I stopped, tray in hand. "ER has a patient being transferred from another hospital, and they are requesting an orderly. Let the aides finish dispensing the meal trays, and you go on over to ER. They want you there when he arrives."

"Sure," I said. "I'll deliver this tray and head right over. Am I to stay there for the rest of the shift?"

"Stay as long as they need you. They will tell you when to return."

I always enjoyed the diversity of working in ER, but couldn't help wondering why they wanted me to be present *when* this patient arrived—perhaps it was another attempted suicide.

I entered ER, and all was quiet. "What's up?" I asked.

"We've been informed that we are about to receive a rather violent psych patient being transferred from Good Samaritan Hospital."

"And just what do you expect *me* to do with a violent patient?" I inquired.

"Well, we would feel better with a little manpower around just in case of trouble," said the charge nurse.

I felt apprehensive as the charge nurse picked up a notepad and read, "Gordon Denny, twenty-four years old, semi-professional football player, suffered a head injury, admitted to Good Samaritan on November 20. Became increasingly difficult to manage and attacked a nurse yesterday, attempting to tear off her uniform. Transferring to Bethesda on November 28."

"I think I just heard a call from 1-West," I said, rising and taking several quick steps toward the door.

"Oh no, you don't!" the nurses chorused together.

I laughed and sat back down. "Well, give me something to do," I said. "I didn't come over here just to sit."

"There's a sink full of used instruments to be cleaned if you would like."

"I like!" I grinned, and headed for the kitchenette.

I was nearly finished with that task when I heard a nurse say, "It looks like he's here."

A moment later I glanced down the hall. My first sight of Gordon Denny was tremendously impressive. He was a powerfully built, athletic man with thick, strong arms, a massive chest, and a jutting overbite that gave him a menacing appearance. He was handcuffed between two uniformed police officers, and they were taking no chances with their charge.

One of the officers announced, "We were asked to safely deliver Mr. Denny into—"

But his speech was cut short by the staccato sound of submachine gunfire! Gordon Denny, in his deranged state of mind, acted as though he held weapons in both hands. In his fantasy, he was pointing them in our direction and giving an impressively realistic imitation of rapid gunfire.

When the patient finally stopped "shooting," the policeman patiently continued. "As I was saying, we are delivering Mr. Denny into your care. Where do you want him?"

"Right this way," responded the charge nurse, and she led the officers into Room 5. This room was equipped with a hospital bed which had rails to fasten the restraints. Once the patient was secured to the bed, it could be moved to any room as required.

Unlocking one handcuff only, the officers "helped" Mr. Denny lie down. His free wrist was then fastened to the bed rail with a thickly padded leather restraint. The second officer released Gordon's other hand and held it firmly while the nurse fastened that wrist to the opposite bedrail. The officer then handed a packet of papers to the charge nurse, tipped his hat to the nurses, gave a nod of acknowledgment in my direction, and bid us good day.

"Should I head back to 1-West?" I asked.

"No way! You're staying right here with us," the charge nurse informed me.

I sat with Mr. Denny and tried to engage him in conversation while the nurses did the necessary paperwork and made some phone calls. There had been some miscommunication as to where this patient would be placed. Until they cleared that up, he would remain with us in Room 5. As I conversed with Mr. Denny, he seemed moody and distant, and time passed slowly.

It was rather late when Dr. Benning arrived. Even then, he did little in the way of examining the patient. However, he did explain that until they prepared a safety room for Mr. Denny on 4-North, he would be admitted to 1-West. This was due to the risk of the patient breaking the floor-to-ceiling window on the fourth floor and jumping out! They were trying to find a room for him on the ground floor.

We finally moved Mr. Denny to 1-West in Room 106, locked in

a Posey™ belt and ankle restraints but with his hands free. As a precaution, we moved his bed four feet away from the wall where the oxygen and suction equipment stood.

In report the following morning, we heard that Mr. Denny had asked to go to the bathroom in the middle of the night, but was given a bedpan. Moments after the nurse walked from the room, she heard a terrible din of clanging, crashing metal. Rushing back into the room, she found that our patient had expertly thrown his bedpan through the open door of the bathroom. He threw it with enough force to waken most of the patients on 1-West as the stainless steel pan ricocheted off the tiled walls and floor!

Because of occasional cerebral drainage from Mr. Simpson's nose, Dr. Glosser finally gave up his hope that the dura was going to heal on its own. Despite his reluctance to perform a second craniotomy, he scheduled Mr. Simpson for surgery. However, the day before surgery, the doctor wanted Mr. Simpson to sit in a chair until cerebral fluid began dripping from his nose. We were supposed to catch the fluid in a glass vial. The lab then needed to positively identify the sample as cerebral fluid to confirm the second operation was justified.

"Mr. Simpson, your doctor wants you to sit in a chair for a bit," I said as I entered his room. "Are you ready?"

"Sure, I'm ready to sit in a chair. When may I get up?"

"Right now," I explained. "The doctor is coming to see you this morning, and he wants you sitting in a chair."

"Okay, sure," he said, lifting himself on one elbow and squinting at me.

I soon had Mr. Simpson sitting comfortably in a chair for the first time in nearly two months. I stood by with the glass vial, watching for the first sign of his cerebral drainage. After twenty minutes, Mr. Simpson asked, "How much longer, Johnny?"

"Well, as soon as we collect a few drops from your nose, you can lie down again."

Eventually, Dr. Glosser showed up to examine his patient.

"Mr. Simpson," he explained, "we are going to be taking you to surgery tomorrow, but I must make certain it is absolutely necessary because of the dangers involved. I need just a few drops of fluid from your nose so the lab can analyze it. Okay?"

"Yeah, sure," replied Mr. Simpson.

The brain surgeon bent close and held the vial in readiness as he asked, "Can you grunt for me? Push as if you were moving your bowels."

"Do what?" asked Mr. Simpson in alarm.

"Put pressure on you head so your nose will drip like it has been doing. We must obtain a specimen of this fluid for an analysis."

Mr. Simpson complied, bending forward, taking a deep breath, and making a loud groaning noise, but not a drop appeared from his nose. After several more fruitless efforts, Dr. Glosser handed me the vial and ordered me to keep trying.

An hour passed, and then another, and Mr. Simpson said, "I'm so tired of sittin' here. Can't I please go to bed?"

"I'm sorry, but the doctor said we must first get several drops from your nose."

A few minutes passed in silence, and then Mr. Simpson said, "Can't get up. Nope, can't have no pillow. Not allowed to go to the bathroom. Can't even sit up in bed! But now I gotta sit up. Nope, I ain't allowed to go to bed. Gotta' stay in this chair." He shook his head slowly and said, "And they think I'm the crazy one!"

I couldn't help but smile at his logic. After two more hours, Dr. Glosser gave up, and Mr. Simpson gladly returned to his bed. His surgery was canceled, and he never again dripped cerebral fluid from his nose. By all appearances, his leaking dura had finally healed on its own. A week later, Mr. Simpson was discharged and returned home. He still squinted, and sometimes talked a bit irrationally, but he was happy to be alive.

During report, Mrs. Stevens announced, "I will be assigning one orderly per shift to personally care for Mr. Gordon Denny during his stay on 1-West. Early this morning, he asked for a urinal. When he received it, he gripped it like a football and threw it, breaking the big window in his room. Maintenance removed all the glass and boarded the opening with a sheet of plywood. Someone must keep a close watch on him. If he's left alone very long, he begins shouting expletives. Visitors in the front lobby could easily hear him." She looked in my direction and said, "See what you can do about that."

Upon entering his room, I saw that Mr. Denny's bed linens were folded on a chair and his bed had not been changed for obvious reasons.

"Hi, Mr. Denny," I said, "how are things going for you today?"

He yawned and said, "Oh, all right, I guess."

"I want to freshen up your bed," I announced, "and make you a bit more comfortable. Does that sound good to you?"

"Yeah, man, I'm so tired of lying on my back."

"I understand. Let me see if we can do something about that."

He perked up immediately and said, "I'm thirsty."

I opened the carafe on his bedside stand and found the water to be room temperature.

"I'm going to get you some fresh ice water," I told him. "I'll only be gone a minute. Sit tight, and I'll be right back."

As I was scooping ice into Gordon's container, I heard obscenities resounding from Room 106 and realized I always needed to close the door when I left his room. I hurried back, closed the door behind me, and asked, "Are those the words your mother taught you to say?"

"What words?" he asked innocently.

"The ones I heard you shouting while I was gone."

"You think they're bad?"

"Of course they're bad! You're a man, and real men don't talk that way."

He contemplated that while I poured a glass of fresh water for him and placed a straw in it. Since he had already distinguished himself as an avid thrower, I held the glass for him. He was thirsty and took a long drink, nearly emptying the glass.

"You and I are going to have to work together to make you more comfortable," I told him.

I unlocked the restraint from his right ankle and had him roll onto his left side. Next, I pulled the used sheets loose and stuffed them tight against his back. I replaced them with the fresh linens and asked him to roll over the hump, which he did. But when I asked for his foot to place it back into the restraint, he refused.

"Nope," he said emphatically, "you're not going to get my foot again."

"Well, I wouldn't want to sleep on that hump in the middle of my bed, but I guess that's up to you," I said. His brow furrowed, and he wiggled his body, trying to flatten the uncomfortable bulge he was lying on.

Then his face brightened. "I know," he said. "Just turn my other foot loose, and I'll get out of bed so you can make it more easily."

"I'll release that foot just as soon as you allow me to fasten this one back where it belongs," I replied.

"Please," he said. "I'll be good. I promise!"

"But," I countered, "If you were good, you would willingly give me this foot so I could release the other one."

After extensive coaxing, Gordon finally submitted to having his right leg restrained, and I was able to finish changing his bed. While I worked, we had an interesting conversation in which he told me he was married and his wife was expecting their first child.

"So, Gordon, when is your baby due, and how is it going to feel to become a father?"

A look of tenderness crossed his face, and his eyes glowed with anticipation as he said, "Our child is due in three months, and I really want to be a good father!"

"That's wonderful," I said. "Will I get to meet your wife?"

"Yes, when she comes. She's a jewel," he sighed.

Several days passed, and I learned how to relate to Mr. Denny. We were learning to trust one another. In fact, we developed a plan where I released the Posey™ belt and one leg restraint, then lowered the rail. This allowed him to stand on his own feet, one of which was still shackled to the lowered bed rail.

On Thursday evening, I met Mrs. Denny for the first time. As I entered Gordon's room, I could feel tension in the air. Gordon was pouting in his bed, and his wife looked sullen. I asked gently, "Is this the wonderful wife you told me about?"

"She brought me a gift, but she won't give it to me!" he complained. This somehow didn't seem to fit the jewel of a wife Gordon had told me about.

As I turned to his wife, she showed me a fruit basket and told me, "I gave him an apple, and he threw it at the TV." She spoke softly, but she was obviously upset. I sensed that not only was she disappointed by her husband's actions, but she was also struggling to come to grips with the severity of his mental disorder.

"She brought me an apple, and I want an apple, please!" Gordon continued.

"Promise me you will not throw it?" I asked.

"I promise. Please!"

Okay," I said. "But if you throw it, then I will take it away. Understand?"

"Sure," he agreed. "I promise."

I turned to Mrs. Denny, who still seemed disturbed by this whole ordeal, and said, "Go ahead and give him an apple."

She hesitated, shooting me a questioning look. "Go ahead," I urged. "He promised."

Mrs. Denny selected a beautiful Red Delicious apple from the basket she had lovingly prepared for her husband. She brought it hesitantly to Gordon's bedside and gingerly held it out to him, no doubt half expecting him to grab the apple and throw it. But he looked lovingly into his wife's eyes as he slowly took the apple from her hand.

"Thank you," he said. Turning the apple in his hands, he selected the choicest place to sink his teeth into. He bit into the apple and chewed slowly, relishing its flavor while I relished the moment. Then, quick as a flash, he flung the apple! It hit the TV and bounced back onto the foot of his bed. He lunged, snatched it, and drew back for another throw, but I intercepted his hand in midair. Locking my fingers about his wrist, I pulled his arm back over the headboard and anchored it there.

"Gordon," I said as he glared over his shoulder at me, "you promised me you wouldn't throw that apple, but you did. Now I'm going to take it away from you." His eyes narrowed, his jaw set, and he squeezed with unbelievable strength. The apple was crushed to pulp in his grasp, and the juice trickled between his fingers and ran down his arm. One at a time, I pried his fingers from the remains of the apple and took it from him. Tears glistened in his wife's eyes, and she left the room to regain her composure.

I reminded Gordon of his love for his wife and their coming child. I explained that he needed to consider her condition and treat her with extra kindness, and Mr. Denny promised he would.

I continued working with Gordon Denny the following week and came to know him quite well, including the quirks of his tortured mind. My heart ached for his faithful wife, who was struggling with her husband's mental illness. Physically, he looked just the same, and yet he expressed a totally different personality than the one she had known and loved. I tried my best to explain that her husband had no control over his thoughts or actions, and we were trying to help him recover that control. She appreciated these explanations but still struggled to grasp her husband's disabilities.

Try as I might, with all the spiritual and moral reasoning I could muster, I was unable to cure Gordon of shouting curses at the top of his lungs. This eventually brought about his transfer. Maintenance felt it was best to board up the window before he had a chance to break it. All furnishings, tables, nightstands, and lamps were removed from his prospective room. When all was readied, Gordon Denny was transferred to his specialized room on the psychiatric ward of 4-North.

CHAPTER 22

Needful Restraints

An elderly lady was admitted to our floor. She was tiny, weighing in at just under a hundred pounds. Her uncut hair swung in a long braid, and she had a gracious personality. Not only was she a delight to serve, but I was also fascinated by the fact that her grandson was famous among America's accomplished astronauts. She became a bit of a celebrity on 1-West.

As I spoke with her each evening, we developed a good relationship, and she came to trust me. However, on one such visit, I detected something was bothering her. I found her staring fearfully at the ceiling and pointing occasionally. So I asked her, "Anne, how can I help you?"

Pointing a gnarled, arthritic finger upward, she confided in a whisper meant only for my ears, "It's them!"

I saw nothing and dismissed her concern out of hand. Later that evening, I checked on Anne again and found her even more restless and distraught.

"Anne," I said, leaning close. "Tell me what is wrong, and maybe

I can fix it for you."

Glancing over my shoulder, she leaned close to my ear and said, "It's them. They are after me. They are trying to get me!"

"Nobody would want to hurt you," I said. "You are such a lovely person!"

"Don't you see them?" she asked in alarm.

Turning, I followed her gaze, and the only thing that broke the monotony of the white ceiling tile was the embedded track for the privacy curtain circling her bed. Being the grandmother of such a famous person, Anne had been given a semi-private room that had been converted into a private room, eliminating the need for the privacy curtain. The curtain had been removed, leaving twenty small, empty hooks still visible in the track.

Upon realizing Anne's fear was the product of her imagination, I leaned close and whispered back, "Do you want me to take care of *them?"* I pointed toward the hooks.

She placed her hand to her mouth in a gesture of fear, but she nodded hopefully. "Yes."

It only took a few moments to climb onto a chair and slide those terrifying hooks around her bed and out of her line of sight. "There," I exclaimed to Anne. "I took care of *them!"*

Anne was greatly relieved and thanked me sincerely. She helped me see that there were times when I needed to acknowledge the *perceived* problems of my patients, and then guide them out of their fears rather than trying to refute their false perception of reality.

I had just clocked in and walked into the nurses' station one morning when the phone rang. Our ward secretary answered and then said briskly, "Yes, I'll send him right up!" I assumed she was referring to me since I was the only man working on 1-West that morning. She spun in her chair and said, "Johnny, 4-North, STAT!" I took off, and she called after me, "It's Mr. Denny!"

I reached the elevator in record time and chafed at its slowness as I rose without interruption to the fourth floor. Racing to the entrance of the electrically locked door, I remembered with relief that although I could enter from the hall, those within needed to be let out by the electric switch activated only from the nurses' station. I jerked the door open and rushed in. The nurse pointed me to Mr. Denny's room, and I dashed through the outer door and made sure he was not holed up in the restroom. In three steps, I reached the second door, which was standing open, and I stopped short! There stood Gordon, without any restraints, alone in the middle of his room.

"Good morning Mr. Denny," I said as calmly as I could at that moment.

"Hi," he said, glowering at me.

I leaned my shoulder against the left door jamb and moved my feet toward the right, blocking as much of the doorway as possible.

"So, what are you up to this morning?" I inquired.

"I am going home," he announced.

"I see," I said. "Has Dr. Benning dismissed you?"

"That makes no difference. I am going home, and nobody's going to stop me!" he sneered.

"Is your wife coming to pick you up?"

"I'll call her."

"What are you planning to do at home?" I asked.

All this time, Gordon was slowly inching toward the doorway where I stood, and I was desperately planning how to avert a disaster. I certainly did not relish the idea of getting beaten to a pulp, but neither could I allow this man to escape his room and possibly attack the nurse or another patient. I whispered a desperate prayer and stood there blocking his exit with raw fear coursing through me.

"You know you cannot be dismissed until Dr. Benning says so. Was he here this morning? Did he talk with you?"

"No! Get out of my way!" he ordered.

"Mr. Denny, you are smarter than that. You know the rules," I said. "I cannot let you go until you see Dr. Benning. So just go back and sit on your bed until the doctor comes."

He took a quick step toward me and drew back his huge fist. I gulped as I remembered the way that giant hand had crushed an apple. Through clenched teeth, Gordon hissed, "I said, get out of my way!"

I continued standing in his way looking dumb while quaking inwardly. Suddenly, he lunged, and my eyes instinctively closed as I waited for the punch that would fill my head with stars and knock me unconscious. When no punch landed, I cautiously opened my eyes, and there was his hard-knuckled fist, an inch from my nose. The moment Mr. Denny saw my eyes open, he pushed with his fist, flattening my nose and twisting his fist back and forth as he pushed my head back. Was he going to flip me over backwards?

Suddenly, Mr. Denny dropped his fist to his side and said, "Man, you're not even scared." If only he knew how deeply shaken I really was!

But taking advantage of his mistake, I said, "Come on, let's talk about it." I strode past him and sat on the edge of his bed, my knees trembling. "Come on," I urged, giving the bed an inviting pat.

Slowly, as if walking in his sleep, Gordon Denny came and sat beside me. I noted his foot restraints were still locked in place on the bedrails. Now that the crisis was past, I could speak more normally.

"How do you like Dr. Benning?" I began.

"He's not bad, but I don't see him much."

"Do you think he is helping you?" I continued. Gordon shrugged and stared at the floor.

"Do you realize some of the things you've been thinking and saying are not like you at all?" I asked him.

"Really?" He looked at me in surprise.

"Well, that is what the doctor and nurses say," I told him. "And I believe your wife has also noticed a change in you. That's why they brought you to this hospital, so Dr. Benning can try to get you back to your old self. Does that make sense? Has he been giving you medication?"

"I suppose so, they're always shoving another pill at me." Gordon yawned and stretched.

"Why don't you lie down and let me relax you with a good back rub?" I suggested.

"I don't need a back rub; I'm all right," he muttered.

"But I give really good ones. Come on, give me a try."

"All right." He stretched out on the bed, face down, and I proceeded to give him a vigorous back rub. I could feel his tense muscles slowly relaxing as I worked the tightness from his back and shoulders.

As I rubbed, I continued talking. "You know, we've seen people hurt themselves or family members simply because they didn't realize they needed help."

He was silent, so I went on. "I would really feel bad if you went home and did something like that just because you didn't understand that you needed our help."

Gordon sighed. "And I know that would make your wife feel absolutely terrible," I said. I ceased rubbing his back, and he sat up. I fluffed up his pillow and said, "Here, lie down." Mr. Denny looked at me for a long moment, and I reiterated, "Just lie down and get a little rest."

With a sigh of resignation, he stretched out on the bed, and after ten minutes, I finally had one ankle back in its restraint. The second one took even longer. The nurse explained that he would need a Posey™ belt and wrist restraints as well. It took a lot of patience and persuasion to get this all accomplished, but I was finally ready to head back to 1-West.

"Mr. Denny," I said, "I'm going to be leaving. I have other people who need me, but I'll stop around and see you. Okay?"

"Okay," he said. "See you."

I spoke briefly with the charge nurse, and she hit the button for the electric lock and let me out. I rode the elevator back to the main floor, and as the elevator doors opened, I heard the ringing of the phone on 1-West. I didn't even get to enter the nurses' station before being told to get back to 4-North, STAT! As I ran, I tried to imagine what could possibly have gone wrong in the few minutes since I had left the psychiatric ward. When I entered Gordon Denny's room for the second time, he was out of three of his five restraints and working diligently on the fourth.

The charge nurse told me later that mere minutes after I left, Mr. Denny had begun thrashing uncontrollably. Jerking and lunging, kicking and pulling with unbelievable strength and stamina, he had extracted himself from several of his restraints.

It took me nearly two hours to get Mr. Denny calmed down and talked back into his restraints once more. Since Earl and I worked with the same patients, I told him about the happenings of the day. He too had worked with Mr. Denny and understood the serious situation I had faced.

Two days later, on Earl's shift, Gordon Denny went berserk again, and Earl was sent to 4-North. He arrived in Mr. Denny's room just as the patient freed one hand and began working on the other. With a flying leap, Earl sailed over the foot of the bed and landed on top of Gordon, forcing him to lie down. He struggled to get Gordon's arm back into the restraint. Suddenly, Earl felt a searing pain on his chest. In his desperation, Mr. Denny had bitten Earl with enough force to break the skin. The patient was eventually subdued and put back in restraints, but Earl had to go to ER for a precautionary tetanus shot.

A week later, Mrs. Andrews said to me, "Remember Mr. Denny? He will be going home soon."

"Really, how's that possible?" I asked incredulously.

"Well, their ward secretary told me Dr. Benning gave him two electric shock treatments, and he has snapped out of his situation."

"That is amazing! I am so happy for him. I am going to pay him a visit to see for myself."

"You'd better do it today because he might be discharged by tomorrow."

I quickly completed my assignments and obtained permission to visit Mr. Denny on 4-North. Upon entering, I saw him sitting among the other patients. I sat beside him and said, "Hi, I'm Johnny, and I heard the good news."

He raised a questioning eyebrow and asked, "Johnny? From where? Have we met before?"

"Yes," I explained. "I took care of you when you were on 1-West."

"1-West?" he questioned. "You say you took care of me?"

"Yes, don't you remember you told me you were going to be a father soon and you were looking forward to being a good dad?"

"Well, I am going to be a father," he said politely. "But what makes you think I would have told you that? I don't even know you."

I was in shock, hardly able to believe how completely Mr. Denny had changed. All those hours we had spent together were totally gone, and he honestly did not remember me at all.

I stuck my hand out, and he took it in his massive one. I said,

"Mr. Denny, may God bless you with a healthy child, and I wish you well."

He thanked me, no doubt still wondering who I was and why I had come to visit. He was a different Gordon Denny from the one Earl and I had worked with.

Mr. Denny later came back for an evaluation and a minor adjustment in medication, and at last report was living a normal, happy life.

CHAPTER 23

A Threefold Cord

The Bethesda Hospital was much like a close-knit village. News spread rapidly among its employees. One such news item was that the hospital was considering the use of a computer for payroll. Any employee who was interested in computer programming was invited to take an aptitude test. Knowing this was beyond my capabilities, the opportunity did not interest me in the least. Lee Schrock, on the other hand, wanted to take the offered test to see whether this was something he wanted to get into.

We were pleasantly surprised when Lee scored higher than any other employees taking the test. So it was that a 1-W voluntary service worker moved from the storeroom into the accounting office. Lee worked with the MS-DOS system and had to learn computer-programming language in his new role. We all felt elated to have one of "our boys" working in accounting. Lee continued working with computers in accounting long after his two years of compulsory service had been fulfilled.

The ER had enjoyed a relatively peaceful evening. At 8:15, however, things began to escalate when several patients arrived in a short time. We were kept busy filling out forms, preparing patients, and calling doctors. Each of these patients had a different doctor, and we often waited an hour or more for the doctors to arrive. Even the on-call doctor was not required to remain at the hospital as long as he left a number where he could be reached.

Then an ambulance arrived carrying two accident victims. One had a three-inch arm laceration requiring sutures. But before that ambulance left, another one arrived, bringing two more passengers from the same accident. This filled every available room, and the last patient was parked in the hallway, lying on the ambulance cart.

"Johnny," said the charge nurse, pausing as she rushed about. "Get the information on that patient in the hall." I grabbed a clipboard with its triplicate form and hurried to the patient.

"Hi, my name is Johnny," I said. "I'm an orderly working in the emergency room. Could I have your name and age, please?"

"My name's Barry Scott, and I'm 17."

"Your address?"

He groaned as though in pain and gave me an address in Dresden, Ohio.

"Do you live with your parents? Do you have a number you would like us to call?"

Barry was becoming increasingly uncomfortable and a bit curt in his responses. He was raising his knees as though trying to find a more comfortable position. "Yes," he said, and gave me the number. "When is the doctor coming?" he moaned. "My legs hurt like crazy!"

"As soon as I can get this information, we will contact the doctor. Can you tell me what happened, and what are your complaints?"

"I was in a car wreck, and my back and legs are just killing me!"

I took this information to the charge nurse, who was hurriedly calling doctors and parents of the carload of youth involved in this accident. I was asked to assist a doctor who was placing a cast on a broken arm. That completed, I checked on my patient in the hallway and found him thrashing his legs about in agony. I placed my hand on his shoulder and said, "Look, Barry, we are trying to get the doctor here as fast as we can, but you have to hold your legs still. Do you realize that if you have a spinal injury, you could do permanent damage by simply thrashing about? I know it hurts, but you have to try to hold still."

"I can't help it!" he snapped. "When you hurt like I'm hurting, you'll move too!"

Two ambulance attendants approached and asked for the cot Barry was lying on. I met their eyes and jerked my head to the side, indicating I wanted to talk to them in private.

Out of earshot, I explained, "I'm afraid this patient has a spinal injury, and we do not want to move him more than absolutely necessary to prevent further injury. I'm sure the doctor will order X-rays as soon as we contact him. When we move him onto the X-ray table, I'll bring your cart, and you can be on your way. Can we do that?"

The attendant glanced at his watch and shrugged. "I guess so. What else can we do?"

"Let me check with the nurse. I'll be right back."

I was back moments later and explained, "Dr. Lister is the on-call doctor tonight and has ordered X-rays. The X-ray department is preparing, and it won't be much longer."

I noticed Barry had calmed down somewhat and asked, "How are you getting along?"

"A little better," he said. "My legs don't hurt quite so much now, but my back hurts terribly!"

"You will be going to X-ray soon, and we will have everything ready when the doctor gets to your case," I told him.

Ten minutes later, the X-ray technician came. "I have an order for X-rays on Barry Scott."

I intercepted her and told her, "This patient may have a spinal injury, and we want to be very careful to prevent possible damage. I'll bring him to you on this cart to eliminate one move. Then I will assist in getting him onto the X-ray table."

I followed her, pushing Barry on the ambulance cart. We carefully transferred him onto her X-ray table, and I returned the cart to the waiting ambulance attendants. I thanked them for their excellent service and especially for their patience. As they left, I quickly cleaned up the cast room in preparation for the next patient. The charge nurse poked her head into the room and said, "Johnny, the X-ray lady requests your assistance to get Barry Scott back onto a cart."

Barry was lying on his side with his face away from me as I entered. The technician silently beckoned for me to move down to the foot of the table, then pointed to Barry's spine. I was aghast, for I had never seen anything like this injury. Very visible in the upper lumbar region, between two vertebrae, there was a five-eighth inch protrusion jutting from his spine. She motioned me to be very careful. Ever so gently, we slid Barry onto the cart, taking special pains not to twist his body in the slightest. Then we carefully transported him back to ER.

One by one, our patients were treated and released. That is, all except Barry. He was admitted to 1-West. Dr. Lister decided on a plan for treating Barry's spinal injury. He asked for my assistance, and we rolled Barry into Room 118. With several people grasping each side of the sheet, we carefully moved him onto the hospital bed. We lowered the foot and head ends of the bed, and Barry lay in an uncomfortable position. He was on his back with his head and feet both fourteen inches lower than his midriff. This placed his spine in a hyper-extended position exactly where his injury had occurred.

Dr. Lister, who was a urology specialist and not an orthopedic doctor, next opened a leather case and explained to Barry, "I have a tool here that may prick you a little. I am going to begin at your feet and move it upward. As soon as you feel any pricking at all, I want you to tell me, okay?"

The tool looked like a cowboy's spurs except Dr. Lister held it by its single handle, and it was made of sharp needles. The doctor began on top of the foot and slowly rolled the wheel of needles upward over the ankle and onto the shin. "Tell me as soon as you feel anything," he instructed.

We watched silently, wondering how severely the paralysis had affected Barry. How could this treatment ever reduce the fracture? Would Barry be confined to a wheelchair for the rest of his life? Dr. Lister continued rolling the wheel while intently watching Barry's face for any reaction. He crossed over the knee and started up the thigh, and I noticed little droplets of blood marking the trail where the wheel had traveled. Not until he reached the upper thigh did Barry feel anything.

I couldn't believe that a competent doctor would leave a person with this type of injury lying in such an unlikely position. Why didn't he perform surgery or apply traction? Just draping the patient over a hump seemed very odd to me. Feeling troubled, I prayed for Barry, his healing, and his future.

I had the following weekend off and went to Minerva to visit Ruth and her family. I had been serving at Bethesda for about a year, and Ruth and I were eager to announce our engagement. We anticipated a spring wedding.

During Christmas break in 1966, Ruth and I began making our engagement cards. We had purchased small, plain, unlettered cards. In her best handwriting, Ruth wrote "Engaged" in her lovely penmanship on the front of the cards. On the inside, I drew a rope of three strands running horizontally across the little card. In the bumps of each twist we wrote the letters M A R R I A G E. On the right side of the drawing, we left a short section of rope not yet twisted together. On these yet-to-be-united ends we wrote "Christ" on the center one, "Johnny" on the bottom strand, and "Ruth" on the upper strand. This was to show that a threefold cord is not easily broken, reflecting the message of Ecclesiastes 4:12. We were very concerned that we would center our home on Christ.

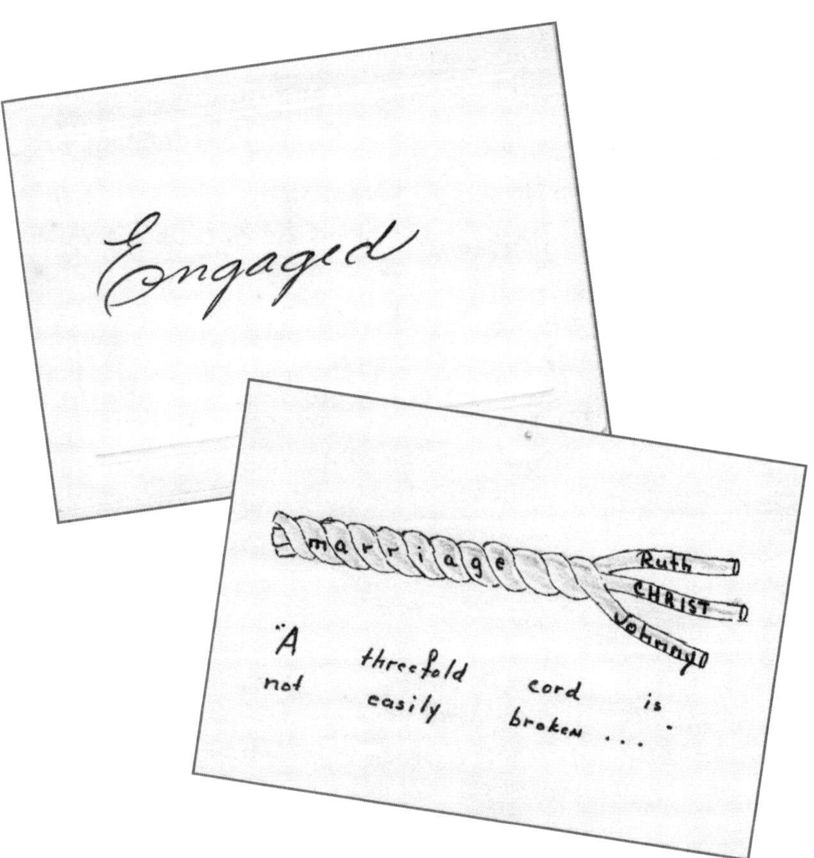

It was a wonderful weekend. Ruth's family already felt like my own. We were enjoying our Sunday afternoon popcorn in the family room with Ruth's ten siblings when I went to the kitchen for a drink of water. As the water was quenching my thirst, I looked out the kitchen window at a scene that produced a deeper thirst than the one I had just quenched. For there were Victor and Emma, my future in-laws, walking together toward the chicken house. They were holding hands as they carried their wire egg baskets. After twenty-two years of marriage, they were still deeply in love. I was profoundly moved and prayed in a whisper, "Lord, that is the kind of marriage I want. Help me to live in such a way that I experience it!" That prayer did not go unheard.

The Sunday service at the Christian Fellowship Church was spiritually uplifting. Their singing was heavenly, and the preaching of the Word captivating and challenging. The brotherly love that flowed through the hearts of the worshippers drew my heart to them. I found myself singing for most of my two-and-a-half-hour drive back to Zanesville. What blessings God was extending to me!

Barry was still lying in the same awkward position, but he certainly was in better spirits. Eating with his head hanging down was challenging, but he joked about it and did surprisingly well. Family members came to visit and encourage him. After a week, his level of paralysis slowly began to diminish, and Dr. Lister was pleased with his progress. After four weeks in the hospital, Barry was fitted with a back brace and ferried to daily physical therapy where he exercised on parallel bars to regain his walking ability. When he was dismissed at the end of his sixth week, my amazement increased, as did my respect for Dr. Lister.

I walked over to the nurses' station bulletin board where the daily surgery schedule was posted along with other important hospital messages. I took a push pin and anchored our engagement card in the center of the other messages. Of course, it created quite a stir and lots of questions.

I was in the treatment room cleaning up a catheter tray while Dr. Donalds was giving his report of an admission on the dictaphone. He seemed to be staring absently at the bulletin board as he spoke. But when he finished, he rose and made his way to the opposite end of the nurses' station. Lifting the flap on our engagement announcement, he stood for a long minute absorbing the message of a Christ-centered marriage. I was glad he had noticed and read the engagement card, but was a little taken aback by the amount of attention he gave it.

Some of the nurses asked me when we were planning to be married. I explained that my fiancée was teaching school, so we would wait until the school term ended in the spring.

One nurse asked, "Is your wife going to work here at the hospital?"

"I certainly hope so," I said. "I want Ruth to share my hospital experience with me."

"Do you think she will like it?" asked another nurse.

"I feel sure she will. Ruth has a physically and mentally handicapped brother who suffers from daily seizures, and a sister who was stricken with polio as a child. Hospitals have already been a part of her life experience. Besides, she used to work in a nursing home."

"I'm sure she will do well," the nurse concluded.

Sandra Andrews, a student nurse, said, "I saw your engagement card and wish to congratulate you."

"Well, thank you," I replied.

"But I do have some questions," she continued. "You are from Virginia, aren't you?"

"Yes, I am."

"Well, I'm dating a young man who is also from Virginia. I really want to know what you mean by a threefold cord not being broken."

"It's like this," I explained. "My love for Ruth is imperfect because I am a flawed human being, and she is too. Our love could be tested until our human capacity to love runs out. But when our human love is intertwined with divine agape love, it is perfected. If Ruth were to really disappoint me in some way, I might not feel as though I could continue to love. But the agape love of Jesus that we have wouldn't stop there. It would carry us through."

"That is beautiful concept," Sandra said thoughtfully. "So what do you do on your dates?"

"We talk most of the time. It seems we never get finished talking about all the subjects we should cover. Often we are not alone." I laughed and added, "Sometimes it feels as if I am dating Ruth's whole family. Also, we almost always have devotional time together."

"Devotional time? What do you mean by that?"

"I mean that we read together from the Bible, discuss it, and pray together."

"Why ever would you do that on a date?" she asked.

"Dating is an opportunity to lay the foundation for our future home. How are we going to have a Christ-centered home unless we invite Him into our relationship from the beginning?"

"But don't you . . . uh, I mean, don't you believe in the physical aspect of love?"

"Certainly we do," I replied. "That is God-designed and is to be reserved for marriage only. You see, Sandra, when a couple reserves physical love for marriage, it's kind of like depositing their money into a bank. Then when they withdraw it at the proper time, it has far greater value—like compounded interest. We are putting that aspect of our love into God's bank."

"I am so intrigued by all this," Sandra said. "I really wish you could talk with my boyfriend."

Three days later, I came to the cafeteria for my break and sat with a group of student nurses with whom I had worked. There was good-natured banter going on around the table concerning our marriage plans. However, our conversation became more serious as I shared our joy in a pure courtship and a Christ-centered marriage. Time passed swiftly, and those who had started their break earlier had to return to work. Only one student nurse remained, and she looked rather downhearted.

"You make me so sad," she said.

"Why?" I asked in surprise.

"Because you and your girlfriend are so happy."

"We certainly are!" I agreed.

"But," she continued very seriously, "I will never be that happy. I was dating a young man I thought I could trust, and I made a terrible mistake. I have a little daughter now, and my boyfriend left me. We never got married. Realizing I can never have your kind of joy makes me very sad."

I hardly knew how to respond, but my heart ached for her. "Alice, there is one thing you can do," I said. "Give your life to Jesus. Let Him lead you. He will guide you in the best way possible."

"I know," she responded, "and I want to, but even that cannot erase the past. Still, I am happy for you."

She returned to work, and I sat alone with my thoughts.

CHAPTER 24

Touched

I was sitting in the nurses' station registering my TPRs when the voice of Marilyn Anthony, our ward secretary, broke through my concentration as she spoke into the intercom.

"Yes, it's my daughter Amy who wanted to apply," she said.

"How old is she?" questioned the ward secretary from 3-East.

"Amy's going on twenty and has completed her schooling. I was sure I could get her a job as an aide here at Bethesda."

"I see. That's neat," broke in the 3-East secretary, "mother and daughter working at the same place."

"That's exactly what I thought, but that's not the way it's working out!"

At this point, a light began to flash on the intercom console and the hall resounded with an intermittent beep, alerting our ward secretary that a patient needed help. However, she continued her conversation without regarding the relentless beeping.

"Well, I do know about the hospital's policy against having family members working together on the same floor," commented the 3-East secretary.

"Oh, I knew about that rule too, but that wasn't what I was asking. All I wanted was to get Amy a job as an aide somewhere in the hospital. I went right to the top and asked Mrs. Deckhart, the assistant head of nursing," explained Marilyn. "She knows me, and I've been working here for over a year already."

"And did Amy get the job?"

"No!" exclaimed Marilyn. "Mrs. Deckhart told me they don't have any openings."

I finished registering my TPRs and headed for the room where the unanswered light was still blinking over the doorway. I turned off the call button and asked, "May I help you?"

"Yes," said the lady in Bed 2, pointing to the patient in the other bed. "Her IV ran out."

"Thank you for notifying us. I'll get the nurse." As I passed the nurses' station, I couldn't help noticing that our ward secretary was still hunched over the intercom chatting with her friend from 3-East.

I went back to my room that night feeling troubled. In making plans for our marriage, Ruth and I had been looking forward to sharing this hospital experience together. I was disappointed to learn that there were apparently no openings for nurse aides.

A week later, I sat nervously in Mrs. Deckhart's office. She was pleasant and most professional as she asked, "And what can I do for you, Mr. Miller?"

"Well," I began. "In looking ahead, I thought I should let you know that Ruth and I plan to be married on May 20. I would like to arrange for some time off then."

"Wonderful, and congratulations. I am so happy for you!" She smiled at me with genuine interest. "How long have you known each other?"

"For nearly four years, but we've lived 500 miles apart for most of that time."

"I'm sure she is a wonderful person," Mrs. Deckhart said. "I suppose she will join you here, and I know you will truly be happy together."

"This is why I requested this meeting with you," I explained. "You know I haven't taken my vacation for this year."

"Yes, that is correct."

Hardly daring, I asked, "If I saved my vacation from this year and combined it with my vacation week from next year, we would have two weeks for our wedding and honeymoon. Is that possible?"

"Hmm, let me see. Perhaps we could accommodate you," she responded pleasantly as she opened a schedule book and turned several pages. She made a notation before telling me, "You may count on that time off, and if I can be of further help, please do not hesitate to ask."

"Thank you, Mrs. Deckhart, I really appreciate this!" I exclaimed in relief.

"You are most welcome," she said. "I am glad to arrange that for you. It's easier to accommodate because you made your request so far in advance. Last minute planning makes things extremely difficult. By the way, is your wife planning to work here at the hospital?" she inquired.

Completely surprised by her question, I faltered, "Well . . . we were hoping . . . I mean, Ruth really wanted to be an aide here, but I heard there are no more openings for aides."

"And just who said that?" she demanded with a frown.

"Well, uh, that's what I heard," I replied lamely.

"Listen, Mr. Miller, if your wife wants to work at Bethesda, you have her come talk with me, okay? Don't forget!"

I left Mrs. Deckhart's office with my heart singing.

"Johnny, have you seen the invitation?" asked Marilyn Anthony as she turned from the intercom and pointed to the bulletin board.

"Not yet," I responded as I walked over to read the card. It read, "Christmas Party! All 1-West employees are invited to Mrs. Stevens' residence. To be held at 8 p.m., December 22. Refreshments will be served."

"You and Earl are coming, aren't you?" asked Marilyn. "They have this every year, and I hear it's lots of fun!"

"I'm not sure," I said, not exactly certain what this party might involve. It seemed best to remain noncommittal.

That evening, I discussed the upcoming party with other VS unit members, and felt it best to find out a bit more about it before deciding whether to attend.

On the job, student nurses were asking, "You're coming to the Christmas party at Mrs. Stevens' house, aren't you?"

"Thinking about it," was my stock reply.

One evening, I was working with charge nurse Marsha Carol. "Say, Mrs. Carol," I began. "Tell me more about this upcoming Christmas party everyone is talking about."

"Well, what would you like to know?" she responded.

"What is this party like?"

"We sing, serve refreshments, and play some games. That's all. You'll enjoy it!"

"Will alcohol be served?" I asked.

"No. Well, it's not *served,"* she clarified. "However, some people may bring their own. But you don't have to worry; no one would expect you to drink."

"You know, I doubt we will be there."

"But why not?" asked Mrs. Carol.

"Look at it this way. Jesus is the Prince of Peace, isn't He?"

"Yes," she agreed.

"How can it be right to celebrate the coming of the Prince of Peace with drinking, which brings anything but peace?"

Mrs. Carol thought for a moment before she said, "I see what you are saying, and I do understand. I actually would have been a bit surprised if you and Earl had come to our Christmas party."

So, although they invited and even pressured us to attend, deep down our coworkers knew our participation would have been inconsistent with our testimony.

I found myself in need of spiritual advice and went to visit Brother Clyde. I shared my heart with him, and I'll forever be grateful for the spiritual direction he gave me that night. Clyde wisely saw that I was trying to punish myself for my failures. I was trying to live the Christian life in my own strength instead of in the power of Christ.

"Johnny," he said, "make absolutely sure all your sins are under the blood of Jesus Christ, and then claim that victory and move forward in it. If you fail, confess your failure to the Lord, ask for His forgiveness, receive it, and determine in your heart to walk closer to Him. That is the road to victory!"

He also shared helpful advice in preparing my heart for marriage. His words were weighted with brotherly love and wisdom which I could not resist. The example and experience he shared with me proved to be a tremendous blessing and drew me close to him.

We were having a busy evening in ER when Carmen's parents brought her in. Dr. Shuman had performed a tonsillectomy on her three days earlier. Carmen was a tender-hearted little nine-year-old with dark eyes, red hair, a cute little pug nose, and a freckled face. Her mother was concerned that Carmen was listless and not feeling well. When Dr. Shuman arrived, he ordered a hemoglobin test.

While waiting for the results, he examined little Carmen's operative site and discovered she was still bleeding! He ordered the needed instruments from surgery and anesthetized the back of her throat. I watched, fascinated, as he wore the physician's concave mirror which directed light on the back of Carmen's throat, but allowed the doctor to see through a center hole. He carefully inserted the cauterization tool to the site where the tonsils had been removed and pulled the trigger. There was a short sizzling sound as the tip of the tool burned the bleeding vein shut. A wisp of smoke curled out of the brave little girl's mouth. Dr. Shuman left Carmen to speak with her parents in the waiting room. He returned after a lengthy consultation and reexamined Carmen, only to discover blood still trickled down the back of her throat. Again, he anesthetized her throat to prepare to cauterize her bleeding veins.

"Johnny, Dr. Donalds will be needing a suture tray set up in Room 2 to attend to an accident victim," said the charge nurse. "Do you have time to set that up for him? The patient will be coming in by ambulance, and we want to be ready."

"Certainly," I responded. "I'll have it ready." One never knew what would be needed when an accident victim was on the way. We needed to be ready for any situation.

The ambulance arrived, and I helped the attendants move Debra onto our cart. She had a bandage of blood-saturated gauze taped across her forehead. The charge nurse removed the bandage to reveal a large cut running all the way across the poor girl's forehead. With the bandage removed, blood gushed profusely from the wound, and the nurse slapped thick wads of four-inch pads over the cut and ordered me to apply pressure to them. Placing my hand under the patient's head for support, I pressed hard while the nurse ran to bring a stretchy sterile bandage.

Upon her return, she had me replace the soaked pads with clean ones and again apply heavy pressure to them. As she began wrapping the bandage completely about the head, she instructed me, "Now Johnny, lift her head, but keep your hand low. Good. Now remove your hand long enough for me to wrap the gauze over the wound, and immediately apply pressure again." Working together, we alternately wrapped and pressed until we had twelve layers pressing tightly against the laceration. But even then, blood continued seeping through.

"I need to report to Dr. Donalds," the nurse told me. "Just keep applying direct pressure. That's the best we can do for the present." She left me with the patient and went to confer with Dr. Donalds and to check on Dr. Shuman and little Carmen.

"Debra, can you tell me what happened?" I asked.

"I was going to a school party with my boyfriend, and a rabbit ran onto the road right in front of us. My boyfriend didn't want to hit the rabbit, so he tried to dodge it. We lost control, and the car went into the ditch and hit a culvert. My head broke through the windshield, and it cut my forehead."

"Were you unconscious at any time?"

"No, and I wasn't even hurt except for the cut. Do you think it will leave a scar?" she asked.

"I certainly hope not. I'm sure Dr. Donalds will take every precaution to minimize scarring. You seem pretty brave about all this. How old are you?"

"I'm fifteen," she said.

"I assume your parents have been notified?"

"Oh, yes, the ambulance driver was very nice. He radioed my parent's phone number back to headquarters, and they called my home. Will Dr. Donalds see me? He's our family doctor."

"I believe the nurse is talking to him at this moment."

I kept steady pressure on her bandaged forehead. My arm ached from the strain, but I had to continue. At the same time, I tried to keep up a steady conversation with the patient to keep her mind occupied and quell her fears.

The nurse returned and announced, "Dr. Donalds has ordered X-rays for Debra. Would you take her to X-ray and ask the technician to bring her back when she's done? I'm helping Dr. Shuman with a third cauterization for that little girl. He's having unusual difficulties with stopping her bleeding. And she's such a darling!"

Dr. Donalds arrived shortly before our patient was returned from X-ray. Thankfully, Debra's skull had not been fractured, and the only treatment required was the closure of the five-inch laceration across her forehead. I adjusted the light as Dr. Donalds cut the bandage from her head. As he gently scrubbed the blood from the area, the doctor closely examined the wound. I opened the suture tray for him as he gloved up.

"I will be needing a scalpel and number 23 blade," he announced as he loaded a syringe with local anesthesia. He laid a sterile drape across the patient's face, explaining, "I'm going to give you a few sticks with a needle to numb the area so I can repair the damage, understand?"

"Okay," she said.

"How are your mom and dad getting along?" Dr. Donalds asked. "I haven't seen them for some time."

"They are doing well, thank you. They just got back from vacation last week." This kind of small talk continued to keep Debra occupied. Dr. Donalds explained that the laceration was a pressure cut with ragged edges rather than a wound made by a sharp object.

"This means," he explained, "that I must cut away the upper and lower edges of this wound and give it a smooth edge to prevent an ugly scar. That is what you want, isn't it, Debra?"

"Yes, it is. I trust you," she responded from beneath the drape.

"You will have to be patient with me because this is tedious, and it will take some time."

"That's fine. Just do what you must do," she said.

Dr. Donalds began probing the wound for any foreign matter. He removed several shards of glass. But then his eyes met mine, and he made a wry face as he lifted bone fragments from the wound. The sharp edge of the breaking windshield had almost cut through her skull!

When the doctor was satisfied that the wound was clean, he began straightening its edge with his scalpel. Suddenly, Debra's hand shot up toward her face, but I grabbed it before she contaminated the sterile field.

"No, no!" cried Dr. Donalds.

"But, my nose itches," said Debra plaintively. "It's driving me crazy!"

"Okay," said Dr. Donalds, "but you will have to scratch that itch under the drape, not on top of it. Mr. Miller, assist her."

I guided her hand under the sterile drape where she gratefully scratched away.

"Thanks!" she said. "That's better."

As the tedious surgical procedure stretched on and on, our patient became fretful and afraid. "May I hold your hand?" she asked. "I'm scared."

With a grin, Dr. Donalds replied, "I'm using both of mine, so you will have to hold Mr. Miller's hand. Will that do?"

"M–may I?" she asked in a quavering voice.

"Of course," I said as I took her cold, nervous hand into mine.

Dr. Donalds did a superb job of cleansing, edging, and closing the wound to prevent a permanent, disfiguring scar. Debra was very appreciative and thanked us for the care given her. She gratefully hugged her parents who had been sitting anxiously in the ER waiting room.

My shift was nearly over when the charge nurse told me, "Dr. Shuman wants to keep little Carmen overnight. He plans to run some tests in the morning. Pediatrics just called, and they have a bed ready for her. Can you take her up?"

I headed for the elevator with Carmen on a wheelchair. Looking at her face as the elevator rose, I saw sweat glistening on her forehead and freckled cheeks. Her eyelids were drooping with fatigue, and no wonder—she had been through so much! I tried to imagine what her throat must feel like after being cauterized three times. The pediatric nurse said, "If you wait several minutes, Mr. Miller, you can save us a trip by taking the wheelchair back to ER."

"Sure," I responded. "I'll wait." The nurse exited the room and nodded that it was okay for me to retrieve the wheelchair. As I entered, brave little Carmen pulled her heavy eyes open for me with great effort as I said, "Good night, Carmen." She didn't respond verbally, but nodded her head and gave me a weak, tender smile.

Years later, I still haven't forgotten that sweet smile. Only an hour and a half after I left her bedside, little Carmen passed from her hospital room into the loving arms of Jesus. Her death rocked the entire hospital. Dr. Shuman even canceled all surgeries for the next several days. Carmen had died due to a misdiagnosis. Apparently, she slowly bled to death over several days following her tonsillectomy, and a simple transfusion could easily have saved her life.

CHAPTER 25

Just an Orderly

The student nurses we had been working with were graduating at last. The ceremony was held in a large church in Zanesville, and we orderlies were invited. A hush filled the sanctuary as we took our seats among the hospital officials, family members, and the head nurses from each department. A speaker addressed the graduating class of 1967 before the pinning ceremony that made each student an official nurse. However, the most impressive part of the service was the graduating nurses singing their pledge together. The meaningful words were taken from a hymn by H.A. Walter:

> I would be true, for there are those who trust me;
> I would be pure, for there are those who care;
> I would be strong, for there are those who suffer;
> I would be brave, for there is much to dare.

Our graduate nurses still had to pass their State Board examinations, but we orderlies realized our relationship to them was changing. After working alongside them for over a year, we would be working under their supervision in the future.

During report, we learned that our ward secretary, Marilyn Anthony, was moving to 2-East, and we would be getting a new secretary in her place. I couldn't help wondering whether her daughter was to be our new ward secretary, or whether Mrs. Anthony had been able to find employment for her daughter since my conversation with Mrs. Deckhart.

Shortly after this, Mr. McKline was admitted for a minor knee operation, and his nine-year-old son was scheduled for a tonsillectomy. They were together in Room 103. I delivered their supper trays to their bedside tables and positioned them so father and son were facing one another. "Enjoy it," I instructed, "because you know there is to be nothing by mouth after midnight."

Mr. McKline smiled and nodded, but his son Tommy asked, "Why is that?"

"It is because the medicine they give you to go to sleep for your operation sometimes makes people sick on their stomach. You don't want that happening in the middle of surgery!"

"Do you enjoy working here in the hospital?" Mr. McKline asked.

"Yes," I responded. "I love it!"

"You do? What made you choose hospital work?"

"Well, I am a conscientious objector, and I am working here instead of doing military service. This is a way I can serve my country with a clear conscience."

"How long have you been working here?" he asked.

"I have completed my first year."

"And how much longer do you have to serve?"

"I am required to work for twenty-four consecutive months to complete my term," I said.

"So, what do you plan to do when your term here is up?"

"I am getting married in May, and my wife-to-be would like to join me in working here. After that, we will be praying about where to go. I am from Virginia, and she is from a rural community in northeastern Ohio. We are not sure yet where we will be living."

"Interesting," he observed. "I wish you and your fiancée the best."

A little later, I entered Room 103 just as Tommy asked his father, "What's a conscience objector?"

His father replied, "A conscientious objector is a person who believes it is wrong to kill another person or even to serve in the army."

"Oh," said Tommy. "I see."

I wasn't sure how much he understood, but as I left the room, I overheard the father continue his explanation.

The evening supervisor, Miss Grey, asked me to follow her to Room 114, the special deluxe room. There, she introduced me to Mr. Wheatly, a wealthy elderly patient who owned several car dealerships in Zanesville. He was remarkably intelligent, but had suffered a stroke that left him partially paralyzed.

The supervisor asked, "How are you this evening, Mr. Wheatly?"

"As good as can be expected," he replied.

"How was your supper?" she asked.

"It was good, but I wasn't that hungry. I couldn't possibly eat everything they brought me."

"Mr. Miller is here to help you become a bit more comfortable," she explained.

Working together, we turned Mr. Wheatly onto his side. Then I gave him a thorough back rub with a soothing cream.

"You do an excellent job," he commented.

When I finished, we propped Mr. Wheatly up in bed and fluffed up his pillow.

"Thank you," he said. "Thank you very much!" Then addressing me, he asked, "Are you the doctor?"

"No," I chuckled. "I'm just an orderly!"

"Well, I appreciate your help, and I want to thank you for coming," he said.

"You are most welcome, and good night, Mr. Wheatly," I replied as we headed for the door. I paused and added, "Don't hesitate to use your call button if you need anything."

I fell into step with Miss Grey as we headed toward the nurses' station.

"Mr. Miller," she began in a somber tone, and I cast about in my mind, wondering if I had done something wrong.

"I want you to know I did not appreciate the way you responded to Mr. Wheatly!"

"I'm sorry," I said, feeling baffled. "What exactly are you referring to?"

"He asked you if you were the doctor, and you said, 'No, I'm *just* an orderly.' I'll have you know, Mr. Miller, you are not *just* an orderly; you *are* an orderly, and don't you ever forget that! Don't belittle your role. It is an important one."

I was flabbergasted by her sentiments and her comments.

In the other private deluxe room, I visited Raymond Byers, a pilot with a broken back. His back had fused, and he had been admitted to Bethesda for therapy. He was given daily whirlpool baths so the swirling water would increase circulation in his legs. On the parallel bars, he struggled to walk with the help of his arms as he tried to regain the use of his legs.

Raymond had told me about his job. Several times a week he had flown over an AT&T transmission line to inspect it. Three inches in diameter, the line was buried eight to ten feet deep and could handle five thousand telephone calls at one time. It crossed several states, and his job was to make sure no one was digging close to the right of way. Upon landing in Ohio, he thought his plane's engine was running a bit rough, so he asked the mechanic to listen to it.

"Let's take her for a spin," the mechanic suggested. "We'll see how she sounds in-flight." They had just cleared the runway and climbed to about 800 feet when the engine sputtered and died. Raymond struggled to circle back and land on the runway, but the plane lost airspeed and crashed. The mechanic, fearing a fire, jumped out and ran as soon as the plane skidded to a stop. Raymond had been trapped in the pilot's seat, his legs paralyzed by a spinal injury.

As I gave him his back rub, I asked, "How was your therapy today?"

"Okay," he responded. "But it makes me feel like a baby when I can hardly walk fifteen feet on the parallel bars before I'm exhausted. I used to play football in school, and running was my thing. Now it takes all my concentration and energy just to place one foot in front of the other!"

"But the important thing is that you are doing it," I encouraged him. "As long as you keep going, you're making progress toward the day when you walk without the parallel bars, right?"

"True. I just wish I were already there," he said.

"I don't blame you," I said as I gave his shoulder muscles a vigorous workout. "I'm sure I would feel the same. But you know, step by step is the road to success. The Christian life is that way too. Little by little and step by step, we learn to walk with Jesus. It isn't always easy, but it is so worth it."

As I completed the back rub, Raymond said, "I have a question. You orderlies are all from the same church, aren't you?"

"The churches we come from are quite similar, but we have volunteers from various churches in Pennsylvania, Virginia, and Kansas."

"So, are you Amish?" asked Raymond.

"My grandfather was Amish, but the church in which I grew up was Mennonite."

"Okay, but you fellows are different. I mean, you believe the Bible, but so do others. What makes you different?"

"We believe the Bible is God's Word, so we want to do everything it commands."

"Like what, for instance?"

"Do you remember that we talked the other day about my being a conscientious objector to war? Jesus taught his followers in Matthew 5 not only to refrain from hating or killing our enemies, but also to bless and show kindness to them.

"Jesus also taught in Matthew 19 that marriage is for one man and woman for life. He forbids divorce and remarriage. So, my wife-to-be will not have to worry that I would ever divorce her and marry someone else. In these practical ways, we take the Bible at its word and live it out in everyday life."

"Okay, that is just what I was getting at. Why do you fellows live this way when other Christians that I know do not?" he asked.

"Well, Raymond," I explained, "in John 3, Jesus taught we must be born again. What that means is that every person is born with a natural urge to lie, cheat, steal, hate, or even kill. We are born with a sinful nature, but Jesus said we must be born again to enter the kingdom of heaven. When we repent of our sins and ask to be forgiven, the sacrifice of Jesus washes away our sins."

"I understand, but that is exactly what other Christians say too. They still watch TV, go to movies, or even smoke, but I know you don't do those things. Why?"

"When people are born again by the Spirit of God, the Holy Spirit lives within them, and they are transformed to live like Jesus. It isn't a matter of living by a set of rules. Rather, it's about a life that has been changed by the power of the Holy Spirit."

"I admire you fellows for the way you live, but I still don't understand the difference."

I straightened up his bedside table, clipped his call button to his bed, and prepared to leave as I explained, "Well, the Bible calls it walking in truth."

"I'll admit it looks like a wonderful way to live," said Raymond. "I'll see you tomorrow. You've given me a lot to think about."

"Johnny," said the ward secretary, "we received a call from 2-East, and they need a catheter for a post-op patient. Do you have time?"

"Sure, I'll head right up there." As I arrived on 2-East and started down the hall toward the nurses' station, I noticed a man sitting on a chair in the hallway. That seemed unusual, but when I arrived at his side, I saw that he was very confused and wasn't wearing any clothing! "Say, mister," I said. "Would you like for me to help you back into your room?"

"No, you don't!" he responded angrily. "Bob's coming to pick me up any minute, and I don't want to miss him."

"Well, let me help you get dressed up for Bob," I said, slipping my hands beneath his arms and trying to help him to his feet. I was relieved that visiting hours were over and the two of us were alone in the hallway.

"No!" he shouted, jerking back. I saw that he was quite agitated, so I simply walked around to the back of his chair. Out of his reach, I tilted the chair onto its back legs and dragged him backwards into the privacy of his own room. I had to grin at all the fuss he was making. I reported to the charge nurse that they had a patient who needed attention in Room 205.

She made a wry face and shook her head, saying, "That man's been way out in left field all afternoon!"

I completed the catheter application and returned to 1-West in time to clock out.

The following evening, Dr. Wise asked me to assist him. In Room 117, he had a patient who was suffering from a collapsed left lung. As we walked toward the patient's room, Dr. Wise paused and explained, "This patient hasn't suffered an accident, as is usually the case with these symptoms. He simply had a fluid buildup in his chest that collapsed the lung. His lung was hanging by the trachea, causing major discomfort and chronic coughing. The last time I drew off fluid, it contained cancerous cells. We have applied nuclear medicine to kill the cancer, and I want to draw off more fluid today and see what's happening."

After prepping the patient and having him sit up, Dr. Wise cleansed a site on the lower back where he inserted a very long needle at the base of the ribcage and began to draw off fluid. Leaving the needle in, the doctor emptied his syringe into a sterile specimen basin as I steadied the patient. The fluid looked like bloodied water to me. As he was extracting the third syringe full, our patient coughed a bit. But the fourth syringe produced a coughing spell that caused Dr. Wise to withdraw the needle, saying, "I believe that is enough for today." He applied a bandage to the puncture, and I helped the patient lie back on his bed as he tried to suppress his cough.

"Allow me to explain what is happening here," said Dr. Wise as he pulled up a chair at the patient's bedside. "Although the fluid buildup has caused your lung to collapse, it is filled with porous pockets containing some air. That makes your lung light enough to float on the surface of the liquid. But as we draw this fluid down, more and more of your lung is hanging on the left branch of your trachea. This places an unnatural pressure on your cough reflex, located at the Y of your trachea, and this produces an involuntary cough. I will send this specimen to the lab, and they should be able to tell me the level of the nuclear medicine still in your system as well as the number of cancerous cells present. I want you to drink plenty of fluids, eat wholesome foods, and get all the rest you need. Okay? I'll be by to see you again tomorrow."

Dr. Wise thanked me for my assistance and headed toward the laboratory with his sample.

Later, as I helped the pilot in Room 112 prepare for the night, we picked up our discussion from the previous evening.

"Johnny," he said, "do all the members of your church believe like you do?"

"Concerning what?" I asked as I freshened up his bed.

"Well, you spoke last evening about being born again and how that changes a person. Do all of your members believe that, or are you, well, different from the others?"

"We believe it is absolute necessary for every member of our church to be a born-again believer in Jesus Christ," I replied. "You see, if someone is a church member but does not have the Holy Spirit living in him, there is no way he will be able to live a Christ-like life. He must be transformed by the Spirit of God."

"This is starting to make more sense to me now," said Raymond thoughtfully. "So that is what makes you fellows different from other Christians I have known."

I worked in silence for several minutes. Raymond was deep in thought, but at last he said, "Maybe some of the Christians I know are not born again." After several moments, he asked, "Johnny, do you think you will ever be a minister?"

"Hmm . . . well, we believe every brother in our church should live in such a way that if God called him into the ministry, he would be ready with the biblical qualifications and would have the ability to minister."

"Does a man simply decide he wants to enter the ministry and that's it, or does he have to get a college degree?"

"No, a person doesn't just decide he wants to be a minister. When a minister is needed for one of our churches, we have a series of special services with preaching that emphasizes what the Bible says about the needed qualifications. To be considered, a brother is to be honest, of good report, well versed in the Scriptures, the husband of one wife, able to get along with people, and humble. He must also have an aptitude for teaching others. Then we ask the congregation to pray and ask the Lord to impress on their hearts who in the congregation meets those requirements. After prayer, they cast their ballot for that person."

"So, it's like an election, and the winner becomes the minister?"

"Not really," I explained. "We hope there are several brethren who would meet the Biblical qualification. We set a minimum number of votes for a brother to be considered."

"And what happens if several people have those qualifying votes?"

"In such cases, the brothers who "share the lot" sit in front of the congregation. In another room, someone places a slip of paper (the lot) into one of several identical hymnals or Bibles. The books are then brought in and placed in front of these brothers. Great care is taken to make sure no one but God knows which book contains the slip. After a minister prays, asking God to direct the brothers, each brother takes a book. The bishop opens each book one by one, and the brother whose book contains the slip is ordained to the ministry."

"I'm impressed," said Raymond. "I've never heard of anything like this before."

"It's not the only way to ordain leaders," I said. "However, it was used by the apostles in Acts 1, and it has also served us well."

"This has been good," Raymond said. "You've answered a lot of questions. Thank you!"

"You are welcome, Raymond. Good night."

CHAPTER 26

Betsy's Crash

Following a weekend visit with Ruth and her family, I found the VS unit humming with news. Fifteen-year-old Betsy Scout had been traveling with a group of friends to a school basketball game. Betsy was anticipating an enjoyable evening with her peers when the driver veered off the road and slammed into a ditch. Screams of fear and pain filled the car as the occupants were flung about. The car skidded to a stop, resting on its side. Chaos reigned as they tried to untangle their bodies and come to grips with what had happened. Someone with the clearest head among them pushed open the door on the upper side of the car. They clambered out and then turned to pull others from the car. Relieved that no one was seriously injured, they began laughing nervously.

Then someone asked, "Where's Betsy?" Kneeling on the frame while someone held the door open, one of her friends peered into the dark interior and saw the shadowy outline crumpled in the back seat. "Betsy, are you all right? Come, I'll help you get out."

She heard crying and a groan as Betsy called back, "I can't move. Nothing works!"

"What do you mean?" cried her friend in alarm.

"My arms and legs," Betsy sobbed. "I don't know. Something is terribly wrong."

It had been a tedious ordeal for the paramedics to extricate Betsy from that car. Suspecting she had suffered a severe neck injury, they first encased her neck tightly in a plastic neck brace, then strapped her to a body board and gingerly lifted her from the wrecked car. They loaded her into their waiting ambulance, and with sirens wailing and lights flashing, they headed for Bethesda Hospital. At our emergency room, an orderly helped stabilize her head as Betsy was carefully transferred from the ambulance cot to the X-ray table and then onto an ER cart.

Betsy's X-rays showed a dislocated fracture between the sixth and seventh cervical vertebrae with her spinal cord cramped in a shallow S. shape. Paralysis affected her arms and hands, restricting normal movement, while her legs had no feeling or movement whatsoever.

Betsy's beautiful brown hair hung past her waist. She cried as they cut off her hair and shaved her head in preparation for surgery.

In surgery, Dr. Glosser drilled a small hole on either side of Betsy's skull and inserted tongs which were firmly fastened into her skull. She was then laid onto a Stryker Frame in Room 109, with fifteen pounds of traction applied to the tongs. The purpose for the constant traction pulling her head in a direct line with her body was to move her cervical spine back into its normal position. Every four hours, a second frame was laid on Betsy, sandwiching her between the upper and lower frames. While a trusted person held her head, the others slowly rotated the movable portion of the frame 180 degrees. The person holding her head carefully turned it to precisely match the rotation of her body. This ensured no further damage would be done to Betsy's spinal cord. One wrong move during this process could cause irreversible damage. Betsy had come to trust our orderlies and insisted that one of us hold her head each time she was to be turned.

With the rotation complete, the new position was locked into place and the top portion of the frame removed. This process not only helped prevent pneumonia from settling into her lungs, but it also gave Betsy two views of her shrunken world. Unable to move her head, she stared at the ceiling during her four hours of face up position, and she studied the floor during her four hours of being face down. Unable to turn her head, she could never see who had entered her room until they came to stand right beside her. When she was face down, she tried to identify medical personnel or visitors by their voices or shoes.

Betsy's family came from their home in West Virginia to visit and encourage her every week. We all realized Betsy would never walk again unless there was a reduction of her cervical spine and healing of her spinal cord.

Dr. Glosser came in daily to examine Betsy. He checked for voluntary movement, sense of touch, and reflexes. Slowly, her arm, elbow, and wrist movements improved. Although her fingers had basic movement, they lacked the fine motor control to pick up objects. She could move her hands where she wanted them to go, but once there, her fingers refused to properly respond. Dr. Glosser found that Betsy could feel absolutely nothing from her waist down. She had no reflexes whatsoever in her feet or ankles.

After four days with no change in his patient, Dr. Glosser ordered the traction to be increased to twenty pounds. Later, that was increased to twenty-five, and finally, thirty-five pounds of traction pulled on Betsy's skull to try to bring her broken spine into proper alignment. But sadly, there was no change.

After three weeks, I realized Betsy was losing hope and depression was beginning to set in. I wanted to let her know we cared.

"Betsy, none of us knows what the future holds for you," I said. "We don't know if you are going to get well or not. Even Dr. Glosser cannot tell you. But one thing I do know—God knows all about your situation. Have you considered where God is in all of this?"

At this point, Betsy began to cry softly. Lying face up and unable to move her head, she tried to blink away the tears that pooled up in her eyes. She was too choked up to respond. I offered her a tissue, and she tried to grasp it, but her fingers were not cooperating.

"My friends and I have been praying for your healing," I continued.

She swallowed hard and said, "Thank you."

"How would you like me to bring you a record player and some Gospel records to listen to?" I continued. "My friends have them, and I am sure they would loan them to you. Is that something you might like?"

"Y–yes," she said, her voice still shaky with emotion.

"I'll bring them over tomorrow and set up for you before my regular hours."

"That will be nice," she responded. "Thank you."

The following day, I set up the record player and held up each record for her to read the labels as I explained a bit about each one.

"This one is by the Diller family, and they sing encouraging Gospel songs," I explained. "And this one is special. It is called *Flight F-I-N-A-L*. It is somewhat like a parable of an inter-world airline flying to heaven. It describes the plane's arrival in heaven. I think you'll like the beautiful singing from this choir."

I set the player on an end table, loaded it with several records, and tuned the volume to play softly. I excused myself and went to begin my shift for the evening. Checking in on Betsy and talking about the records provided opportunities for further discussion of spiritual matters.

As time passed, Betsy's hair began to grow back. It was soon a quarter inch long, and it itched, especially around the point where the tongs entered her skull. At times she would ask for help to scratch those areas because her partially paralyzed fingers just couldn't scratch.

Betsy was hopelessly bored while lying face down with her forehead and chin supported by the canvas of the frame and the traction holding her head steady. There was nothing to see except the shelf fourteen inches below her face and the tiled floor beyond.

As I observed Betsy lying face down, an idea popped into my head. I brought her a tablet and pencil. Placing them on the shelf below her, I said, "Betsy, I want you to write something for me. I think writing will exercise your coordination, and perhaps this will improve the fine motor control of your fingers."

I squatted down beside her and watched as she made her first attempt at writing. "Oh," she said. "This is horrible! I don't want anyone to see these scribbles."

"Good," I teased. "I won't look." She was having a difficult time, and it took tremendous concentration just to form a letter. The pencil slipped from her grasp and clattered to the floor out of her reach.

"It's no use!" she exclaimed. "I can't do it."

"It will come. Just keep trying," I said, retrieving the pencil and placing it back into her fingers.

"I've got to run now and care for my other patients, but you keep writing. I'll tell you what! Write my girlfriend a note. Her name is Ruth. I told her about you, and she is praying for you. See what you can do. I'll stop by later."

Two hours later, it was time to turn Betsy. I held her head firmly as two nurses locked the second portion of the frame over her back and rotated her into a face up position. I discovered the pencil had again slipped from her impaired hand, and she had given up writing.

As I thought about Betsy's dilemma, another idea occurred. What if she had a really fat pencil? Maybe that would be easier for her to grasp, and it might increase her ability to write. Not only was I concerned about her fingers, but Betsy also needed something to occupy her mind other than worry and self-pity. Betsy needed hope, and writing to others could become a means to that end.

Back at work the following day, I wrapped bandage tape around the pencil, layer upon layer, until it was over half an inch thick. The woven surface of the tape was much easier to grasp than the smooth surface of the thin pencil. We started over again with Betsy's writing lessons. However, even this specialized pencil occasionally slipped from her grasp, and it could be thirty minutes before anyone checked on her and retrieved her pencil. It took so much effort to accomplish so little that Betsy became disheartened.

"Betsy," I said as I appeared at her bedside holding a roll of tape, "I'm going to tie this tape across the lower edge of your writing table with the sticky side up. If your hand gets tired or you drop the pencil and it rolls toward the edge of your shelf, the sticky tape will catch and hold it until you can retrieve it on your own. You want to try?"

"And you think that will work?" she asked doubtfully.

"If not, then we'll figure out something else. We won't give up," I told her.

When I checked on her later, Betsy had written half a page in a reasonably legible scrawl, and I praised her efforts.

"But who can read it?" she cried.

"Ruth will be happy to receive this from you," I assured her. "In fact, she will love it! I'll mail it with my letter tomorrow." And I did. However, I added an explanation to my letter, asking Ruth to share Betsy's note with her sister Vera[1]. Vera was suffering from polio, which affected her breathing and walking. The disease had paralyzed Vera's arms, making writing quite difficult. I asked Vera if she would please write an encouraging note to Betsy.

A week later, I received a letter from Vera, addressed to Betsy Scout. Betsy was thrilled! "Look," I said, as she finished reading Vera's letter. "Her writing is shaky and hard to read. It's because she has no arm movement, but that doesn't stop her. Write her a response, and I'll send it for you."

Thus began a correspondence between fifteen-year-old Betsy and seventeen-year-old Vera, both struggling with insurmountable disabilities. Vera's letters were a tremendous encouragement to Betsy.

On Saturday, Floyd Randall was admitted into Room 119. He was a twenty-six-year-old farmer from Adamsville, Ohio, who had been helping his neighbor move. Floyd was tall, slim, and strong. He had been carrying furniture into his friend's new home and had just returned to his pickup truck for another chair when he heard a car coming up the street. Standing in the street and hearing an approaching car, he thought it best to move out of harm's way and stepped between his truck and another parked vehicle. The screeching of tires alarmed him a split second before there was a tremendous crash and searing pain as the oncoming car crashed into the vehicle behind him, slamming it into his truck in front of him. His lower legs were crushed between the two bumpers, pinning him helplessly in place.

Sections of bone in both legs were smashed to small fragments. That night, the doctors debated whether to amputate both legs

[1] Vera's life's story of struggle and triumph, *Against the Odds,* is available through TGS.

immediately or try to save them. A younger doctor argued for saving Floyd's legs and won out against the opinions of older and more experienced doctors. Floyd had surgery to remove the bone shards from his legs to prevent decay and the resulting infections. Afterward, his legs were set in temporary casts.

As I entered Floyd's room, he was feverish and jumpy. "Oh!" he said as he jerked awake. "I'm sorry. I'm so nervous, and I feel horrible. I hardly know what to do."

"No need to apologize," I said. "I'm sure I would be the same in your situation. I'm an orderly. My name is Johnny, and I'm here to serve you. This is your nurse's call button." I demonstrated by pushing the button marked "Nurse." There was an intermittent beep, and the voice of the ward secretary said, "Yes, may I help you?"

"It's just me, Johnny," I explained. "I'm showing Mr. Randall how to call when he needs help. Thank you."

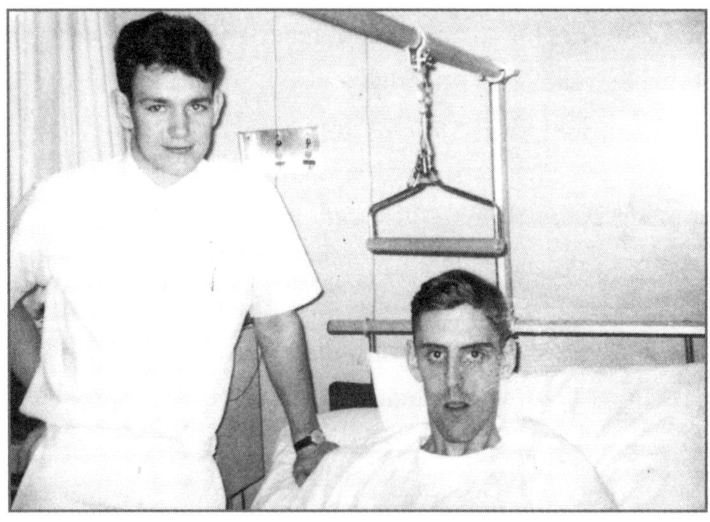

Floyd Randall's lower legs were crushed. Nine months later, he praised God for new bone growth. He used the trapeze bar to pull himself up in bed or into a sitting position.

"You're welcome." The intercom clicked off.

"I want you to call anytime you need anything." I told Floyd. "I am at your service."

He sighed resignedly and sank his head into the pillow. "Thank you," he said. "Thank you very much."

Weeks passed, and Floyd's doctors fitted him with walking casts and released him to go home. Their faint hope was that just maybe new bone would grow and bridge the gap left where the shattered bone fragments had been removed.

Nine months later, I was pleasantly surprised to find Floyd Randall back on 1-West. Floyd was determined to continue providing for his wife and child. His old casts had been replaced several times, and he was driving his tractor and farming with both legs in casts from mid-thigh to toes. I couldn't even imagine how difficult that would be.

On this occasion, he had come in for a minor operation to straighten his toes. They had curled over the edge of his casts, and he could no longer straighten them. He lay on his bed and beamed up at me, his casts removed and steel pins protruding from the ends of his surgically straightened toes.

"Johnny," he said, "watch this!" He lifted his right leg. I felt nauseated as his leg sagged several inches, bending unnaturally at mid-calf. Floyd smiled widely as he asked, "Did you hear that?"

"Hear what?" I asked, stepping closer.

"Listen!" Again, he raised his leg. This time, I just barely heard a dull clunk. He did it again, and each time there was that little clunk. I was baffled.

He explained happily, "Johnny, new bone is growing in my leg! It has almost bridged the gap left where my bones were shattered, and the doctors say it is a miracle. It's the miracle my wife and I have been praying for!"

"I am so happy for you!" I said sincerely. "I never heard of such a thing before."

"Johnny, I'm so thankful," said Floyd. "God had been so good to me!"

Floyd was not alone through his suffering. He faced the uncertainties of his future with a faith in his Redeemer that could carry him through the bitterest experiences. Not only did Floyd have a new bone, but he was also a new creation in Christ Jesus.

CHAPTER 27

The Twitch

My fiancée, Ruth Overholt, was asked to chauffeur visitors to the Zanesville area. While they were visiting friends, she had the afternoon free. I couldn't take off from my work, but Ruth came to 1-West to visit Betsy. As they were getting acquainted, I flitted in and out to see if anything was needed. When it was time to turn Betsy, I helped hold her head like usual. She would remain face down for the rest of my shift. After the turning process was completed, I asked Ruth to borrow a chess set from the White House. I set it up on Betsy's writing shelf, and Ruth, sitting on the floor by her side, taught Betsy how each chess piece moved.

"Here is how I want you to play," I instructed. "Ruth, if Betsy drops a chess piece or knocks one over, you are not allowed to pick it up for her. She has to exercise those fingers and pick them up by herself."

"Oh, come on! You're so mean," teased Betsy good-naturedly.

"Seriously," I responded, "this will be excellent exercise for those damaged nerves. Look at how much they have already progressed. I'm hoping you can eventually regain full use of your hands, and this exercise will help you."

I went about my work, and for the next two hours, Ruth and Betsy talked as they played chess. Betsy loved it even though she frequently fumbled the pieces. It took extreme effort to force her unresponsive fingers to set those fallen pieces back into position. By willpower, she was forcing her damaged nerves to respond. Sometimes she and Ruth became so engrossed in conversation that neither could remember whose turn it was. This was especially true as Ruth described her sister Vera's innovative ways of overcoming her polio-related impairments. It proved to be a wonderful time for both. It was therapeutic for Betsy, both physically and emotionally, and it also gave Ruth a meaningful taste of hospital work.

Ruth Zimmerman had reached out to Nora Smith, a young, single nurse who was searching spiritually. Nora worked as a floater and at times was assigned to my floor. Ruth shared with our small fellowship that she had invited Nora to her apartment for Bible studies. Ruth asked us to pray for Nora.

Following several months of interaction and Bible studies, Nora made a commitment to the Lord, and we rejoiced. We desired to fellowship with her and to see her grow in her walk with the Lord. However, she seemed to reach a plateau in her spiritual progress, and I was puzzled. There was a reservation in Nora which I could not understand. However, Ruth faithfully continued ministering to Nora's spiritual needs.

"Did you hear there's a huge snowstorm predicted for this evening?" asked the ward secretary.

"Yes, I heard about it," I replied.

"They're forecasting up to fourteen inches," she continued. "I'm glad I live nearby. Some of the workers live way out in the country and may have to stay here overnight. If we get as much as they are predicting, it would be dangerous to be on the roads."

As I moved from room to room working with the patients, I glanced outside at the dark, foreboding clouds. Soon after darkness fell, so did the snow. The heavens dumped snow so fast that the maintenance trucks with their blades, tire chains, and flashing lights were waging a losing battle for the hospital parking lot.

An announcement was made that all workers who were able should leave as soon as their responsibilities were completed instead of waiting for the official shift to end. They were warned to be extra-cautious as this snow was wet, heavy, and extremely slippery. Driving conditions were treacherous.

Nora Smith was working our floor for the evening, and she was weighed down with the major responsibilities of 1-West. Calls began filtering in from workers for the oncoming shift. One nurse's car was stuck in a snowbank. Another slid off the road and had called for a tow-truck. Still another would not be coming; she could not even get out of her driveway.

The nursing supervisor announced, "We have already heard from a number of workers who are unable to come in due to the road conditions. We are asking for volunteers to work a double shift and help us through this crisis."

"Miss Grey, I can stay if you need me," I offered.

"Certainly, we need you. Thank you!" she said, making a notation on her clip board.

Nora said, "I am so scared of driving in this weather, but I just can't work a double shift. I can't! But if I can get out of here a little bit early, I think I can make it home."

The results of the snowstorm that necessitated Johnny and Ruth working a double shift.

Ruth near the left, working a double shift. Notice the clock reads 12 midnight.

At 10:30, one of the patients needed a special medication. Nurse Nora unlocked the medicine cabinet and signed for the medication. It was in dry powder form in a sealed, sterile vial and needed to be dissolved in sterile water. I watched as Nora began the mixing process. She was in such a nervous haste her fingers trembled as she cleansed the rubber stopper with an alcohol swab. Stabbing the needle through the rubber stopper, she tipped the vial up to submerge the needle in water. Nora pulled on the plunger to withdraw the water, but it wouldn't come. Desperately grasping the vial and syringe with one hand, she pulled harder on the stubborn plunger but only succeeded in obtaining a few drops.

I had encountered similar problems in my work, and noted that when fifteen to twenty cc's of water had been extracted from a sealed vial, a vacuum was created that had to be overcome before more water could be extracted.

"Uh, Miss Nora," I began, "you need to . . ." but I was curtly rebuffed. Since I was an orderly and she was the nurse in charge, I could only watch helplessly as Nora struggled.

In her anxiety, she was not as careful as at other times, and the needle slipped from the vial and became contaminated. With an angry exclamation that should not be uttered by a follower of Jesus, Nora hurled the syringe into the trash. I was stunned. Nora, nearly in tears, opened a fresh syringe with trembling hands and was about to jab its needle through the top of the vial when I stepped to her side and held out my hand. She gazed questioningly at me for a long moment.

"Let me do this for you," I said, and she slowly placed the syringe into my hand. I pulled back the plunger and filled the syringe with air before releasing it into the vacuum of the vial. Retracting the needle, I repeated the process. It was then easy to draw the sterile water from the vial. With a sigh of relief, Nurse Nora quickly mixed the medication and administered it. She clocked out a few minutes later to brave the snow-choked roads as she headed home.

Two weeks later, Nurse Nora was going off duty during shift change, and there was a scurry of last minute tasks. The nurses' station buzzed with activity, and as I passed by, Nora opened her purse on the counter in front of me. She retrieved something, and then turned away, leaving her purse open. In plain sight within her purse lay a pack of cigarettes! I blinked in surprise, deeply disappointed. I thought Nora was sincerely trying to follow Jesus.

Contemplating Nora's life, I realized whenever people live in deceit or hide sin, it damages their relationship with Jesus Christ. Their lives spiral deeper and deeper into sin. I desperately did not want this to happen with Nora. Yet I realized God allows all people to choose the path they will take. I prayed for Nora's victory.

Report was completed, and I began going from room to room to check on patients. I entered Betsy's room and asked, "How are you this afternoon?"

"Oh, I don't know," she sighed.

"What do you mean, you don't know?" I asked as I brought a fresh glass of water with a straw and offered her a drink. Betsy seemed restless and frustrated.

"I just—well, it feels like my legs hurt."

"Now, Betsy," I bantered. "You know you can't feel anything in your legs. Dr. Glosser said you can't. There's no way they could hurt, right?"

"Yeah, but you know, sometimes I almost feel like I could move them."

"Okay, Miss Betsy," I smiled teasingly. "If you're so smart, let's see you do it." I flipped the covers off her feet.

Lying flat on her back with her head anchored in traction, there was no way Betsy could see her feet. "Go ahead," I said. "I'm watching."

I had regularly massaged her feet to enhance blood flow and muscle tone, and now I stood looking for any sign of movement. I glanced briefly at Betsy. Her eyes were closed, and her fists were clenched. She took a deep breath and strained to make her paralyzed feet move, but there was not the slightest movement.

"Relax," I suggested. "Take a couple of deep breaths, close your eyes, and let every muscle relax. Pretend you are sound asleep." She complied as I waited. "Now give it all you've got! Let's see if you can move your feet."

Betsy twisted her shoulders and strained with all her might. In absolute amazement, I saw the big toe on her right foot twitch a fraction of an inch. Masking my surprise, I said, "Betsy, you are going to have to do better than that. Rest a minute, and I'll get the other orderly to see if he can detect any movement. I'll be back in a minute."

I rushed out to find Joe Hertzler. He was in Room 115 helping a cancer patient back into bed with a lift. "Joe," I said urgently. "I need you in Betsy Scout's room as soon as you are free. She thinks she might be able to move her feet, and I think I saw a slight movement. I want you to verify that I'm not just seeing things."

"I'll be there in about five minutes," he responded.

When he arrived, I said in Betsy's hearing, "Joe, Betsy says there are times when she feels like she could move her feet. We are going to put her to the test and see if she can." I removed the covers from her feet and said, "Are you ready? Okay, go for it!"

With a deep breath and intense concentration, Betsy strained every fiber of her being, willing her feet to respond. Again, there was that unmistakable little twitch in her right big toe. I glanced at Joe, and our eyes met. He acknowledged with an almost imperceptible nod that he had witnessed that tiny movement too.

"Okay, Betsy, you relax a bit, and we'll try again a little later," I said. Tired out physically and emotionally from her unusual exercise, she willingly rested. Not wanting to raise false hopes, I hid the fact that we had both seen movement. Small though it was, we were elated.

An hour later, I asked the charge nurse, Marsha Carol, to accompany me into Betsy's room. I explained once again that Betsy wanted to try moving her feet. We bent over the end of the Stryker frame and watched closely as Betsy strained. And there it was, just a tiny twitch!

Nurse Marsha exclaimed, "Betsy, you moved your toe! This is wonderful! It is only a very tiny movement, but after two months of nothing, this is exciting. I'll have to record this movement in your chart for Dr. Glosser to see. I'm sure he is going to be interested."

After Dr. Glosser read the report and examined Betsy's slight movement, he burst our bubble of hope. "This is not a conscious movement," he explained. "Here is what is happening. Betsy is straining with extreme effort, and as she does so, it produces a spasm, somewhat like a Charlie-horse. The muscles in her leg involuntarily tighten, causing this little flick of her toe, but this is not a conscious movement. It is meaningless, and it has no value."

How were we to respond to this announcement? Should I continue encouraging, massaging, and exercising? I concluded that if there was any movement, it should be exercised.

Betsy's parents and her older brother, Roger, who seemed to be the spokesman for the family, had faithfully visited her. They came again that Saturday evening and were present as we turned Betsy to her face-up position.

"We have some questions for you when you have a minute," Roger began politely.

"Sure," I responded. "I'll be glad to answer them if I can."

"Betsy tells us you've been helping her exercise her feet every day."

"Betsy, you've been telling on me again?" I interjected, grinning.

"Well, you have," she responded defensively.

Roger continued, "We know that Dr. Glosser says Betsy's small movement is of no importance. What do you think?"

"I'm not a doctor," I said. "So I obviously can't answer from a medical standpoint. But if I were lying on my back as Betsy has been for the past two months, and I managed a small movement, I would want to exercise that as much as I could. I would try everything to increase it. Did she tell you we are now up to a quarter inch of movement with the right toe? And the left one gives us an occasional tiny movement as well. Whether it is spastic or conscious, Dr. Glosser can say, but it is undeniably movement. To me, that is exciting!"

"Well," said Roger, "we are thrilled with this development, and we want you to know how much we appreciate what you have been doing."

"Betsy, do you feel up to showing your family what you can do?" I inquired.

"Sure!" she said.

I pulled back the covers and massaged her feet with lotion, flexing her feet, toes, and ankles. Once we had completed this ritual, I called the family to join me at the foot of the bed.

"Okay, Betsy, take a deep breath and get ready." Betsy inhaled deeply. "Get set, GO!" Betsy bit her lip, clenched her fists, and strained as though she were lifting heavy barbells. Everyone standing nearby saw her toe twitch a quarter of an inch.

"You did it!" exclaimed Roger. "I'm so proud of you, Betsy."

"Mom, did you see it?" asked Betsy eagerly."

"Yes, darlin', I saw it!" her mother said as she leaned over and hugged her daughter.

Her father, although more subdued, was all smiles. He too had seen the movement.

When a patient was hospitalized for a prolonged period, workers sometimes tended to shift their focus to the trauma and urgent needs of incoming patients. At times, the needs of long-term patients seemed to become less important. I noticed that as nurses became more accustomed to having Betsy Scout in their care, they were less careful about keeping her turning on schedule, and they tended to interact less with her.

I tried to watch the clock and be available every four hours to help turn Betsy at the prescribed time. Our nurses seemed to lose interest in Betsy's slow progress at moving her toes. On the other hand, I felt led to help all I could and found time on every shift for an exercise session with Betsy. Of course, this was an extracurricular activity not ordered by Dr. Glosser, who still insisted the movements were merely spastic.

I sat with several graduate nurses eating supper in the cafeteria one evening, and Betsy's situation came up in their discussion.

Miss Gerhart asked, "Johnny, do you agree with Dr. Glosser that Betsy's toe movements are involuntary? You have exercised those movements more than any of us."

"Yes," added another nurse. "I've seen it, but I do not know what to make of it."

"Tell me something," I responded. "How would you evaluate Betsy's movement if you had never heard it diagnosed as spastic?"

"Fair enough," chimed in Miss Andrews. "But you must realize that Dr. Glosser is a neurosurgeon."

"I'm aware of that, and I am most respectful of Dr. Glosser's expertise," I assured them. "However, the question here is whether the movements we have witnessed are voluntary or involuntary. They have progressed measurably since we have been exercising them. How can that be spastic?"

"I think you need to be careful, Johnny. I'm afraid you are becoming overly involved with your patient," said Miss Andrews. "We were taught in nursing school never to allow ourselves to become emotionally involved with our patients."

"What?" I exclaimed incredulously. "Do you think I am becoming romantically involved with Betsy?"

"Of course not!" chorused several of the nurses together.

Miss Peters explained, "We were taught that a nurse must not allow emotions to interfere with her ability to work objectively in the patient's best interest. And it looks to us like you care, well, perhaps a little too much about Betsy's situation. That's all."

"I do see your point, but I cannot help caring," I said. "I don't call it emotion. Perhaps empathy or compassion would best describe what I feel."

"The progress Betsy has made is surprising, but be careful," Miss Andrews warned as she rose to head back to her floor.

"I'll be careful," I promised.

Later, in thinking over their warning, I realized the love of Jesus in my heart caused me to care at a different level than a professional nurse was taught to care. I believed Christ's love should flow through our hearts to the hurting so they would see Jesus in us.

While working an evening shift in ER, and knowing Betsy was to be turned at 7:00, I asked permission to dash over to 1-West and help since no orderly was on duty to hold her head. But when I arrived, a nurse told me they were busy with admissions and would not be turning Betsy until later.

I retraced my steps to ER, and returned after another hour, only to find that they still were not ready. When I showed up for the third time, Nurse Oakland got right in my face and yelled at me to back off. Not accustomed to being shouted at, I felt shocked and hurt. But what hurt even more were the hot words that flashed through my mind. Even though I did not speak them, I realized my carnal nature had spoken. Yes, I thanked God I had not uttered them, but I still felt defeated.

Thirty minutes later, our elderly nurse aide, Dotty, showed up in ER and said, "Johnny, I have Betsy ready. If you can come help, we'll get her rolled." I walked back with her and passed Nurse Oakland sitting in the nurses' station charting. We turned Betsy without any problems.

Although Nurse Oakland never apologized directly for her harsh words, she later mentioned that during that evening, she had dealt with three admissions and a death. Obviously, she had been overwhelmed. As followers of Jesus, we do not wait until someone asks before extending forgiveness. I had forgiven Nurse Oakland, and we worked congenially together many times afterward.

On another occasion, we VS workers dealt with an unexpected blow from the ER charge nurse, Mrs. Keller, with whom we had worked amiably for over a year. She was a good nurse, and we highly respected her ER skills. However, the nursing supervisor explained that Nurse Keller had registered a complaint with the head office, saying she would no longer work with the 1-W orderlies whom she considered *incompetent*.

Sincerely desiring to have a positive testimony for our Lord, we were concerned. Eventually, we discovered that Nurse Keller's husband was a member of the military reserves. He had been shirking the required monthly training sessions, choosing to play golf instead. His superiors realized this and had recently called him into active duty. He was forced to leave his wife behind and was sent to a supply post in Hawaii. Nurse Keller was reminded each day she worked with us that her husband was overseas while we, as conscientious objectors, were exempt from military service. She felt this was a great injustice and notified the head office that she would no longer work with us. From then on, our ER work had to be scheduled around Nurse Keller's work schedule.

CHAPTER 28

The Challenge

ER was dealing with the normal minor injuries one afternoon. Then Mr. Johnson came in complaining of abdominal pain and nausea. Dr. Moore examined the patient and asked the usual questions. After performing several tests, he determined that he needed to insert a tube into Mr. Johnson's stomach. I helped get things ready. After the doctor explained the procedure to the patient, he began inserting the tube through the patient's nostril, carefully threading it down his throat and into his esophagus.

I stood by with a glass of water, which Dr. Moore ordered the patient to drink. Swallowing would help direct the tube into the stomach as the doctor continued pushing. The patient dutifully drank several swallows of water, and then, without warning, he forcefully vomited. Ducking to one side, Dr. Moore shouted, "Keep swallowing! Keep swallowing!" The poor patient panicked, feeling as though he was drowning, and the procedure had to be postponed. Ten minutes later, Dr. Moore successfully inserted the tube into the patient's stomach and began explaining.

"You are suffering from a twisted intestine which blocks food from moving through the intestinal tract," he said. "We want to connect this tube to our vacuum system and remove the contents of your stomach. Visualize what would happen if you twisted a water hose until it formed a kink. This is what has happened to your intestine. If it remains in that position too long, the blood flow will diminish due to the compressed blood vessels, and gangrene will set in. Then you will really have a problem. We want to prevent that by performing corrective surgery tomorrow morning. I will admit you now so we can start an IV and do your bloodwork. I will see you before you go to surgery in the morning, okay?"

"Well, I guess, if you say so," replied Mr. Johnson.

"We really don't have much choice, do we?" asked Dr. Moore as he prepared to leave.

Things became quiet after Mr. Johnson was transferred to his room on 3-East. Then the phone rang, and I overheard the nurse say, "Yes. Okay, I'll send him."

Wondering if I was needed for a problem psych patient on 4-North, or a catheter patient on some other floor, I waited for my orders. However, the nurse gave me a quizzical smile and explained, "That was the front desk, and they say you have a visitor in the lobby."

"What?" I exclaimed.

"That's what they said. We only have one patient right now, so you may go."

I strode to the end of the hallway and arrived at the elevators where the traffic from ER, 1-West, and the lobby converged in a congested crowd. I scanned the faces, and there stood Norman Swartzentruber, a minister from my home church. I was stunned, but I had to wait several moments until the crowd thinned so I could reach him. I'm sure he read my questioning expression, for as we greeted each other, he chuckled, "Don't worry, there's nothing wrong."

Norman had married my first-grade school teacher, and had later been ordained to the ministry. I appreciated his dedication and example. Having just completed a week of revival meetings in a neighboring area, Norman had taken time out on his way home to stop and visit me.

I still had an hour left on my shift, so Norman sat in the ER waiting room and then accompanied me to the VS unit. We had a wonderful time catching up on the news from my church and family back in Virginia. I shared some of my hospital and VS unit experiences. Of course, I had to tell him all about our marriage plans. In fact, I had hoped he could preach our wedding sermon, but a scheduling conflict meant he needed to apologetically decline. Norman's visit was a blessing, and I appreciated reconnecting with him.

Back on 1-West, I continued to fit Betsy's exercises around my regular duties whenever possible. Through our intense exercise routine, all ten of Betsy's toes began to move. Some moved more than others, but they all *moved* as she exerted downward pressure.

"Okay, Betsy, this afternoon we are going to do something different," I announced. "Instead of only pushing your toes down, we are also going to try pulling them back up. What do you think of that?"

"But I don't know if I can," she said doubtfully.

"Well, neither did we know you could move your toes at all until we tried, right?"

"Yes, I guess that is true. You know what? I do want to try."

"All right, let me finish massaging your feet, and then we'll give it a go. Can you feel this?" I asked as I flexed her toes downward and then bent them far back.

"Feel what?"

"I was just wiggling your toes to see if you could feel them."

"No, I can't actually feel that. I mean, when you massage my feet, I feel the bedframe shake a little, but I don't feel anything in my legs or feet."

"Did I tell you my minister from Virginia stopped in to see me?" I asked.

"No, you didn't."

"It was a complete surprise. He lives 500 miles away and was just passing through. I invited him to our wedding, but he won't be able to come. Betsy, are you going to come to our wedding?"

"Yeah, right! Me and my one-inch hair. I'd really be a sight, wouldn't I?"

"Hey, just be thankful you have hair," I told her.

"I am thankful, believe me!"

"Are you ready?" I asked.

"Yes."

"Okay, toes down!" I commanded, and Betsy grimaced. "Harder!" Betsy put all her concentration and energy into moving her toes, and every one of them curled down beautifully.

"Wonderful!" I exclaimed. "That is farther than I have ever seen them bend. Now pull your toes back as far as you can. Pull harder! PULL!" When I saw that nothing was moving, I said, "Okay, relax. I want to show you something. Raise your arm and make a tight fist. Good, now open your hand as wide as you can. You see, the muscles you use to open your fingers are in your forearm. And the muscles that lift your toes upward are in your lower leg. It is going to take some practice to get those muscles to obey you. It's kind of like they are asleep, and you have to wake them up. Do you want to try again?"

"Sure," she said.

"Okay, down! Now up, Betsy. Up!" Nothing happened. "Well, we are not quite there yet," I told her, "but I believe we will get there.

Do you want to know why I believe that?"

"Yeah, why?"

"Because I saw the tendon on the top of your foot tighten slightly, and that makes me think those muscles are beginning to sense what you want them to do. Can you give it another try?"

"Oh, I just want to walk again!" she blurted in desperation.

"I know you do, and this is the way to get you there. Get ready to try again. Ready? Down, now up. Relax. Again, down and up. Okay, rest. Your toes come back on their own to their resting position, but no farther."

"But I tried as hard as I could!"

"Oh, I know you did," I assured her. "However, I did notice something else. When you curl your toes down really hard, your whole right foot moves downward a fraction of an inch. That's not just toe movement, that's foot movement, and that will be extremely important to walk again. We are going to keep working on that. But for now, I've got to run. Rest up, and we will do more later."

In making rounds and seeing to the needs of our patients, I checked on the eighty-year-old man whose last name was Yoder. He was in Room 120, Bed 2. "How are we doing this afternoon?" I asked.

"Just fine," he responded.

"I'm Johnny, and I am here to help you."

"Oh, are you a nurse?"

"No, I am an orderly, and I'm here to get you some fresh water. I will also need to empty your catheter bag and measure your urine output."

"Okay, you just do what you gotta do. It's all right by me."

"Do you understand that the doctor doesn't want you getting out of bed? That's why he wants you to have a catheter, so you don't have to get out of bed to use the toilet. If you need the bedpan, just push your nurse call button, and I will come help you, okay?"

"Okay," he said. "I see on your name tag that you are a Miller. Did you grow up in Ohio?"

"No, I am from Virginia."

"And you came all the way up here to Ohio to work?" he asked.

"Well, yes," I replied. "I'm a conscientious objector to war, and I'm working in the Bethesda Hospital to serve hurting, sick people instead of being in the military. I am a 1-W worker."

"Are you Amish?" he asked.

"No, I am actually Mennonite, and I am part of a church-sponsored voluntary service unit here in Zanesville."

"I think that is wonderful," Mr. Yoder said. "I grew up in an Amish home, but I left when I was very young. Do you know *Deitsh* (Pennsylvania Dutch)?"

"Yes, a little," I responded. Of course, he had to test my language skills immediately, which showed how rusty I actually was. Mr. Yoder was thrilled to find someone who could speak a few words of his childhood language. Even though he had left his roots long ago, he seemed pleased to meet someone who embraced many of the Biblical truths he had been taught as a boy. At eighty, Mr. Yoder was experiencing heart issues, and he had come in for tests.

The following day, when I entered Mr. Yoder's room, he said, "Say, do you know this song?" And he began to sing a German hymn. His voice was cracked with age as he slowly sang through the verse. Suddenly, I recognized it as a hymn we used to sing in my childhood from the German hymnal in my home church. I chimed in on the chorus and sang with him, "Give to our God, give to our God, give to our God His honor."

Mr. Yoder sang the second and third stanzas, and I helped him on each chorus. It meant a lot to him to share this with me. As I turned to leave his room, I met an unexpected audience of nurses and aides in the hallway who were intrigued with our mismatched duet.

Four days passed, and my evening shift was just ending when the intercom called for assistance in Room 120. I rushed there to discover that Mr. Yoder was not in his bed, although both bedrails were still in position. The patient in Bed 1 had awakened to see Mr. Yoder staggering toward the restroom, and he had called for help. Mr. Yoder had forgotten he could call on his nurse button and receive a bedpan. Instead, he had climbed out over the footboard of his bed. The fact that he needed to make this trip was most evident by the trail left on the floor. I had just finished cleaning and scrubbing the floor when Mr. Yoder emerged from the restroom, oblivious to the activity he had caused. He greeted me like an old friend. His catheter tubing, which he had pulled from the collection bag, was neatly wrapped about his neck. As he strained to take each step, a bit more urine dripped from the tube onto his soaked hospital gown. I lowered the rail for him to sit on the edge of his bed, where I washed him and dressed him in a clean gown for the night. After reconnecting his catheter tube to his bedside bag, I bid him a pleasant good night.

My attention spiked when Mr. Yoder's name came up several days later in our morning report. "Simon Yoder, Room 120, Bed 2, has been 'farming' all night long. He is about worn out," explained the night nurse. "I don't think he slept a full hour all night."

With report over, I made my way into Mr. Yoder's room and found him flat on his back with an intense look in his eyes. His feet were in constant motion, his covers lay rumpled at the foot of his bed, and his hands were picking imaginary items out of the air. He was breathing heavily with exertion as I broke into his imaginary world. "Mr. Yoder, good morning!" I began. "What are you up to?"

"I have to—" *pant, pant,* "—pick up all these potatoes!" he exclaimed, looking past me. His hands never faltered as he continued with the task in his mind.

I left him in his "potato field" and got a warm washcloth from the restroom. "Here," I said, "your hands are getting dirty from picking up all those potatoes. Let me wash them for you." But even as I washed the right hand, his left one continued picking up imaginary potatoes.

As the day progressed, Mr. Yoder must have completed his task, for he fell into a deep sleep. He awakened after several hours with his mind back in reality. He was prescribed medication for his heart condition and finally dismissed to return home.

Our supervisor, Miss Grey, asked me to accompany her in checking a patient in our private deluxe room. In this case, it was a Mr. Marshall who was experiencing breathing difficulties. He was diagnosed with chronic asthma and was taking positive pressure treatments daily from our inhalation therapy department. The mist he inhaled in these treatments contained medications to dilate the blood vessels and air sacks within his lungs.

Miss Grey introduced herself. "Mr. Marshall, I am the nursing supervisor, Miss Grey, and I want Mr. Miller, our orderly, to meet you as well."

I said, "I'm pleased to meet you, Mr. Marshall, but I'm sorry it has to be in the hospital."

"Well," said Mr. Marshall, "a hospital is a rather nice place to be when you need help, and I guess I need help right now."

"And we are here to help you," replied Miss Grey. "In fact, Mr. Miller will be on duty until 11:00 tonight, and he will be available should you need any assistance. He is also authorized to give you positive pressure treatments when no one from the inhalation department is available. Do not hesitate to call."

Mr. Marshall was a strong, large-framed man with massive arms and chest, and he spoke in a rumbling bass voice. "Well, I'm a bit chilly and would like to have a heavier blanket if I may."

"I will bring you one," I offered. It took a few minutes to retrieve a heavy blanket from the linen storage at the far end of the hall. I spread it over his bed and made the necessary adjustments.

"Mr. Miller, the nursing supervisor informed me that you are a conscientious objector and you are serving here in lieu of military service," Mr. Marshall said.

"That is correct," I responded.

"Well, I served in the U.S. Army as a company commander in Europe during World War II," he said. "I had several noncombatant fellows in my company. And you know, I have nothing but good to say about those boys. They were conscientious and sincere in their beliefs, and I respected them. I wished I had more like them."

I wasn't sure how to respond, so I said, "I am very grateful for the opportunity of working here in the Bethesda Hospital to help people in need."

"Do your best, my boy. That's what I always say, do your best!"

"That is what I want to do," I replied.

Miss Grey glanced at her watch. "Isn't it about your suppertime?" she asked. I acknowledged that it was.

"Why not join me?" she invited.

I fell in step with her as we headed for the cafeteria. She was a dedicated nurse who had never married. Miss Grey had spent most of her adult life in the nursing profession and had attained the status of a shift nursing supervisor.

As we sat eating, Miss Grey glanced across the table and asked, "Mr. Miller, how do you like working in the hospital?"

"I enjoy working with patients very much," I replied.

"When will your term of service be complete?" she wondered.

"Well, my required twenty-four months of service will end in mid-February 1968."

"What are you planning to do then?" she asked.

"I think I'll be working for my father-in-law in construction, but with the hard winter we're having, I've toyed with the idea of staying on here for an additional month."

"Well, I have observed you at work," Miss Grey said. "Not only are you dedicated, but you also learn new skills well. Have you ever thought of furthering your education and becoming a doctor or something in the medical field? You seem to like it well enough."

"Oh, I am sure I would like the medical profession," I said. "It's not that. But you see, in my life, God will always have first place, my family will be second, and my profession will be third. I have noticed something while working here. The people who are very good at medicine almost have to marry their career. It occupies a higher place in their lives than I am willing to give."

Miss Grey contemplated my words for a long moment before replying slowly and thoughtfully, "I see."

I thank God that verbalizing those values to Miss Grey that evening caused them to crystallize in my heart for a lifetime.

CHAPTER 29

A Moving Hope

In another week, I would be leaving for our wedding, and I was thrilled by this new step. Our lives were about to change, but it was a change we had long anticipated, and we rejoiced in knowing God was leading us together.

Nurses and doctors wished us well and asked many questions. Will it be a big wedding? Where are you going on your honeymoon? How long will you be gone? Where will you live when you return? Is your wife going to work here in the hospital with you?

I needed to consciously focus on the needs at hand so I could faithfully fulfill my hospital and VS responsibilities. Preparations for our life together had to wait for my off hours. One of these was the small apartment that would be our living quarters. Although it was one of the houses purchased by the hospital with their future expansion in mind, the VS unit had arranged to use it for housing. However, it was in dire need of some sprucing up.

Even in that flurry of activity, I could not forget Betsy, her paralysis, and her future. I made quick trips into her room to communicate, encourage, and to keep her exercising.

On one such visit, I asked, "What do you say, Betsy; are you ready see if we can get those feet moving?"

"Of course I'm ready," she replied. "I was hoping you would have time to help me before they roll me face down again."

I stood so Betsy could see me and explained, "I'm going to roll up this blanket and place it under your ankles. That will lift your heels off the bed and make it easier for you to move your feet, Okay? Let's see what you can do today."

With her heels clear of the bed, Betsy pushed hard and both of her feet moved nearly half an inch downward. "Great!" I exclaimed. "You actually moved your feet down. Now let's see you pull them up. Pull!"

Betsy strained, her toes straightened, and both feet moved slightly upward. "Super! You're getting there," I praised. "You pulled your toes back quite a bit, and your feet also moved up a little. Let's see you do it again. Ready? Down! Good. Now up!" Once again there was not only the curling and straightening of her toes, but Betsy was moving her entire foot about a half inch down and then up. I was elated, and we repeated the exercise over and over until Betsy was nearly exhausted.

"S–so they really are moving?" asked Betsy, her voice thick with emotion.

"Yes, Betsy, they certainly are moving."

"My family is going to be so surprised," she exulted. "My brother is coming with my mom and dad on Friday, and I'm going to show him too."

"You know," I said, "you don't have to wait for me to be here to exercise; you can do that whenever you think of it. Just push and hold your feet and toes down for a few seconds. Then concentrate on pulling them back up and holding that position for several seconds before relaxing them. It's while you're holding them in a stressed position that your muscles and nerves get the most benefit. The more you exercise, the more you progress. Keep it up, and don't forget, we are praying for you."

The exercises continued daily, and although Betsy's progress was slow, there was measurable improvement. Still, Dr. Glosser insisted the movements were merely involuntary, and he offered no hope that Betsy would ever walk again.

I had much to contemplate during my two-and-a-half-hour drive to Minerva. This would be my final trip as a single man before I took on the responsibility of a wife, home, and marriage. I arrived two days before the wedding to help with preparations.

We were married on May 20, 1967 in the Amish Mennonite church at Minerva, and it was indeed a blessed day. We did not know our future, but we had a deep faith in God who had led us together. We pledged our lives before God and witnesses to a committed marriage for as long as we both should live. Family and friends packed the church to capacity, and we held our reception in the Minerva Grange building.

Ruth and I visited the Smithsonian in Washington D.C. and drove along Skyline Drive and through the Blue Ridge Mountains. The Blue Ridge Parkway paved the way to the Smokey Mountains, Cherokee, North Carolina, and Gatlinburg, Tennessee, where we spent most of our honeymoon. As we wrapped up our travels, we spent a weekend with my family in Virginia Beach.

We had planned one extra day after returning to Zanesville before I would report for work at the hospital. This extra day became most needed when our 1960 Corvair blew its engine and left us stranded within sixty miles of my old home in Virginia. We borrowed a car from my father and used that extra day to return to Zanesville, arriving in time for me to start back to work. We left our car in Virginia for the engine to be replaced, glad this catastrophe had not occurred in the mountains hundreds of miles from my helpful family. However, it did strain our meager finances to the utmost.

Ruth and I began our married life in the small house where a center wall had been installed to create a duplex. This provided us with a sitting room and a bedroom. Tim and Ruth Good would soon occupy the other portion of this small house, and we would share a common bathroom with an indicator light in both apartments. There was no kitchen. Since we ate our meals with the rest of the VS unit when off duty and in the hospital cafeteria when on duty, there was no need for a personal kitchen.

Shortly after we were settled in our little two-room apartment, Ruth, feeling a little apprehensive, went to see Mrs. Deckhart and filled out a job application. Within a week, Ruth was cutting and sewing blue uniforms for herself and beginning orientation. After her physical examination, Ruth became not only a member of our VS unit, but also a Bethesda Hospital employee. She was assigned to surgical post-op on 2-East. Although we seldom saw each other during working hours, we felt blessed to care for the sick and witness for Jesus together.

Ruth loved her work and told me all about caring for her patients. Helen was a mother who was suffering from a perforated bowel. Thankfully, Helen knew the Lord and felt drawn to Ruth. Peritonitis had set in, and a deep opening into the abdomen had developed at her operative site. Helen was far too weak to withstand another surgery, and her survival was in serious doubt.

Helen and Ruth frequently shared their spiritual experiences and prayed together. Ruth had gained a deep compassion through her earlier work in a nursing home. She readily adapted

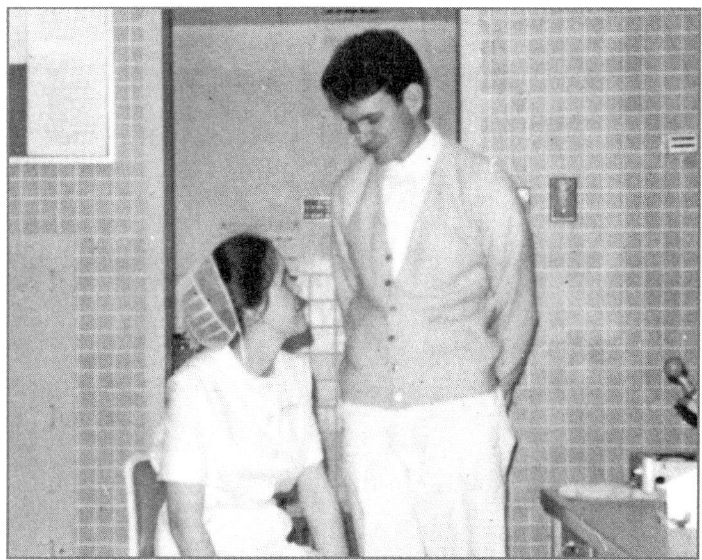

Johnny and Ruth, happily married and working together at the Bethesda Hospital.

to working in the hospital. During the changing of Helen's dressing, she once saw undigested carrots being removed from the operative site and became concerned that Helen would not survive. But through prayer, medication, and good nursing, Helen slowly began to improve.

I quickly fit back into the hospital routine of working on 1-West, ER, and occasionally in intensive care. Howard Willard had been admitted into Room 101 with tingling and partial paralysis of his hands and feet. Tests confirmed that he had contracted the debilitating disease known as Guillain-Barré syndrome.

"Hello, Mr. Willard," I greeted him as I pushed a loaded cart into his room. "Your doctor has ordered a trapeze bar installed so you can pull yourself up in bed. He wants to make your stay with us as comfortable as possible."

"That's sure nice of him," said Howard. "I can see that you do all you can for us. You know, when I first felt my hands and feet gettin' numb, I didn't know what was goin' on. Kind of scared me. But my wife and I have been thanking the good Lord for watching over us. And we are really glad we came to this hospital. You all have treated us good!"

I attached the bar on the footboard and headboard. Next came the overhead bar, and then the adjustable chain swing with its solid bar for grasping. "Okay, I want you to try this out," I said. "Just grab that little swing handle and try pulling yourself up in your bed."

Mr. Willard tried, but his fingers, already weakened by paralysis, just slipped from the handle. It was a shock for him to realize the disease had already weakened him to this point. But Mr. Willard was not one to give up so easily, and draping his wrists over the rigid handle, he hitched himself up in bed, saying, "There, that'll work!"

Very little effective treatment was available for Mr. Willard, and we watched helplessly as the numbness and loss of motion crept relentlessly up his arms and legs. Unknown to him, an iron lung left over from the polio epidemic of the 1950s was retrieved from the old hospital and reactivated. It was positioned in the hallway near his room, and I was instructed to monitor Mr. Willard's breathing as I worked with him. Labored breathing would indicate that life-threatening paralysis had affected his breathing reflex. If that happened, he would have to be encased in that huge white cylinder with only his head protruding. Its alternating negative and positive pressure on his torso would force him to breathe despite his paralysis.

Each day, we observed and charted the progression of Mr. Willard's disease. Thankfully, his paralysis slowed when it reached his upper arms and thighs. As the weeks passed, feeling and normal motor control slowly ebbed back into his impaired limbs, eventually reaching all the way to his fingers. The huge iron lung was quietly removed, and after days of physical therapy, he was well enough to be dismissed. Howard Willard thanked us profusely as he said his goodbyes. He was one happy man, thanking the Lord for his recovery and for the care and compassion he had received at Bethesda Hospital.

In the meantime, Betsy had perfected her toe and foot movements with her determined exercises. "I want to add another step to your exercises," I told her.

"What now?" she wanted to know.

I placed the rolled blanket under her ankles and asked, "Are you ready? Okay, down!" Betsy worked hard to get her feet to respond. As I watched, her toes curled slowly, and her feet began to move downward. "Now, up!" I commanded, and back they came again. "Now try moving only your right foot down. Oops, Betsy, just the right one."

"But how do I do that?" she wondered.

"While you are concentrating on moving your right foot," I explained, "make everything else relax." Knowing Betsy had no feeling in her legs and feet, I couldn't imagine how frustrating it was for her to try moving limbs she couldn't feel.

But little by little, Betsy's determination paid off as she mastered moving her feet individually. Soon I was telling her, "Left foot down, right foot up!" Next it was, "Right down, left up," and Betsy followed the commands. I was thrilled by the promise those movements held for her, and we practiced until she could do it flawlessly.

Three days later, following a new set of X-rays, Dr. Glosser strode into Betsy's room and announced, "Well, Betsy, we are going to discontinue your traction and get that hardware off your head. What do you say to that?"

Betsy hardly knew how to respond, but finally stammered,

"Th–thank you, Doctor."

She could scarcely believe it when those cruel-looking tongs were finally removed from her skull. I saw her repeatedly gliding her fingers through her two-inch long hair, thrilled with the feeling of freedom.

A week later, I placed a rolled pillow under Betsy's knees. "Okay," I instructed, "when I say 'go,' I want you to lift your right foot up off the bed. Do you think you can do that?"

"I don't know, but I will certainly try," she said eagerly.

"Okay, are you ready? Go!" Betsy grimaced and strained, but there was absolutely no movement. Again and again we tried, but nothing moved. Since I had other obligations, I removed the pillow and said, "Now, don't you be discouraged about this. We'll try it again later. I'm sure you can do it."

The following evening, we tried again. I got everything set with the pillow rolled tightly under her knees. "Betsy, I want you to concentrate and give it all you've got, okay?"

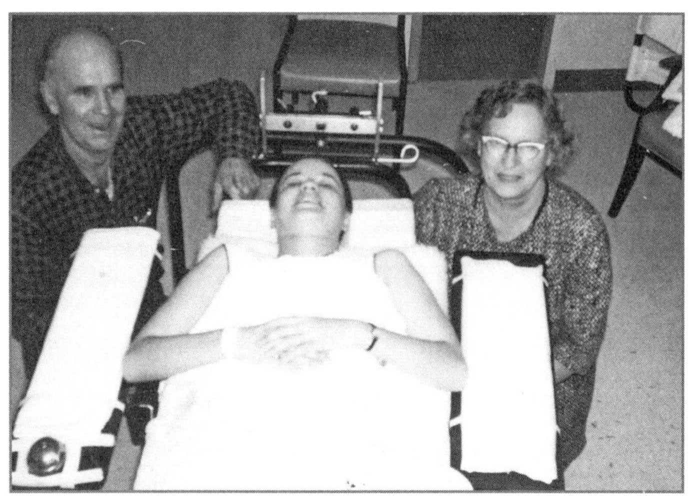

Betsy Scout on her Stryker frame, finally free of traction, rejoices with her parents.

"I'm going to try with all my might!" she responded. Taking a deep breath, she closed her eyes and squeezed her hands into fists.

"Go," I commanded, and Betsy strained until her limbs trembled with effort and her forehead creased with concentration.

My eyes widened in joyous surprise as I saw Betsy's right foot rise a quarter of an inch clear off the bed! It hung there for just one trembling moment before dropping back on the bed.

Betsy's eyes flew open, and she bit her lower lip. "Did it move?" she asked hopefully.

"I'll say it did! This much," I said, showing her with my fingers.

"That's all?" she asked a bit dejectedly.

"Betsy, that's just the beginning. It's a baby step, but I'm sure there will be many more. You rest a bit, and when I get back, we'll try the next step, okay?"

A smile spread over her face as she nodded enthusiastically.

The following evening found us trying again, and we were even more successful. By concentrating on only one leg at a time, Betsy managed to raise her foot high enough that I could slide my hand beneath her heel. "Keep it up, Betsy. Don't let it down yet," I encouraged. "Come on, you can do it!"

When I saw her leg begin trembling with fatigue, I retracted my hand and said, "Relax."

In the weeks that followed, Betsy was able to lift her feet fully six inches off the bed and hold them there for fifteen seconds. We were all proud of her accomplishment.

On Friday, Betsy's family came for another visit. They had arrived several hours before my shift began, and Dr. Glosser had met briefly with them. The atmosphere was noticeably charged as I entered Betsy's room. There was a tense, somber feel in the air, and Betsy's brother Roger asked, "Could we speak with you in private?"

"Sure," I said, and quietly closed the door.

"We are leaving!" Roger burst out. "We are signing Betsy out of here. We want to get her into the Children's Hospital in Columbus. Do you realize that even with all the movement Betsy is capable of, Dr. Glosser still insists it's involuntary? He says he is ready to dismiss her and send her home as she is! I'm totally convinced that Betsy's movements are conscious, voluntary actions. Why does he keep insisting her progress means nothing?"

I tried to mask the disappointment I felt as I replied, "If I may advise you, please don't sign Betsy out yet. There are legal implications involved in such a course of action. If Betsy developed complications, or if you were in an accident, Dr. Glosser could legally refuse to see you. Remember, he is the only neurosurgeon in Zanesville. I think you should sit down with Dr. Glosser and explain that you want to see if anything more can be done for Betsy. Tell him you have heard good reports about the hospital in Columbus and would like to get a second opinion there. Ask if Betsy can stay here at Bethesda until you can arrange to transfer her."

"But what if he becomes angry and refuses to give his consent?" asked Roger.

"Then you have no recourse but to sign her out anyway, but at least you will have tried."

"I can see your point," said Roger. "Mom, Dad, do you understand all this?" After conferring together, they all agreed they would meet with Dr. Glosser to seek his approval before transferring Betsy.

Rising to leave, I rumpled Betsy's shaggy two inches of hair and asked, "Betsy, what do you think?"

"You leave my hair alone!" she said in mock anger, but then she added with deep longing, "I just really want to walk again."

I glanced at Roger, and he nodded knowingly.

A week later, the family was visiting Betsy again, and Roger was all smiles. "I must say, you gave us sound advice," he began. "We met with Dr. Glosser, and he was very understanding."

"Really? What did he say?" I asked.

"He said he has no objections to our getting a second opinion, and that it was up to us. However, he made it clear that he thought it would be useless for Betsy."

"But you can go with his approval, and you don't have to sign her out?"

"That's right," Roger confirmed. "We have everything ready to transfer Betsy on Tuesday."

"Betsy," I said. "If I give Roger our address, will you write and tell Ruth and me how you are getting along? I would really like to keep in touch."

"Sure, I'll do that," she replied.

Following report on Tuesday, I walked into Room 109 and stood gazing at the empty Stryker frame, wondering what would become of Betsy. Would she ever walk again? Had our demonstration of Jesus' love impacted her heart? Would she ever learn to walk with the Lord?

CHAPTER 30

Winning Truth

Ruth and I had enjoyed about five months of married life in the VS unit when there was a change in the leadership. Clyde and Miriam Wagler, along with their children, Myra and Brian, moved back to their home in Hillsdale, Michigan. They had faithfully led us through the process of starting the VS unit, establishing our worship services, and finding our niches in the Bethesda Hospital.

David and Ruth Mast became our new unit leaders. Under David's leadership, a church would eventually be established. David also worked in the hospital. Both our leaders filled a vital place in our lives as we labored together.

A new fad was making its rounds among the young women in America. Many opted to cut their hair short because they said it was so much easier to manage that way. But then they purchased a partial wig of the same color as their hair. These "falls," as the wigs were called, were quite expensive and often twenty-four to thirty inches long. The more expensive ones were made of real human hair.

The VS unit with our new unit leaders, David and Ruth Mast.

This fad was adopted by some workers in our hospital. One such worker was Beth, an aide who worked on 1-West. She came to work with long, flowing, elegant hair, but when the shift ended, she removed it and drove home with her own very short hair.

I enjoyed ribbing her a bit at her expense. Although we had been working together for six months, I would greet her by saying, "I'm pleased to meet you. My name is Johnny. Have we met before?" This usually got a rise out of Beth because she understood I was poking fun at her ever-changing appearance.

One evening as shift was ending, Beth took off her fall and laid it across the counter. I asked, "Is that real human hair?"

"Yes, it is," she proudly assured me.

Absently, I felt a strand of hair, moving it up and down between my forefinger and thumb. "Hey," I said. "This is synthetic material. This is *not* human hair."

"It most certainly is human hair!" she declared. "You ought to see what I paid for it."

"Well, I'm sorry, but you were misled," I persisted. I took a single hair of her expensive fall and demonstrated by sliding it back and forth between my thumb and forefinger. The hair moved forward and backward in both directions. "I'll show you the difference," I said, and pulled a hair from my own head. "Now watch closely." I demonstrated the action again. "See, real hair will always creep in the direction of its root when it is pinched and rubbed forward and backward. That's because real hair is made up of tiny platelets arranged like a string of Vs with all their points aimed at the hair root. When they are rubbed back and forth, they move in that direction."

"Well," sniffed Beth. "I guess I know human hair when I see it."

"Okay, whatever you say," I conceded. "Just don't say I didn't tell you."

Ruth was finding it difficult to get off at the close of her shift, and I frequently found myself waiting for her to finish. One evening, she told me that the ward secretary, Marilyn Anthony, often assigned her the most difficult and time-consuming jobs. When a patient accidentally soiled the bed, Ruth was usually the one sent to clean things up.

Marilyn Anthony had worked on 1-West before being transferred to 2-East where Ruth now worked. I remembered how she had wanted her daughter to work as an aide at Bethesda, but had been told there were no openings. I wondered if she had a grudge against Ruth, who had been warmly invited to work as a nurse's aide.

Ruth was standing by the door in her crisp uniform one day, ready to go to work, when she broke down. "Johnny," she said with a catch in her voice, "I–I just can't take it anymore!"

"Why, what's wrong?" I asked, immediately concerned.

"It's Marilyn Anthony. She treats me like dirt!" Ruth said as she

Ruth, dreading another evening of disparaging treatment at work.

shook with sobs. "Last night I had so much work to do, and other workers were just standing around chatting in the nurses' station. We were told that a patient had soiled the bed so badly that she needed a complete bath, and the bed had to be scrubbed and changed. Marilyn ordered me to do it, and I did.

"But that put me so far behind that I was still working a half hour after the rest of the shift had clocked out and gone home. It looks to the oncoming shift like I am lazy and can't get my work done. This kind of thing has been going on ever since I started working, but it is getting worse. I can't take it anymore—I can't! It's getting to the point where I dread going to work!" She buried her face in her hands and let the tears flow.

I gently placed my arms about my sweet wife. "Honey, don't cry," I begged. "I know you are a willing worker, and this is hard to take, but please listen to me. I am here with you instead of in Vietnam with people trying to kill me. We are truly blessed, and God's grace will carry us through the unfairness. Just do your best as unto the Lord, and allow God to work it out."

"I want to," she cried. "I really do want to. And I'm so ashamed of my feelings, but I can't help it!" I produced a hanky, and Ruth wiped her eyes and gave me a feeble smile.

"Perhaps you might want to wash you face before we head for the hospital," I suggested. "It's almost time to leave."

As we walked across the expansive lawn toward the back of the hospital, we discussed the issue further. I told Ruth, "You know, we really dare not complain. Don't say a word about your mistreatment to anyone, and neither will I. Just hold you head high, do your best, and let truth float to the top."

"What do you mean by that?" Ruth asked.

"Well," I explained, "truth is lighter than falsehood, and given enough time, it will float to the top. We don't need to push it there."

"Hmm . . . you think so?"

"I know so."

After work that night, I again waited twenty minutes past quitting time until Ruth was finally free. The other VS workers on our shift had nearly finished their snack by the time we arrived in the dining hall. We prayed together that night, asking God to give Ruth the grace to face her pressures with a Christlike attitude.

As the weeks passed, Ruth felt the pressures become even more intense. Yet we were determined to say nothing and allow God to deal with this situation.

Each nurses' station in the entire hospital received a private call asking all personnel to be on the lookout for a psychiatric patient who had slipped out of 4-North while visitors were coming in. For obvious reasons, such an announcement couldn't be made on the public-address system. Minutes after the alert went out, the nursing supervisor showed up on 1-West and sought me out. “Mr. Miller, “we fear this patient has left the hospital, and we *must* find him!” she said gravely. “I want you to run toward Route 60 and watch for him out there. But be careful. He can’t be trusted.”

I exited by way of the front lobby and ran until I was out of breath. The night was chilly, and I wished I had taken the time to put on my jacket. What would I do if I found the patient? I certainly wasn’t going to tackle him, but I might try to engage him in conversation. Maybe I could explain that he needed treatment which only the hospital could give. I would try to persuade him to return peaceably so we could care for his needs. Half an hour passed, but I didn’t see anyone who matched his description. I watched and waited for another fifteen minutes before giving up and returning to 1-West.

I asked our ward secretary, “Would you please call the night supervisor and tell her I was not able to locate the patient?”

“Oh, they found him wandering around in the basement near the cafeteria about ten minutes after you left,” she said. “He is safely back in 4-North.”

With a sigh of relief, I said, “That’s good! I can chalk that one off my list.”

I started refilling carafes with fresh water, giving back rubs, and preparing patients for the night. When I entered Room 110, Larry Harding reminded me his dressing had not yet been changed. I reported his need to the charge nurse, but she was quite busy and asked if I would change his bandage.

“Sure,” I replied.

“You’ll need to use sterile technique. He has a deep, infected wound,” she reminded me.

I gathered the necessary items and headed for Mr. Harding’s room. “So, how did you receive this injury?” I asked as I cleansed the area with an antiseptic solution and sterile pads.

"I was traveling on a country road one evening, and it was a bit windy," Larry explained. "Suddenly, there was a crash as a dead limb snapped off a tree and fell through my windshield. A portion of it hit me here in the hip joint."

"When did this happen?" I asked.

"Almost seven years ago."

"What?!" I exclaimed. "And it's still not healed?"

"Unknown to the doctors, there were bits of wood broken off next to the bone," he said. "The fragments festered and needed to be removed surgically, and that's when I contracted this staph infection. I have been hospitalized numerous times, but it just will not heal."

"I see. And it keeps draining?"

"Yes, that small hole needs to be cleaned out every time we change the dressings. You do have sterile cotton swabs on your tray, don't you?"

"Yes, I have them right here."

"Okay, you'll need to push them to the bottom of my wound to clean it out."

I carefully opened the sterile cotton swab with its long stem, dipped it into the disinfectant solution, and then twirled it slowly as I pushed it through the small opening of the skin and into the wound. The swab was over an inch into the wound when Mr. Harding said, "Oh, you've got to go much deeper than that. It's way down in there!"

Afraid of hurting the patient, I advanced the swab slowly, deeper and deeper until it was well over two inches into his leg.

"That's more like it," he said.

I retracted the swab, covered in thick, yellow pus. I repeated this process until the wound was clean, and then applied antibacterial ointment and re-bandaged the wound.

After cleaning up and safely disposing of the soiled bandage materials, I was nearly finished with my shift. Several of us clocked out and walked toward the elevator together. As we stepped into the elevator, I saw that Beth had removed her fall and had it draped over her arm. On a whim, I placed it on my own head. It must have looked hilarious, for they couldn't quit laughing. When Beth caught her breath, she said, "I dare you to go meet your wife like that."

In response, I reached over and pushed the elevator button to take us to the second floor. My companions could hardly suppress their emotions as the door opened on 2-East.

Wearing my crepe sole shoes, I moved very quietly, thinking, *Won't Ruth be surprised! She'll get a kick out of this.* I ran on tiptoe as I neared the nurses' station. All was quiet, with patients mostly asleep. The outgoing and incoming nurses were having report behind the closed door of the conference room. Suddenly the thought hit me, *What if some doctor is making late rounds—I'd better check before walking into the nurses' station with nearly waist-length hair.* I peeped stealthily around the doorframe, and Ruth was staring straight at me!

She had been left all alone in the nurses' station during report. As she waited for report to end so she could join me, she rehearsed the evening's work. *Hmm,* she thought. *I never did hear whether they found that psych patient. Is he still roaming around somewhere?*

The silence of the floor with everyone asleep was eerie. Then she heard a soft scuffling sound. *Is that the mental patient?* Her heart began to race as she swiveled her chair to face the door. At that moment, a man's face with long, flowing hair cascading on each side slowly peered around the corner.

What happened next produced the greatest embarrassment of my two years in 1-W service. Ruth shot straight into the air with a piercing scream, her chair flipped over with a loud crash, and she landed in a heap on the floor, simultaneously crying in fear and laughing with relief. During her short flight, she had realized the face encased in all that hair was not an escaped psychiatric patient, but her own beloved husband.

Shocked and surprised by Ruth's reaction, I spun about and made a dash for the elevator, saying in a loud stage whisper as I ran, "Down, push the down button!"

The ladies on the elevator were choking with suppressed laughter, but I could not share their mirth. I was deeply embarrassed by the commotion I had caused. I had never intended to scare Ruth, and I knew I had to somehow make amends for what I had done.

"What on earth was all that noise about?" the nurse asked Ruth. She explained truthfully, and I was deeply humbled. As a young person, I was learning the exercise of wisdom is far more valuable than having a bit of fun. It was a lesson well learned.

* * * * *

On 3-East, our Christian neighbor man lay dying of emphysema, and I went to visit him. Gilbert Hall had come to know the Lord ten years earlier. He and his wife were committed Christians, and she welcomed my gentle knock at the door.

Her husband had oxygen pumping through a nasal cannula, and yet he was gasping for breath as if he had just run a mile. His lungs were incapable of properly absorbing oxygen. This poor brother had been a heavy smoker for years before he repented and surrendered his life to Jesus Christ. He had quit smoking and concentrated on living the rest of his life in obedience to the Lord. However, becoming a Christian did not erase the effects of years of tar and smoke damage.

Gilbert nodded as I entered, indicating he welcomed me, but he needed oxygen so desperately that he couldn't spare any breath for conversation. He was taking forty breaths a minute, but his damaged lungs could only absorb a small fraction of the life-giving oxygen. The rest was being exhaled. I didn't stay long at Gilbert's bedside, but I laid a hand on his arm and explained that we cared and were praying for him. His wife expressed her thanks, and Mr. Hall nodded gratefully.

Two days later, Gilbert Hall left his wife behind and passed into the presence of the Lord. I learned that the heart races when the body is short of oxygen, and over a prolonged period, the heart grows fatigued and finally gives out.

The picture of this loving husband's struggle to breathe was indelibly etched into my mind, and it produced in me an aversion toward tobacco that would last a lifetime.

Several weeks passed, and Ruth shed a few more tears due to the mistreatment she suffered at the hands of her ward secretary. Through it all, she maintained her sweet, Christ-like spirit, and we continued praying.

It was now becoming almost routine for me to go up to 2-East after clocking out to wait for Ruth. On Friday evening, I finished on 1-West and again made my way up to Ruth's floor. All the personnel were already gone except for two nurses having report in the conference room and another one updating patient charts. Ruth was busy finishing up her late assignment once again.

I strode into the treatment room and glanced at the time clock. The nurse noticed me and asked, "You're Ruth's husband, aren't you?"

"Yes, I am."

"So, you are waiting for her?"

"That's right."

She wrote in silence for several moments. "How does your wife like her job?" she asked with genuine interest.

"Oh, she loves taking care of patients," I responded.

"What does she have to say about her working conditions?"

"Well, not too much," I said lamely.

The nurse glanced about to make sure there was no one within earshot. She pursed her lips and squinted at me with a determined gaze. "I've been noticing what's going on around here," she said emphatically. "Believe you me, it is going to stop. It's absolutely ridiculous!"

I was uncomfortable, looking for a graceful way to end this conversation. Ruth and I were both determined not to complain, so I didn't know how to respond. Just then, Ruth breezed out of a patient's room with a load of soiled laundry. She flashed me a cheery smile and said, "I'm almost done."

A few minutes later, Ruth was beside me. As we passed the nurses' station, we wished the sympathetic nurse a hearty good night.

The following week, Ruth came home happy but perplexed. She said, "I don't know what has gotten into our ward secretary, but she has certainly changed!"

"What do you mean?" I asked.

"She is treating me with so much respect. And you know, she even asked me to share my cake recipe with her. She has quit assigning me those last-minute jobs too. So far this week, I haven't gotten off late even once. I find myself looking forward to going to work again. Her change of heart has made such a difference."

"Ruth, do you think just maybe the truth has finally floated to the top?" I asked.

She flashed me a knowing smile. "I guess it has."

CHAPTER 31

Conflict and Death

Ruth continued working with Helen whenever possible. For some time, it appeared that Helen was going to succumb to the massive infection caused by her perforated bowel. Heavy doses of antibiotics administered through IVs were barely able to keep her acute abdominal infection at bay. She told Ruth, "I'm so tired of being here in the hospital away from my little girls. Please pray that I can be patient and get well enough to go home. I miss them so much!"

Ruth ministered to her suffering through personal prayers and spiritual encouragements. The volume of food particles appearing in her opened operative site began to diminish, and as the weeks passed, they ceased altogether. The infection was slowly being conquered, and healing had begun. Little by little, Helen gained strength until she could sit up. Before long, she stood for short intervals and even took a few steps. The day came at last when Helen felt she could go for a short walk. She took Ruth's arm as they ventured into the hall with an air of triumph. As they slowly shuffled past the nurses' station, Marilyn Anthony and the nurses came out to celebrate and to congratulate Helen. For one who had lain in bed for so long, too weak to even sit up, this was indeed a victory walk that celebrated faith and perseverance.

Midway through our afternoon shift, I was called into the nurses' station by Nurse Oakland. She said, "We've just received word that a Mr. Powell was admitted to 3-East two days ago. He is emotionally unstable, but he holds a prominent position on a newspaper. If he had been admitted to 4-North, the publishing company feared his psychiatric problems would become public knowledge. The repercussions of such a leak could be devastating. 3-East is asking for help with a confrontation going on right now. Nurse Shepard is on duty, and she will explain what is to be done."

I left immediately for 3-East, reflecting on my deep distaste for being involved with these kinds of conflicts. When I reported to the nurses' station, Nurse Shepard said, "Thanks for coming. Just wait here until the others join us."

Within minutes, two of my fellow orderlies arrived, and she began briefing us. "Last evening, Mr. Powell became belligerent and combative. This was very unusual because he is such a fine gentleman. The Powells have been close friends of ours for many years. But this afternoon, he became angry and unmanageable. He chased his wife down the hallway, cursing her and kicking her repeatedly. I called my husband, and he is in the room with Mr. Powell right now, trying to calm him down. We have been listening in through the intercom, and it's not getting any better. That's why I called you fellows. The patient is adamant that he's leaving the hospital, and we absolutely cannot allow that. It would be dangerous for himself and for others. His doctor has prescribed a hefty sedative, along with orders to transfer him to 4-North. That's where he should have gone in the first place. Let's go. This way, please."

We followed her down the hall to Room 319, where we stood listening to the uproar from within. "Jim!" an angry voice shouted. "I said I'm not going to transfer. I'm going home! Get that through your ______ head!"

"Harold, stop and think what you have been doing," came the soothing voice of Mr. Shepard. "You tried to beat up your wife, and that's just not like you. You love Janie and would never hurt her. You're acting erratic. You're not yourself, and that's why your doctor admitted you—so we can help you."

"I am out of here!" the deranged man insisted. "Who do you think you are? You are trying to hold me here against my will, and that's not legal. Get out. Get OUT!"

There were more curses before the door suddenly opened and Mr. Shepard emerged, looking quite stressed as the door slammed behind him. Nurse Shepard introduced us to her distraught husband, and Jim began explaining, "Fellows, this isn't going to be easy. I see no recourse but to manually subdue him. I have tried talking with him for half an hour." He shook his head and took a deep breath. "He's a close friend of mine, but I have not been able to talk any sense into him at all. He's just not himself and won't listen to anything I say."

Orderly Mose Stoltzfus asked, "So you want us to subdue him so he can be sedated and transferred to the psych ward. Is that our goal?"

"That is what his doctor recommends," Nurse Shepard confirmed. "Engage him if necessary, sedate him, but get him safely into 4-North."

"Okay," said Mose. "Let's see what we can do. Are you ready?" He glanced at Earl and me.

Ready? I would never be *ready* for this kind of confrontation. I detested it!

"Just a minute," said Mr. Shepard. "I recommend that you take off your name pins and glasses and let my wife keep them for you until you're finished." We complied, and then Mr. Shepard quietly pushed open the door and motioned for us to follow.

We filed in silently. Mr. Powell was trying to use the phone and looked up in surprise. "What do you want?" he snapped.

"Harold, these are my friends who work here at the hospital. They are here to help you transfer to the other floor," Jim said evenly.

"Jim, I'm leaving! I'm calling a taxi right now."

Mose spoke up. "We understand you have been through a lot of stress, and we want what is best for you. That's why we came," he explained kindly.

"Thanks, but I won't be needing your help," Mr. Powell snarled. "I am leaving in just a few minutes." Mose strolled to the far side of the room, getting closer to the phone and to Mr. Powell while sizing up our patient. He was well over six feet and powerfully built. He had broad, well-defined shoulders. Earl and I stayed between the patient and the door, and Jim Shepard faded into the background. Mr. Powell stood with his back against the wall, and again picked up the phone. I edged closer while he concentrated on dialing. I noted he was left-handed, and I felt fear settling in the pit of my stomach. The tension in the room heightened perceptibly, like a spring being wound ever tighter. Something was about to snap.

As Mr. Powell was distracted with the phone, I eased up till I was right beside him, wondering if I dared make a grab for his right arm.

"Yes, operator, give me the sheriff's department, please. My name? Harold Powell. Yes, I'll hold." Suddenly, he realized we were standing uncomfortably close, and he shook that heavy receiver menacingly and warned us, "The first ______ that touches me will get it!"

A few seconds later, he jiggled the phone impatiently and said,

"Operator, operator!" I gave Mose a knowing look and grabbed the patient's arm in both my hands, praying that Mose would pin the arm holding that receiver. Mr. Powell looked at me incredulously as I ducked my head, fearing what might happen next. With unbelievable strength, he flung me across the room. I landed face down on the bed, but I hadn't lost my grip on his arm, so he had been pulled along with me. He landed beside me on the bed. Mose had grabbed his other arm and landed on top of the patient, and Earl piled on to helped secure Mr. Powell as well.

"My arm, my arm!" he shouted. "You're breaking my arm!" I quickly moved to relieve the uncomfortable angle of his arm, but then recalled the nasty bite Earl Nisly had received from a disturbed patient. I quickly placed my arm below Mr. Powell's chin so he couldn't bite anyone.

"You're choking me!" he shouted. "Get your hands off of me!"

I made sure I wasn't restricting his breathing in any way and said, "Mr. Powell, I am not choking you."

"Yes, you are!" he argued.

"You're talking, aren't you?" I countered. "That means I can't possibly be choking you."

At that moment, the nurse arrived with a syringe loaded with a sedative. She gave a quick injection, pulled the needle from his arm, and said, "Okay, you can let him up."

I looked at her in utter disbelief. Let him up after all we had been through? What made her think this injection was going to take effect in ten seconds?

Earl removed himself from the bed, and then Mose followed, but as they did so, I felt Mr. Powell's fingers digging painfully into my arm. He intended to stand up, but he was not about to let go of me. I had a sinking feeling that this might not turn out well. As Mr. Powell rose from the bed, he gripped my arm with both hands, quickly spun around, and pulled my arm up over his shoulder. I realized he was going to body slam me over his shoulder and onto the concrete floor. In his mind, I was the source of his problem since I had been the first one to take hold of him. Mr. Powell was also still convinced that I had choked him.

He crouched low to get leverage to swing me up and over his shoulder. I went completely limp to make his intended maneuver more difficult, and then brought my knees up under him. He tried twice without success, and then, still clutching my arm, he spun around and drew back his left fist to smash my face. With a sudden jerk, I freed my arm, jumped back, and threw up my forearms to intercept the blow.

At that moment, Harold's longtime friend, Mr. Shepard, sprang into action. He leaped between us, his eyes blazing. Drawing back his fists, he shouted, "Harold, you do that again, and I will flatten you!"

Mr. Powell began shouting, "I'm going to get all of you fired! I know the people who run this hospital, and I am going to report you. I'll sue you! And you," he said, stepping in my direction. "You choked me, and you are going to lose your job!"

I saw that my presence was only adding to his irritation, so I quietly exited while he was distracted. Nurse Shepard informed me Dr. Benning was on his way. She told me to go to 4-North to be available just in case there were further problems. On the fourth floor, I waited outside the psych ward, out of sight but keeping an eye on the elevators. Twenty minutes later, I followed the orderlies and Dr. Benning as they led Mr. Powell into the psychiatric ward. He was still loud and blustering, and he kept pacing in extreme agitation. I remained out of sight to avoid upsetting him further. They were having a difficult time persuading Mr. Powell to enter his room where he could be secured.

Things eventually settled down. Noting that I was no longer needed, I decided to leave. Just then, a visitor opened the one-way electrically locked door from the outside. Knowing this door closed slowly, I made a beeline for it while it was open. As I ran, I heard Mr. Powell shout, "There he goes! That's the one who choked me! Get him!" I dashed through the door and pushed as hard as possible against the resistance of the slow closure to get that door latched between me and the onrushing patient. A moment after the lock clicked, I watched through the small, safety-glass window as Mr. Powell slammed into the door, still intent on getting me. But thank the Lord, the door had locked! I quickly stepped out of his line of sight, and when I no longer heard him shouting, I entered the elevator, picked up my name-pin from Nurse Shepard, and headed for the calmer atmosphere of 1-West.

As a 1-W conscientious objector intent on living out the teachings of Jesus Christ, I was troubled at having to use even benign force on a patient like Mr. Powell. True, we could never become angry at such confrontations, and striking or harming a patient was out of the question. Yet, keeping a person from harming himself or injuring others was necessary, and at times this became my duty. Despite the necessity, I found it distasteful and unsettling.

I was back in ER on the afternoon shift when an ambulance, its siren screaming, sped through the parking lot and screeched to a stop at the entrance. Within moments, the ambulance team rushed inside with a patient on their cart. Hurrying beside the patient was Dr. Thomas. He was performing mouth to mouth resuscitation and external cardiac massage. This was obviously a desperate situation, and Dr. Thomas' white shirt was soaked with perspiration. He appeared haggard and fatigued as he momentarily raised his head and shouted, "No, not ER! Take him straight to ICU."

"Johnny, go with them," instructed the ER charge nurse.

I dashed ahead and opened the large door leading to ICU. As we entered, there was a moment of hesitation from the head nurse until Dr. Thomas shouted, "We need a bed!" All normal protocol was dropped, and we hurriedly transferred the patient from the ambulance cart onto a hospital bed. In all this flurry of activity, Dr. Thomas never stopped filling the patient's lungs with life-sustaining air nor stopped his heart compressions to circulate live-giving blood.

"Code Blue, Code Blue! ICU for Code Blue!" blared over the PA system, and moments later, James Wesson arrived with a crash cart. Dr. Thomas waited until James had the mask and bag ready, and then he quickly moved aside so James could place the mask over the patient's nose and mouth. All the while, Dr. Thomas continued his rhythmic heart compressions without a pause. James suggested I give Dr. Thomas a break, and I moved into position so we could make the switch without breaking the rhythm of heart compressions.

Dr. Thomas took a deep breath and wearily wiped the sweat from his face. "This is my next-door neighbor, Mr. Tiller," he panted. "I was on my front porch, and Mark was pushing his lawnmower. I was looking right at him when he collapsed, and I immediately ran to him. He wasn't breathing, and he had no pulse. I began immediate resuscitation and heart massage."

"And you continued that until now?" asked James.

"Yes, I continued during the ambulance ride and through ER. I know Mark well. At my recommendation, he came in two weeks ago for a complete physical examination. We did all his bloodwork, EKG and everything, and I gave him a clean bill of health. His collapse is quite a shock to me." For a long moment, no one spoke. The sound of James' pumping airbag and the heart compressions filled the cubicle where we worked desperately to save Mark Tiller's life.

A technician arrived and hooked up the leads to the heart monitor. I could see the effect of our compressions on the monitor, so we knew we were keeping Mark's blood circulating. After five minutes, Dr. Thomas said, "Miller, pause for a moment." I did, and there was nothing on the monitor but a flat line. Mark's heart was still not beating!

Dr. Thomas broke the ensuing silence with a brief, "Carry on, boys. I'll be right back." He ducked around the curtain, returning in several minutes to closely examine the patient. "His color is good," he observed. "You boys are doing a fine job. Keep it up. I've ordered the defibrillator from surgery, and we will apply electric shock to get his heart beating again."

A surgical technician rolled in with a large machine, positioned it at the patient's bedside, and plugged it into a wall receptacle. The machine whined as it built up a surge of electrical current while we hurriedly slipped a grounding plate coated with a conductive lotion under the patient's bare back. Watching the gauges closely, Dr. Thomas barked the order, "Pull the monitor leads!"

The leads were snatched from the patient's chest to avoid blowing the heart monitor with a surge of current. Dr. Thomas smacked a disc electrode directly over the heart and ordered, "Stand clear!" as he lowered his thumb onto the trigger. He glanced about to make certain all personnel were clear of the bed, and then he pressed down.

Whump! Mark's entire body gave one huge contraction and then relaxed as the voltage surged through his muscles and his heart. "Leads," commanded Dr. Thomas, and the monitor leads were hurriedly affixed to Mark's chest. The heart monitor reactivated. All eyes were glued to the line as it raced across the face of the monitor.

We willed it to begin its up and down movement, but there was not a flicker. The monitor contained only that ominous flat line.

"Resume resuscitation," ordered Dr. Thomas. James and I traded places, so he was now giving the heart compressions while I applied one deep breath from the bag for every four compressions. Four in, four out. Four in, four out. We worked like a well-oiled machine.

Following ten minutes of continuing resuscitation, Dr. Thomas ordered another heart shock, but again, the monitor showed no sign of any heart activity. Despite that hopeless flat line, Dr. Thomas was not about to give up. Fearing acid build-up in the blood from non-functioning kidneys, he ordered sodium bicarbonate injected by IV to reduce that danger.

As James and I continued with the heart compressions and breathing, Dr. Thomas contemplated a Xylocaine injection directly into the heart to get it going once more.

Just then, a heart specialist, Dr. William Chenny, stepped into our cubical. Taking in the resuscitation in progress and the defibrillator standing by, he asked, "Say, Jerry, what's going on here?"

Dr. Thomas began rehearsing all that had transpired, including the complete physical only two weeks before. Dr. Chenny, wearing his neat bow tie and chewing his beloved gum like he always did, listened intently. Then he asked, "How long ago did he collapse?"

"It's been nearly two hours," Dr. Thomas said. "But I've given him sodium bicarbonate by IV, and the only interruption to the resuscitation was about one minute during the heart shock. We ought to be in pretty good shape, don't you think?"

Dr. Chenny chewed his gum thoughtfully as he gazed at Mark lying on the bed. We continued breathing and compressing his heart for him. Without a word, Dr. Chenny walked to the head of the bed. Taking a penlight from his vest pocket, he lifted Mark's eyelid and looked deeply into the pupil of his eye. He repeated the process with the other eye. Slowly, he replaced his penlight.

Dr. Thomas asked, "What about Xylocaine straight to the heart? What do you say, Bill?"

"Jerry," said Dr. Chenny in a low, respectful tone. "You can do Xylocaine if you like, but you are working on a *dead* man."

I felt sorry for Dr. Thomas as that thought slowly registered, and the truth hit home. He suddenly deflated like a child's balloon. His shoulders sagged, and he suddenly appeared old and worn out. In a somber voice, he said, "You boys can quit now." But even as we did, he gazed for a long moment at the monitor. It stolidly confirmed Dr. Chenny's diagnosis.

I had much to share with Ruth as we walked home that night, but deep down, my soul was acknowledging that life is in the hands of the Creator rather than the created.

CHAPTER 32

Costly Mistakes

Ruth and I were thrilled to receive a letter from Betsy Scout one day. Eagerly, we read together:

Dear Johnny and Ruth,

How are you? I am fine. I miss the Bethesda Hospital and the wonderful people I learned to know there. Here at Children's Hospital, things are very different. The care is wonderful, but the people are not so friendly as in your hospital. How much longer are you and Ruth going to keep working at the hospital?

Two young doctors have been assigned to me, and they took a bunch more X-rays and have been studying them a lot. I see one of my doctors nearly every day. They have been watching my toes and feet move, and they are planning to operate on my neck. They have talked with my brother and Mom and Dad. They are saying that my broken bones have grown fast to each other even though they are in the wrong position. They are hoping if they break them apart and fasten them in the right place, maybe my nerves can heal enough so I could actually have feeling come back in my legs and feet, and maybe someday even I might be able to walk! I am very excited about this, but I'm kinda scared too. What if something during the operation would go wrong? I would love to see you again. Maybe you can come see me here.

Your friend,
Betsy Scout
P.S. Please excuse my scribbles. I know my writing is terrible.

Having a deep interest in Betsy's future and wanting to maintain contact, I responded with a letter. I answered her questions, asked about her and her family, and wondered whether her new doctors felt her foot movements were only reflexes. I assured her we would continue praying for her.

I learned in report that Bruce Wagner, Room 120, had been in surgery that morning and returned from the recovery room at 2:30. When the supper trays arrived at 5 p.m., I noticed there was no tray assigned for Room 120. "Mr. Wagner, how are you feeling?" I asked. "I heard you were in surgery today. How did it go?"

"Not too bad, not too bad," he responded with a good-natured grin. "A bit woozy I am. Wouldn't want to run any races just now, but I might feel up to it tomorrow."

"Well, they didn't send you a supper tray because they didn't expect you to have an appetite so soon after surgery. Also, the kitchen didn't know when you were returning from surgery."

"What!" he exclaimed. "No supper? Man, they didn't let me eat any breakfast this morning, I was in surgery over lunch, and here they are keeping back my supper! You don't think they'd try to starve a fellow, do you?" he chuckled.

"Hey, if you have an appetite, I'll get a supper tray brought up for you, okay?"

"Seriously, I'd appreciate a little something," he said.

"Good, I'll get it for you. I'm pretty sure it will be chicken broth, some crackers, some Jell-O, a little fruit, and maybe a cup of tea or coffee."

"Okay," he smiled. "That would be just fine. I wouldn't feel good on a heavy meal."

I soon returned with his supper tray of light food and moved several items from his bedside table to make room for the tray. As I did so, I noticed a bundle of metal rods, plates and screws. "What is this?" I asked in surprise.

"That's my hardware," Bruce said with a grin.

"Hardware? What do you mean?" I asked.

"That's what they took out of me today."

"All of that!" I exclaimed incredulously.

"Yep, they've been bothering me for some time, and since I didn't need them anymore, the doctor thought it best to get rid of them. When I was young, I got me a job working in the coal mines near my home in West Virginia. We were drilling holes for blasting deep in the mine. We had this V-8 engine rigged up on a cart with wheels, and it ran a long shaft with a big drill bit on the end of it. Well, one day when I was drilling, I guess I got a little careless and got against that rotating shaft. It grabbed my clothes and began to wrap me all about that shaft. It flung me round and round, beating me against the floor of the mine. It broke me up pretty bad, and those metal pieces are what they used to put me back together."

"Wow, Bruce, it's a miracle you weren't killed!"

"I would have been, but there was Someone looking after me, that's for sure."

"Do you mind if I take a look at the hardware?" I asked.

"Of course not. Go right ahead."

"What did they do with this one?" I asked as I lifted a half-inch stainless steel rod nearly a foot long and deeply fluted on each end.

"Oh, that's the one they took out of my leg. My thigh bone was pretty much busted up. And you know, every time it was fixing to rain, that thing would commence to ache like everything!"

There were five smaller rods, two steel plates, and a handful of screws. I lifted the entire lot of them and commented, "You must have lost two pounds since this morning."

Bruce chuckled. "That's kind of an expensive way to lose weight, isn't it?"

Report also notified me of Norris Smith in Room 104, an eighteen-year-old from West Virginia who was a patient of Dr. Morgan. He had a crushed left hand. He was a chunky, talkative youth with an Elvis Presley hairstyle. It appeared that every hair was anchored in place by some type of slick hair product. He was sitting in his chair with his injured hand propped up, ready for someone to talk to. His bandaged hand was the size of a softball, and it had obviously sustained considerable damage.

I introduced myself and asked, "What happened to your hand?"

"I was with a little traveling circus and was working on their merry-go-round," he said. "I had my hand on them big gears underneath, what makes it go around, you know? The other worker thought I was done and started her up, and that thing just grabbed my hand in them gears. It took 'em a while to turn the thing backwards and get me out. Since it wasn't that far to Zanesville, they drove me over here to git fixed up." He grinned cheerfully.

"My, that must have been painful," I observed.

"Oh, it hurt right smart till they gave me that shot in the 'mergency room, then she commenced to feelin' better. And in surgery, I didn't know nothin'. Knocked me plumb out so they could get them busted up bones in place. I'm feelin' much better now. Say, ya don't know where a fellow could get a bit of Crisco, do you?"

"Crisco?"

"Yeah, ya know, just plain old Crisco. Ever try it?" asked Norris.

"I can't say that I have," I said, remembering that my mother used it in making pie crusts.

"Best thing I ever used on my hair. Makes her stay in place all day long. I use it all the time traveling with the circus. But if I got to stay here long, I don't know how I'm gonna get some—unless I can get a hold of my folks."

I finally extricated myself from Norris Smith's room and went about my duties, perplexed by this young man who seemed more concerned with keeping his hairstyle intact than the fact that he was facing life with a seriously impaired hand. But then I thought, *How often have I been overly concerned with things that are temporal while neglecting those that are eternal?*

I entered the nurses' station just in time to hear Nurse Carol exclaim, "These new felt-tipped pens are driving me crazy! If you lay them down for a minute without the cap on, they dry out, and you have to shake them to get them working again." She shook the pen and began charting again, only to stop in frustration to give it another shake.

"Here, let me fix it for you," I offered. She handed me the stubborn pen with a look that said, "Okay, let's just see *you* fix it!" Being confident that my experience in the daily routine of shaking mercury down in thermometers would work for this ink pen, I really went at it, giving my wrist that extra snap with each shake.

Somewhere around my seventh or eighth snap, Nurse Carol began shouting, "Stop, Johnny! Please stop." I stopped in surprise, wondering what brought on her shouting fit.

"Look!" she exclaimed as she pointed. Speckled all across the floor, up over the desk, on the glass surround, and even on the white ceiling, was a six-inch-wide path speckled with fine ink droplets. I was aghast at what I had done, and I spent the better part of an hour humbly scrubbing off the marks of my overconfidence with an alcohol-soaked rag.

Near Mount Perry, Ohio, John A. Miller was having a difficult time starting his John Deere A. He spun the flywheel again and again, but it only made an occasional pop before coasting to a discouraging stop. After many tries, that familiar *po-pop, po-pop, po-pop-pop* began, and the engine was running! He let it warm up a bit before climbing onto the seat and adjusting the throttle. Putting it in gear and slowly engaging the clutch so as not to stall it, he drove his tractor to the gas tank to fuel it up for the job ahead.

Remembering his difficulty in starting the tractor, John decided to let it run. He removed the gas cap, stretched the hose high, and began filling the tank. Just then, Daddy's "helping hand" climbed up on the side of the tractor. Seven-year-old Mintie loved her daddy and wanted to help. And John was delighted to have his oldest daughter with him.

"Daddy, let me fill it," she begged.

He handed the spout to her, warning her, "Be very careful."

Mintie felt important as she held the nozzle and directed the gas into the tank. But not wanting it to run over, she stretched to look into the tank. In doing so, she unconsciously pulled the nozzle just outside the lip of the tank. Suddenly, gas spattered onto the outside of the tank and ran down over the running engine.

BOOM! A terrific explosion engulfed little Mintie in a sheet of flame. She gave a desperate, imploring look at her father as she screamed and jumped to the ground with her dress on fire. Her little hands tried vainly to beat out the flames. Her father rushed to her, grabbed her burning dress in his strong hands, and ripped it in two. He threw the burning fabric away from his precious daughter and beat out the rest of the flames.

Mintie was terrified and screaming with pain as her father scooped his daughter up in his arms and ran for the house. Mintie's little legs and abdomen were covered with angry red burns. Her mother quickly administered a soothing home remedy and gave Mintie aspirin to ease the pain. But what should they do next?

Being New Order Amish and not owning a car now posed a problem. Although Mintie had calmed down some, they still felt she needed medical attention. John went to the shed, started his other tractor, and sped over to their neighbors, Clarence and Lilly Rockwell. He told them they needed to get little Mintie to the hospital quickly. True to his generous nature, Mr. Rockwell said, "Sure, I'll be there in a minute!"

A sober mother and father tenderly wrapped their little daughter in a clean bedsheet and carried her to Mr. Rockwell's car for the trip to the hospital.

LPN Betty Miller was on duty when a white car stopped at the entrance of the ER. An Amish couple climbed out, with the father carrying a little girl wrapped in a sheet. He approached the nurse's desk.

"May I help you?" the nurse asked. The lines of concern on the father's face told her this was serious even before he spoke. "My little girl was burned when gasoline exploded from our tractor. I believe she needs to see a doctor," he explained. The girl's mother stood anxiously beside her husband.

Grabbing a clipboard, Miss Miller quickly directed them into Room 1 and began gathering information. Esther and John A. Miller were from a fairly new Amish community about half an hour southwest of Zanesville. As she carefully unwrapped the sheet, the nurse saw that little Mintie had second and third-degree burns covering her legs, her hand, and her abdomen.

They began gently swabbing the burned areas with a mild solution of sterile water and pHisohex to disinfect the damaged tissue. As she realized the extent of the child's burns, the nurse called the doctor and described the seriousness of Mintie's situation. The doctor prescribed pain medication and an IV, and gave orders to admit her to pediatrics. He would be coming to review her situation shortly.

His orders were quickly carried out, and Miss Miller wheeled the little girl up to pediatrics, where she wrapped her in sterile sheets and placed her in a bed. As she was leaving, Mintie's mother lamented, "I was hoping Mintie might be treated and released, but the doctor wants her to stay for the night. I was certainly hoping she wouldn't have to stay so long!"

Nurse Miller's heart went out to this mother who was soon expecting another child. It was easy to see that she cared deeply for Mintie

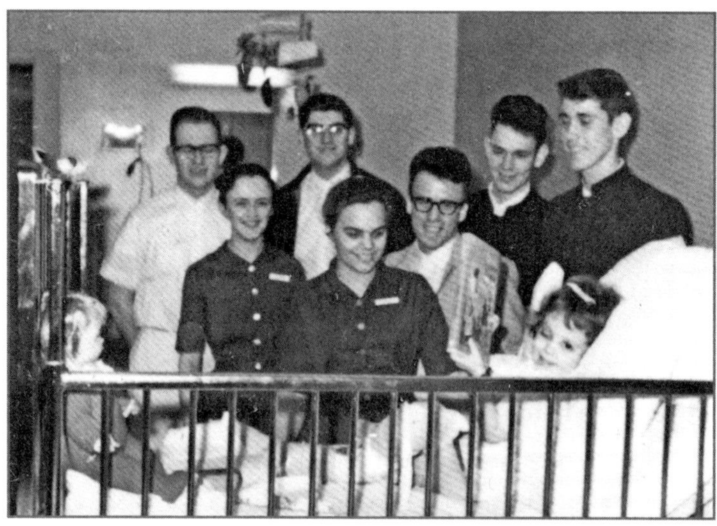

The VS unit workers enjoyed bringing cheer to patients in the hospital. ***Back–L to R:*** *Joe Hertzler, Nolan Brunk, Earl Nisly, Johnny Miller, Joe Weirich.* ***Front:*** *Elmeda Graber, Rhoda Stoltzfus*

and wished to have her at home so she herself could care for her daughter. However, Nurse Miller understood from previous experience with burn patients that it would be weeks before this little girl could return home. She wisely refrained from telling Mintie's mother what she knew.

Following Dr. Donalds' examination, the nursing supervisor pulled LPN Betty Miller from ER to assist her in pediatrics. They donned masks, gowns, and gloves, and scrubbed the little girl, beginning at her feet and cleansing her entire body. After patting her dry with sterile towels, they wrapped her burnt legs and abdomen in Furacin gauze to prevent infection and reduce fluid loss. They moved Mintie's legs as gently as possible, but they knew their brave little patient was enduring tremendous pain. Although Mintie resembled an Egyptian mummy when they were finished, she barely even whimpered during the entire ordeal.

Betty shared Mintie's situation with our VS unit about and asked that we pray for her and her family during this difficult time. During the next few weeks we regularly prayed for the little Amish girl's needs.

Nearly a year before, I had met Mintie's father as he was recovering from an appendectomy. I now wanted to meet his wife and daughter and made my way up to pediatrics. A nurse informed me that I had to wear a mask and gown to enter Mintie's room. We had to be extra careful to avoid introducing any infection to our little patient. I was pleased to find both John and Esther with their daughter. They had numerous questions about the hospital and medical procedures which I was able to explain.

The days dragged into weeks, and we continued visiting Mintie and her family members. A thoughtful member of our VS unit brought a tape player for Mintie. She became very fond of the hymns, "I'll Be Somewhere Listening for My Name," and "Out of the Ivory Palaces," and she wanted them played over and over.

On September 23, Mintie's mother was admitted to the Bethesda Hospital's OB facility, and soon Mintie had a new baby brother named Titus Paul Miller. Excitement and joy filled the Miller household despite Mintie's continued hospital stay. Just a week later, Dr. Donalds felt Mintie was well enough to go home and help care for little Titus Paul.

This brave little Amish girl had won the hearts of the nurses and aides, and they would miss her. They bought her a stuffed toucan with a large yellow beak. Mintie loved that stuffed toy, which the nurses autographed for her as a keepsake. When the day finally came for her release, Mintie made sure that precious toucan was packed with her belongings.

After thirty-one days in the hospital, Mintie said goodbye to the workers. She left with lots of scar tissue, some of which would remain for life. However, innumerable memories of love and kindness filled her heart. Those memories would be a lifelong blessing.

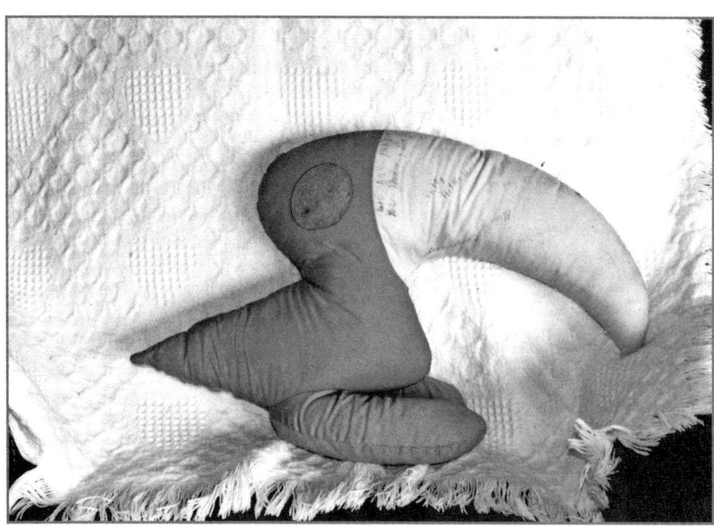

Mintie still has the stuffed toucan as a reminder of her kind nurses.

CHAPTER 33

The ER Sermon

Michael Richardson was driving his tractor on a steep hillside. Suddenly the tractor began to slide. Michael quickly tried to correct the problem, but just then, the downhill tire dropped into a dip, and his tractor began to roll. He tried to jump clear but was hopelessly pinned by his left shoulder and arm under the massive weight of the tractor.

A young cousin was nearby and ran to the house for help. Michael's wife, Amy, made a desperate call for an ambulance and then rushed to the field.

Blood was oozing from under the tractor when Amy reached her husband's side. She began asking about the accident. Did he think he had any broken bones? How were they going to lift the heavy tractor? She had the presence of mind to keep him alert and talking. That huge tractor wheel had narrowly missed his head! She shuddered at the thought of what could have been as she lovingly stroked her husband's hair and prayed while they waited.

Soon the wail of a siren echoed up the valley, and what a sweet sound it was! Michael was in shock and weak from loss of blood. Pain dulled his senses as the paramedics arrived and began working to free him. In a blur of activity, Michael soon found himself in the back of the ambulance with his wife holding his hand. It was so comforting to have her near. An IV of normal saline was dripping into his good arm; the bag swayed as the ambulance sped around the curves.

In the emergency room, Dr. Capp ordered two units of blood to be typed, cross-matched, and readied. X-rays disclosed extensive damage. Michael had suffered multiple fractures of the radius, ulna, and humerus. However, the more serious damage was his crushed clavicle, scapula, and shoulder.

Dr. Capp did a superb job of engineering a two-way traction with the patient in a reclining position on his hospital bed. A drop from an overhead bar suspended his arm with his elbow bent at right angles. Both lateral and vertical tractions were applied. Portable X-rays declared the doctor's feat of engineering a success, but blood and fluid continued to seep from Michael's mangled shoulder.

Michael's loving wife stayed with him day and night, supportive in every way and ensuring her husband received the best of care. This young couple had only been married for two and a half years, but their loving commitment was beautiful to see.

On the fourth day it became apparent that Michael required an enema. The trauma and pain he had experienced had completely upset his digestive system. A student nurse was assigned to care for Michael. However, she was hesitant to administer the enema because of his sensitivity and his awkward, reclining position and restrictive traction. She spoke with the head nurse, Mrs. Stevens, and asked if an orderly could administer the enema for her. I was extremely rushed and feared I wouldn't be able to complete my assignments with the seven patients assigned to me that day.

However, when Miss Susan explained the situation, I said, "Sure, I'll help you. Go ahead and order your enema up from pharmacy and let me know when it arrives."

Fifteen minutes later, Miss Susan found me making my last bed for the day and delivered the enema. I grabbed several chux pads to protect the bed, along with a fracture pan designed for these situations. I hurriedly made my way into his room. Visitors were seated in the far corner of the room, engaged in serious conversation with Michael's wife. I nodded my hello as I drew the privacy curtain about Michael's bed in one swift movement that seemed to startle him. I then set the fracture pan, pads, and the enema on the edge of his bed and slipped on a glove, ready for action.

"Michael, I'm here to give you this enema," I announced.

A look of fear crossed his face, and he exclaimed, "What are you doing?"

"I'm giving you an enema, that's all," I replied.

"What's this?" he shouted.

"Johnny, wait. Please, wait a minute!" came the desperate cry from his wife. I stopped all proceedings and ducked outside the curtain. "He is so upset and jumpy," said Amy. "He can't tolerate anything being done quickly, especially if it's a procedure he does not understand. Please slow down and explain exactly what you need to do. I think Michael will settle down when he understands."

I was embarrassed that in my hurry, I had failed to explain. I had assumed Michael would understand common hospital procedures. Ducking back inside the curtain, I apologized and then kindly explained each step of the procedure. I showed him that the enema contained a stool-softening compound which would greatly benefit him. Just as his wife had predicted, Michael was willing to cooperate once he understood, and we were successful in alleviating his difficulties. God used this and many similar experiences to teach me a lesson. Speed and impatience breed questions and mistrust in the hearts of those we are trying to help.

About two weeks into Michael Richardson's stay, a foul odor developed in his room. Careful examination indicated it was originating from the head of his bed, and in spite of his injury, we realized we had to change his mattress. This was going to be extremely difficult since he was fastened to traction that could not be released. We would have to carefully raise him a little and slide the used mattress out from under him as we slid the fresh one into its place. We would have to do all this with as little movement as possible.

With several workers coordinating our movements, we slowly changed the mattresses with Michael still occupying his bed. We managed it without adversely affecting his extensive injuries. I saw that blood and fluids from his injuries had soaked all the way through the mattress we removed, staining several square feet. We sent the used mattress to the basement, where it was fed to the incinerator. The replacement mattress was covered in plastic that could easily be cleaned.

Michael was young and strong, and he eventually recovered. After some physical therapy, he was finally released to go back to his farm.

Our evening was nearly finished when I got a call. "Johnny," said the charge nurse, "Dr. Yang has ordered a catheter for a patient on 3-East. I know it's nearly quitting time, and doing the catheter would make you late. I can call and tell them to wait until after the shift change so the night duty personnel can do it if you prefer."

"Oh no, I'll be glad to take care of that," I responded. "I'll go right away."

On 3-East, I received my instructions from the charge nurse.

"It's Mr. Smith, and he is in Bed 1 in Room 311. The tray is in the treatment room."

I found the sterile tray ready on the counter. The catheter was in its own sterile package, and I opened both with care to avoid contaminating either. Then adding the rest of the necessary items, I folded the autoclaved tabs back over the tray, set my glove pack on top, and headed for Room 311.

"By the way, Mr. Miller," said the nurse. "Mr. Smith has been confused for several days, and you may have trouble getting him to cooperate. Don't hesitate to press the call button if you need assistance."

I thanked her and went to find Mr. Smith. He was dozing with the head of his bed partially elevated.

"Hello, Mr. Smith. How are you feeling tonight?" I asked as I began drawing the privacy curtain. I smiled and nodded to the man in Bed 2, and he returned my smile.

Slowly and deliberately, Mr. Smith said, "Oh, I guess I'm pretty good. Are you the doctor?"

"No, I'm the orderly, and I have come to give you the doctor's orders."

"Really?"

"Yes, the doctor says he wants you to stay in your bed until you get well. He doesn't even want you getting up to go to the bathroom. I think he's afraid you might get dizzy and fall, and if that happened, you could break a hip or an arm. That would be too bad."

"He never told me about this," said Mr. Smith.

"I know he didn't, but he wrote the order on your chart, and we want to follow the doctor's orders, don't we?"

"Well, I suppose so," he murmured thoughtfully.

"Mr. Smith, let me explain what the doctor has ordered. He doesn't want you getting out of your bed, so he wants me to put this little tubing into your bladder and attach it to this plastic bag that I will hang on the side of the bed. This will eliminate your need to get up to go to the bathroom in the middle of the night. You'll be able to rest so much better and it will help you recover. Perhaps you will even be allowed to go home sooner. What do you say?"

"I don't know. But if you say so, I guess we will have to do it."

"Now I don't want to hurt you in any way, so I am going to ask you to help me, okay?"

"Okay," he agreed.

"First of all, I want to lower the head of your bed a bit so you can relax better. Next, I will show you each item I have in this pack." I held them up one at a time, explaining their uses. "As this tube reaches a point just before the bladder, you are going to feel a bit of resistance, but don't be alarmed. I'm not going to hurt you. At that point, I am going to pause and ask you to take a couple of deep breaths, and that will relax you even more. When we have it inside the bladder, I will fill a little balloon with sterile water, and that will keep the tube right there doing its job until the doctor is ready to remove it. Do you have any questions?"

"Well, I don't guess so, but this is all new to me."

"I'm sure it is, but it is going to be a big help to you. Are you ready?"

"I s'pose so."

In moments, the process was underway. I said, "Okay, Mr. Smith, I want you to give me several deep breaths and just relax." Mr. Smith sounded like a diver getting ready to take a plunge as he gulped huge drafts of air.

Moments later, I inflated the balloon and connected the catheter to the tubing and bag. "There you are, Mr. Smith," I said. "We are all done, and now you won't have to get up during the night. I'm going to hang this collection bag on the frame of your bed, and the nurses will empty it after each shift."

"Oh, okay," he responded. "Thanks. Thanks a lot."

"You're most welcome!" I told him. "And here is your call button fastened right beside your pillow. If you have any questions or need help, just press the button marked NURSE, and she will be glad to help you. Now you get a good night of sleep, and don't you worry about needing to get up for the bathroom. I've taken care of all that for you. Good night, Mr. Smith."

"Good night," he replied slowly as I pushed back his privacy curtain and prepared to turn off his light.

"Excuse me," interjected the man in Bed 2. "Do you have a minute?"

"Sure," I responded without shutting off the light. "What can I do for you?" I assumed he probably wanted fresh water or a blanket.

"I have a question if you don't mind," he said.

"Yes?" I queried.

"Why are you working in this hospital?"

I wondered what was behind the question as I replied, "Well, I am conscientiously opposed to war, so I am working here instead of participating in military service."

What he said next caused my heart to skip a beat. "I fought in World War II," he began thoughtfully. "I fought in the Korean War, and I served in Panama. The military has been my career. Tonight, I have a son fighting in Vietnam."

I experienced a moment of apprehension about what might come next.

"This elderly gentleman in the next bed has been so confused," he continued. "Terribly confused. All day long, I've been watching him try to make sense of what was happening. He just couldn't understand. But you treated him with such kindness and respect and were so gracious in the way you spoke to him. You explained everything to him and went out of your way to help him understand. I know you didn't have to, but you did. And I want you to know I deeply appreciate that. As far as I'm concerned, you're doing as much good right here in this hospital as you could ever do on the front lines in Vietnam."

For a moment, I was speechless. This was not at all what I had anticipated. As I gazed into this military man's face, I saw a gleam of sincerity that warmed my heart. He had meant every word.

"Well, thank you," I responded self-consciously. "Thank you very much. I love my work, and I feel it is a way to pay some of the debt I owe to my God and my country."

"Well, I am impressed and applaud what you are doing," he said.

"Is there something more you need?" I asked.

"No," he said. "I only wanted to commend you. Good night."

"Good night, sir," I said softly as I snapped off the light, picked up my tray, and stole quietly from the room. That night as I walked home later than usual, the warmth in my heart dispelled the midnight chill of spring.

Our two years of 1-W service were drawing to a close. Earl Nisly was making plans to head back to Kansas where he would be helping his father on the farm. The nurses and aides of 1-West were planning a little farewell party.

I was asked to work in ER, but when I arrived, Nurse Truby said, "Johnny, you missed it!"

"Missed what?" I asked innocently.

"You really missed it! Nurse Keller was working the day shift, and I came in a bit early to relieve her. Well, she was giving me instructions about the patient who was waiting for Dr. Barker to give him a lower bowel examination. Wouldn't you know, the nurse aide from 1-West, Dotty, came by just then. She had a coffee can with a slot cut in the lid and held it out for Nurse Keller to make a donation to buy ice cream and cake for Earl Nisly's farewell party.

"Believe me, that was the wrong thing to ask of Mrs. Keller! You know that since her husband was shipped overseas, she has refused to work with you 1-W orderlies. Well, she completely lost it! I mean, she cursed and swore about you fellows getting off scot-free while others are defending our country.

"I think she knew the man waiting for Dr. Barker had been in the military, and she probably thought he would share her sentiments. But when she walked into his room, you should have heard the sermon he preached to her!"

"What did he have to say?" I asked.

"He said, 'Ma'am, how dare you talk that way? Do you have any idea of the contribution those young men are making? Have you ever seen them in action? Let me tell you something. I observed one of those young men helping a poor, confused patient in my room the other night. He was so kind and courteous, and he took the time to explain every detail to this poor suffering soul. He did his work in a very professional manner, reassured the patient, and gave him confidence and hope. Yes, I am a military man myself, but I told that young gentleman he is doing as much good right here in this hospital as he could ever do in Vietnam! What you have said is false—totally false—and I resent it!'"

"Wow! What did Mrs. Keller have to say to that?" I asked.

"She murmured an apology, marched to the hallway, donned her coat, and clocked out, looking quite subdued."

CHAPTER 34

Despair and Hope

On 1-West, a patient was admitted into Room 103 by Dr. Lance. He ordered twenty-five pounds of pelvic traction for Mrs. Amber Masters. The charge nurse ordered the pelvic belt and asked me to install the traction and hook it up on the patient. But when I installed the traction bar onto the bed, I realized this lady was indecently dressed, and I was to administer her traction belt.

I said, "Mrs. Masters, as soon as you change into your hospital gown, let me know, and I'll finish hooking up your traction." I left and went about my other duties.

The charge nurse asked, "Johnny, do you have the pelvic traction installed for Mrs. Masters? I need to chart it."

"Well, I have everything installed, but haven't hooked her up," I responded. "She wasn't quite ready, but I'll do it right away."

"Okay, thanks. Let me know as soon as you are done. I'll keep her chart out till then."

I circled backed to Room 103, only to find Mrs. Masters just as I had left her. Again, I said, "Mrs. Masters, I'd like to hook up your pelvic traction as soon as you have changed, okay?"

An hour later, the nurse said, "Johnny, you have that traction hooked up now, don't you?"

"I'm sorry. I haven't done it yet," I apologized.

"*Please!*" she said in a tone that didn't allow me to put it off any longer.

Praying that Mrs. Masters would be properly dressed by now, I entered her room to discover she had changed nothing. I was incensed by her brazenness! Steeling myself, I quickly installed her traction as she tried to engage me in conversation.

"Do you like working here in the hospital? I suppose you've had lots of training, right? Are you the only one who works with traction? Are you married?"

I answered her questions with a curt yes or no as required and completed my task as speedily as possible. I added the appropriate weight, hooked up the straps, and walked out.

I looked up my older nurse aide friend, Miss Dotty.

"Dotty," I began. "Could you to do me a favor?"

"I sure could," she responded.

"Look, the new patient in Room 103 will not dress appropriately. I asked her several times to change so that I could hook up her traction as I was ordered to. But she just wouldn't cooperate. The charge nurse was getting upset with me because I kept putting it off. I finally had to go ahead and finish applying her traction, and she tried too hard to be friendly. Dotty, I do not feel comfortable around that woman. If she turns her call light on or asks for help, would you please take care of her? I don't want to go back into her room at all!"

"Sure, Mr. Johnny. You go on and take care of the others, and I'll see to it that you won't have to go into her room anymore."

"Thanks, Dotty, I appreciate that."

"You can forget it, Mr. Johnny. I will take care of Mrs. Masters," she assured me.

Several days later, I passed by the open door of Room 103. Mrs. Masters saw me and immediately called out, "Oh, hi there, Mr. Miller. Aren't you going to stop in and say hello?"

I said, "Hi," nodded, and kept right on walking.

A police car pulled up to ER, followed by an ambulance. Two officers helped roll in the ambulance cart. As they entered, we heard loud shouting and cursing. The drunken man on the cart seemed berserk. He kicked and screamed like an angry child, although he appeared to be about thirty years old. His arms were crisscrossed below him, handcuffed to the cart rails, and he was face down. He had kicked and fought so hard that there was no longer any cloth covering on the cart's thin foam mattress. His hoarse crying and horrible curses were mingled with tears and nasal drainage that made a horrible mess.

The police officers had to raise their voices to communicate with the nurse above the shouting. The man of the cart raised his head, drew in a deep breath, and screamed a string of profane curses at the officers until he was completely out of breath. When he opened his mouth to scream, I saw a large gap where his upper front teeth should have been. Then he began to cry again and blew his nose, adding to the polluted vinyl surface of the mattress. My stomach heaved as he laid his face in that mess and swiped his head back and forth. He sucked in another breath and screamed obscenities at everyone until the younger of the two officers smacked his hand against the back of the patient's head, pushing his face into the mattress to shut him up.

I shivered at the officer's callous response. At the same time, I realized the officer had probably suffered so much of this verbal abuse that he had no sympathy left for such a person. The patient reminded me of the man who lived among the tombs before he met Jesus.

The cart was pushed into a room and the door closed so the officer in charge could speak intelligibly with our charge nurse.

"He was fighting and endangering others, so we arrested him, and he went ballistic," explained the officer.

"Why exactly did you bring him here? What do you expect me to do with him?" asked the nurse.

"We were ordered to bring him here so you could medicate him and admit him. We don't know what to do with him."

"Neither do I," replied the exasperated nurse. "But I will place a call to the doctor and see what he says."

"Fair enough," replied the officer.

In a few minutes the nurse returned and explained, "The doctor ordered a drug to calm him down, but he won't admit him. We aren't equipped to handle such patients in this facility."

"Thanks for trying," said the officer. "I guess there is nothing left to do but lock him in a jail cell."

A nurse administered the medication while the patient raved and fought. He was loaded back onto the ambulance, and the police escorted him to the city jail.

The nurse asked, "Johnny, do you know what a wino is?"

"Well, I suppose it is an alcoholic who drinks wine," I said.

"That is correct, but for some reason, it seems to affect their minds more than other forms of intoxication. That man is a wino."

This incident was deeply troubling. I had seen the demoralized depth a man can sink to without Christ. I reflected soberly on the horrible mess the poor man had made of his life.

Two younger men and an older man came into the emergency

room. The older man and the younger boy were handcuffed together. The youth had a cloth bound around his wrist.

The older man was in charge and explained, "This is Jared, and we are from the boys' camp for troubled youth. Jared here has a problem that a doctor should see." The nurse escorted them into an examining room and removed the cloth from Jared's hand, revealing a deep slash across his wrist. Thankfully, the main artery had been spared, and the smaller vessels had mostly stopped bleeding.

The handcuffs were removed, and the nurse gently cleansed the wound. She ordered me to set up a suture tray and left to call the doctor. Jared was sullen and silent, but as I worked, I engaged him in conversation.

"Jared, how old are you?"

"Seventeen," he muttered.

"How did you cut this?" I asked, pointing to his wrist.

"With a razorblade," he replied.

"Why did you do that?"

"Because I'm sick of life," he said defiantly.

"Really? Why?"

"All I've ever had in life was trouble!" he spat.

"How's that?" I asked.

"Man, I've been in trouble all the way through school, and in my neighborhood, and in my home. My mom and dad don't even want me. I have an older brother, but I don't see him very often."

"What's your older brother like?"

Jared gave a sarcastic laugh and said, "He's the one who taught me to fight and steal. Nothing big, just shoplifting and stuff like that."

"And were you ever caught?"

"Caught? Man, I have been in jails, correction facilities, and boys' camps since I was thirteen years old. This is my third time in a hospital. Nobody cares about me, and I don't care about nobody. I'm sick of life!"

"Jared what are these marks on your arms?" I asked.

His laugh sounded hollow as he explained, "Them's cigarette burns from playing chicken when I was in jail."

"So you and another person see who can stand the most pain from a burning cigarette?"

"Yeah."

As I finished setting up the suture tray, I reflected that Jared and his brother actually had no home life. They had fended for themselves without the guidance of godly parents. Heavenly values and the purpose for living had passed them by, and the result was a seventeen-year-old boy already sick and tired of life. He was just waiting for a doctor to sew up his self-inflicted wounds. The scars on his arms would follow him for life, but the scars on his soul would follow him into eternity unless he came to know Jesus and His power to save.

The doctor arrived and sutured Jared's wound before admitting him to the psychiatric ward on 4-North.

We rejoiced to receive Betsy's second letter from the Children's Hospital in Columbus.

Dear Johnny and Ruth,

Thank you for your letter. The doctors did my operation last week. Everything went well. They put my sixth and seventh neck bones back into their proper place, and already my legs are beginning to tingle a little. It kinda stings, but I'm glad I can feel it. They fused my bones together and told me that my neck won't be able to bend as far as normal, but all the time I was in traction I couldn't bend it anyhow. Next week I am supposed to start physical therapy. I am so ready for that! Just lying here day after day is driving me nuts! I want to be able to get well, to go home, and get back to school.

Thank you for being my friends. Tell Vera to write to me.
Your friend,
Betsy Scout

We wrote back, telling Betsy we would soon be moving to Minerva, Ohio, but we would continue to write to her and pray for her. The huge question in our minds was whether Betsy's operation would be a success or a failure. Would she ever walk again? We would continue to hope, trust, and pray!

Two days later, I met Dr. Glosser making rounds and asked, "Dr. Glosser, have you heard anything from the Children's Hospital in Columbus about Betsy Scout? Do you know whether they are planning to operate?"

"No, I've heard nothing at all," was his terse comment. It appeared that he was reluctant to discuss Betsy or her prognosis.

During our last month in Zanesville, Ruth transferred from the hospital to the kitchen of the VS unit. This move was made because we were expecting our first child. Our little bundle from heaven was scheduled for delivery the middle of August, and we were beginning to plan for life after 1-W service.

One day, I was called to the head of nursing office for a meeting with the nursing supervisor.

"Please sit down, Mr. Miller," she began. "You have been with us for the past twenty-four months, and I want you to know we deeply appreciate your contribution to Bethesda Hospital. However, I would like to know your future plans. Would you have any interest in continuing to work here?"

"I must say that I dearly love working here at Bethesda, and these two years have been such a blessing for me," I said. "This whole experience has taught me so much. However, we are planning to move to Minerva, Ohio, where my wife's parents live. I'll probably get a job in construction."

"We wish you well, and if you need a job reference, we will be happy to supply that for you. Again, I want to thank you," she said as she rose and extended her hand.

"Thank you," I murmured around the lump that was forming in my throat as I took my leave.

On my very last evening of working in the Bethesda Hospital, I moved about from floor to floor, saying goodbye to the personnel. Ruth came from the VS unit to find me and join in this farewell. I got choked up several times as I explained that we were leaving and didn't know if we'd ever see these people again. I saw tears in the eyes of several I had worked closely with during the past two years. These were our friends and coworkers, and we had labored together for the good of others. But now our time together was at an end.

The following day, Ruth's father arrived with his farm truck to ferry our wedding gifts of a rocking chair and bookcase back to Minerva. We packed the rest of our belongings in the back seat of our 1960 Corvair and started out. The debt I owed my country had been paid with two years of 1-W service, but the debt owed to my God could never be paid in a lifetime.

Leaving the Bethesda Hospital and the voluntary service unit behind, we headed north into an uncertain future while looking to God who had called us. We knew He would guide us, "For He hath said, I will never leave thee, nor forsake thee" (Hebrews 13:5).

Afterword

The Conservative Mennonite Mission Board formed the voluntary service unit in Zanesville, Ohio, where I performed my 1-W service. This unit operated from 1966 until the draft ended in 1972. It provided a solid spiritual framework for the thirty young men who served God there with a free conscience as they fulfilled their obligation to the United States government. The conscientious objectors worked as accountants, stockroom employees, orderlies, groundsmen, and maintenance workers.

During those years, forty-two young ladies also joined the VS unit. Some served as nurses or nurse aides in the Bethesda Hospital, and others were domestic workers. Several wives of the 1-W men worked in the unit part-time as well.

The relationships formed during that time were appreciated by former workers and patients alike. Mr. Bruce McHenry overcame his heart ailment, maintained contact with some of us, and continued farming for several more decades.

Betsy Scout's surgical reduction of her dislocated fracture relieved the debilitating pressure to her spinal cord. The subsequent physical therapy was hard work, but Betsy was determined not to turn back after coming so far. After several months, she was able to leave Children's Hospital with scarcely a trace of a limp. Praise God, Betsy had the privilege to live a normal, productive life.

Ruth and I visited the Carl Dalton family forty years after the events in this book. For eight years after Jerry's accident, Carl and his wife had tenderly cared for their son in his comatose state until he passed away. As we discussed that fateful night when Jerry suffered his devastating temperature spike, his father said with deep feeling, "Johnny, this thing nearly destroyed my faith in God."

Mintie, the little Amish girl, fully recovered from her severe burns. She later married John G. Troyer, and they were blessed with six children. They attend the Little Creek Mennonite Church near their home in Frankfort, Ohio. When Ruth and I visited them, Mintie still had her stuffed toy toucan, autographed and presented by her nurses fifty years earlier.

The training, discipline, and spiritual growth experienced by those who served in Zanesville has enriched their lives. Twelve of the thirty 1-W workers became ordained ministers. Several served as foreign missionaries, and others helped establish conservative Mennonite churches throughout America.

Canaan Mennonite Church was established in Zanesville in 1968 through the vision and efforts of VS workers and their unit leader, David Mast. Today, this church is part of the Nationwide Fellowship. It has relocated five miles west of Zanesville and has sent missionaries into numerous countries.

God wove the threads of our Zanesville voluntary service experience so that our hearts have bonded like one large family. Friendships thus woven can never be forgotten.

—Johnny Miller

ADDENDUM I

Zanesville VS Unit Guidelines

Prepared by the Conservative Mennonite Fellowship Mission Board

We are happy to present this booklet for your examination. It was compiled to give you a detailed description of our objectives in VS, and the requirements made of those who wish to participate.

As you read this booklet we hope that you will consider the great responsibility of guidance and care which must rest upon someone when young people leave their homes, communities, and churches to serve others in VS.

When we see so many youths of today going away from home into service and then losing out in Bible convictions, and perhaps leaving home to never return, we make no apologies for any part of our objectives or discipline. We are concerned that our youth who serve in 1-W or VS may come back to our home churches and be a greater asset, and of greater service to the Church of Jesus Christ, than ever before. We want our youth to be safeguarded, as well as nurtured. With these concerns, we have prepared this booklet. By God's grace it shall serve as a guide for us in upholding a thoroughly Christian standard.

Read this booklet prayerfully. If you are interested in service, pray for God's leading, discuss your desires with your parents and your ministers, and then make your decision. If you come to our unit, we expect your full cooperation and support.

OBJECTIVES

We are concerned about at least two types of objectives in our Voluntary Service Units.

First: Objectives for Spiritual Growth

- To encourage daily personal fellowship with God.
- To develop a thorough working knowledge of the Bible.
- To help each member live a consistent, disciplined Christian life.
- To strengthen convictions on all Bible doctrines.
- To help each member recognize and withstand false doctrines.
- To provide opportunity for each member to express his faith to other Christians.
- To provide a variety of experiences for each member for the development of his spiritual gifts.
- To help train each member in the spiritual arts of presenting the Gospel to the unsaved.
- To help each member maintain and safeguard the convictions and standards of his home congregation.

Second: Objectives for Christian Witness

- To confront the people of this area with the Gospel of Jesus Christ as experienced and taught by Bible-believing Christians.
- To lead people into a saving faith in Jesus Christ which results in faithful Christian living.
- To establish and maintain a conservative Mennonite church in the area.
- To provide a home-like atmosphere at the Unit where men and women can feel a Christian warmth.
- To encourage on-the-job witnessing.

- To conduct cottage meetings, street meetings, and engage in other witnessing activities to reach the unsaved.
- To cooperate in witness and fellowship only with those who present a thoroughly scriptural message.
- To be busy in the Lord's work, however never at the expense of any of the above *Objectives For Spiritual Growth.*

STANDARDS OF DISCIPLINE AND PERSONAL REQUIREMENTS FOR SERVICE

Part of the commitment to service involves consistency and uniformity in presenting ourselves to the community. The Gospel which changes men's lives is expected to bring about careful living. Each person associated with this VS Unit is expected to observe the following practices which we believe are consistent with scriptural principles and conducive to good Christian testimony.

1. Members shall not indulge in the world's methods of pleasure-seeking, amusements, and entertainments by patronizing or taking part in fairs, parades, circuses, theaters, mixed swimming, dancing, card parties, competitive sports, or any form of gambling, lottery, and such like. We urge the young people to take part in our church activities which foster Gospel evangelism, instead of literary societies.
2. Cars driven by workers shall be of one solid conservative color. Cars shall be of conventional design and not unnecessarily decorated. Sporty equipment, loud mufflers, white sidewall tires, and motorcycles are not permitted. Cars shall have no radio aerials in working condition. Courtesy shall be practiced upon the highways, and obedience to traffic regulations is mandatory.
3. Brethren shall be faithful in wearing the regulation plain-cut coat, particularly when participating in Christian activities. All other items of dress are not to be of a sporty type, neither form fitting nor immodest.

No short sleeved shirts are permitted, except for hospital personnel who work with hospital patients, and then only while on duty. Neckties shall not be worn. Dress shoes (off the job) shall be black and hose in dark solid colors, and hat wear shall be consistent with our unassuming attire. The hair shall be combed neatly and modestly, avoiding popular and fashionable styles.

4. Sisters are expected to wear clothing suitable to women professing godliness. Dresses shall be of modest design, in solid color and texture, mid-calf length, at least ¾ length sleeves and shall include the cape without trimmings (unnecessary buttons, rick-rack, etc.). The covering shall be of sufficient size to adequately cover the hair. The hair shall be put up so the covering will cover it. The hair shall not be cut. The hair and dress shall exemplify humility and meekness. Foot wear should be of plain types, not fashionable (dress shoes shall be black), and no anklets will be permitted. Sisters shall wear black hose of at least 51 guage-30 denier. Nurses and nurse aides may wear the hospital required white hose when on the job. Sleeves on uniforms must be of elbow length. These may only be worn while on duty. The nurse cap shall not replace the prayer veiling. The veiling shall be worn during all waking hours. When a weather protection is needed, the bonnet or hood shall be worn when leaving the Unit or hospital grounds. If scarves are worn on the grounds, they shall be of black and non-transparent material.

5. The wearing of gold or any display of worldliness is forbidden by the Scriptures. Therefore, we will avoid the use of decorative metals such as pins, ornaments, silver or gold metal watch bands, rings, or wedding bands.

6. Unit members are forbidden to belong to secret societies or labor unions. They are asked not to have life insurance nor are they allowed to take part in anything contrary to the nonresistent position.

VOLUNTARY SERVICE RESIDENCE LIVING

1. All workers are expected to be punctual at rising time, morning devotions, meals, and retiring time.
2. All must be considerate and respectful of the rights of others. Each must remain quiet while others are reading, studying, sleeping or during devotional periods. Because of differing shifts of work at the hospital, this becomes very important.
3. Schedule:

   Rising time.................. 5:30
   Breakfast 6:00
   Worship........................ 6:20
   Late breakfast 8:30
   Dinner 12:00
   Supper.......................... 5:00
   Lights out.................. 10:30

4. No one may leave the unit (except for work) without signing out, and no one may leave the area without permission from the Unit leader, and that only twice per month.
5. Each worker is expected to work 4 hours a week for the unit if needed, in such work as gardening, lawn care, maintenance, cleaning, etc. Married women are expected to work only 2 hours per week.
6. Three week day evenings plus Sundays are closed for church and witnessing activities as arranged by the Unit leader.
7. Dating at the Unit shall be limited to once a week and with persons of high Christian character. The date must be cleared in advance with the Unit leader. Christian courtship practices are a must.
8. Allowances: All single workers will be paid $25.00 per month for the first year and $35.00 for the second year. All married couples will be paid $50.00 per month (if the woman works at the unit) the first year and $70.00 for the second year. Registered Nurses and Licensed Practical

Nurses receive $75.00 the second year. All earnings above 40 hours a week may be kept by the workers, but total hours at the hospital shall not exceed 60 hours per week. No time cards shall be punched at the hospital on Sundays. All Sunday work is donated to the hospital.

9. Allowance per meal for workers that need to eat at the hospital may not exceed 70¢. If less than this is used the balance shall be credited to the next week.
10. Minor medical expenses will be paid by the Unit.
11. To married couples: The husband's allowance is $25.00 per month if the wife works at the Unit or hospital. Allowance for wife working 40 hours per week is $25.00 per month. Women working 25 hours per week will be paid $12.50 per month. No allowance will be given for less than 24 hours of work per week. Women not working at the hospital or Unit but getting meals at the Unit will reduce their husband's allowance to $15.00 per month. In case of pregnancy: During the last three or four months the women are excused from work at the Unit. The family then is free to prepare their meals at their home. The Unit will pay the $45.00 per month, rent, all utilities (not including phone calls), plus the $25.00 per month allowance. All other expenses will be assumed by the couple. Only sickness or pregnancy will excuse the couple from eating at and participating in the activities of the Unit.

CONCERNING BOOKS AND LIBRARY

We desire to provide a good variety of wholesome Christian literature. We are equally concerned that we avoid the current abundance of poor reading material. To this end we have adopted the following policy for all reading materials:

1. All books selected for our program or used by our workers shall be approved by two of the committee (Mission Board, Bishop, or Unit leaders) appointed for this work.

2. The King James Version shall be used for all public and private study and worship. Other versions may be used for study purposes if they are approved. The Scofield Reference Bible shall not be used because of its strong Calvinistic teachings.
3. The promotion of false and questionable teachings will not be tolerated in any form.
4. All literature for distribution or for use in the unit shall have been approved by the committee. Literature for distribution shall be chosen to teach clearly the way of salvation, Christian living, and Bible doctrine.
5. We assume the right to question any literature or books brought into the unit.

IN-SERVICE RESPONSIBILITIES

Any effective witness includes many facets. It means being born again; it means a zeal to do the will of God. But it also means a thorough-going consistency and obedience to the Spirit and Word of God. When you come to a VS Unit, we want you to realize several responsibilities which you must assume.

1. The responsibility of maintaining unity and love within the Unit. This may mean that you will give up your own rights in favor of others. You will need to be respectful, kind, and loving. We want a unity of goals and purposes. We want to present a common front under the blessing and power of the Spirit.
2. We want you to maintain a good work record on the job in which you serve. We expect you to maintain above average work habits and attitudes on the job. This is directly connected with your testimony and the witness of the whole Unit.
3. We believe that the Holy Spirit can and will work through you as individuals. We believe in the power of fellowship among believers. Each individual is responsible to help and counsel with others in the Unit. Each, however, is to be careful that criticism or encouragement is given in the spirit of Christian love.

4. It is your responsibility to respect the more conservative convictions of others. Workers will come from many parts of the Church and with varied backgrounds. Therefore it is necessary that we respect each other's convictions. We want no one to "lose out" in convictions while at our Unit. Those convictions which are even more conservative than that which the Unit upholds shall be respected. If your home congregation is more conservative, we expect you to be obedient while away from home.
5. The subject of eschatology shall not become a devisive issue. Persons holding either view shall respect another's view even though it may differ from his own.

We believe that it is important to maintain a positive witness. We need not apologize for any part of our Christian life or practice. Serving in this Unit should be a serious decision, one that involves your personal dedication. All of the fore-going regulations are for the guidance and blessing of the membership. Applicants shall accept these and conform to them as soon as possible. Those who do not willingly accept them cannot be received. If the members become proud and vain or show evidence of vanity and worldliness, they are to be visited and questioned as to life and conduct. If after a reasonable time they still remain obstinate, they become subject to censure.[1]

[1] Earle Zimmerman, *Reflections from the Zanesville Mennonite Voluntary Service Unit 1966–1972,* Silverline Publishing & Bindery, Lititz, PA, 2006, pp. 699–705.

ADDENDUM II

History of Exemption Programs

Nearly fifty years have passed since 1-W days. During that era, thousands of young men were compelled to give twenty-four months in service for their country. Those two years came in the prime of their lives, and their plans for the future had to be put on hold. The men who were involved with the 1-W program understand the work and sacrifice it required. Today's generation, especially those whose fathers were not required to serve, may be unaware of what 1-W service entailed.

The 1-W program followed the CPS program of the World War II era. Prior to that, no alternative programs to military duty were available for conscientious objectors (COs). During World War I, conscription laws provided for noncombatant service, but offered no options for those who conscientiously opposed taking any part in warfare. Conscientious objectors during WWI faced harsh treatment in army camps and military prisons, because they refused to wear military uniforms, take up arms, and participate in drills. They endured physical abuse, short rations, and solitary confinement because they were faithful to New Testament teachings.

The government did not want to repeat the difficulties COs had faced during World War I. When World War II threatened, government officials advised church leaders to create a plan for alternative service. That plan was the Civilian Public Service, or CPS, which went into effect in 1941. The CPS men were required to leave home and move into camps. More than 150 camps and units were established across the country. From 1941 to 1947, thousands of CPS men were drafted.

The government arranged for the CPS work projects, housing, and transportation. The churches were responsible to supply the physical needs, such as food and health care. CPS men did public work such as fighting fires, planting trees, building dams, and working on dairy farms. Others served as aides in psychiatric hospitals.

For a short time after World War II, the draft was no longer compulsory. This lasted for about one year, from 1947 to 1948. Then a new draft law was passed, but exemption was given to COs. However, because of public resentment to this ruling, it was amended in 1951. The amendment required all young men to serve equal time, twenty-four months, either in the military, in civilian work, or in work approved by the local draft board.

When the Korean War began, Congress rejected the proposal of reestablishing camps for COs. The Selective Service consulted with government agencies and church leaders. The result was the 1-W program, which began in 1952 and continued until American troops were returning from Vietnam in 1973.

As the Vietnam War dragged on into the late 60s, with an uncertain outcome and questionable purpose, President Nixon desired to bring closure to the conflict and withdraw American troops. Hundreds of thousands of lives had already been lost, both of soldiers and of Vietnamese civilians. However, Nixon felt that bringing closure would require more recruits being sent to Southeast Asia. Men ages twenty-one and up had already been called. Obtaining more recruits would require lowering the draft age to nineteen. That is why the 1-W men who served later often began service at a younger age than those who went earlier.

As never before, the media informed the public of what was happening in an overseas war. The willingness of Americans to supply more troops was ebbing. The public resentment toward the Vietnam War was perhaps why there was very little ill feeling toward COs who performed alternate service. Hospitals and other places of employment appreciated the work ethics of boys who came from stable homes, boys who had been taught to work and to obey their employers.

During the l-W era, it was relatively easy to be exempted from military service. Usually if a young man was a member of a Mennonite or Amish church, or some other church group which historically taught against military training, he could get the CO exemption. While in some ways a blessing, this lack of opposition did not build deep conviction. The trials COs faced during World War I had required them to take a firm stand against any military involvement.

The Selective Service used various terms to classify draftees. First, they were classified as 1-A, which meant they were available for military service. 1-A-O status meant that a young man could be excused from actual fighting, but was willing to serve in noncombatant military service. However, those who chose for conscience' sake to be exempted from all forms of military training were classified as 1-O, meaning they were available for alternate service. The term *1-W* applied to the time spent actually performing those duties, usually in a hospital. Quoting from the Selective Service System Form 110, a 1-W was a "conscientious objector performing alternate service contributing to the maintenance of the national health, safety, or interest in lieu of induction into the Armed Forces of the United States." At the completion of the two years of service, a classification of 4-W was given.

The Selective Service did not require registration from 1973 to 1980. Since then, the laws of the United States dictate that young men register with the draft board when they reach their eighteenth birthday, but compulsory service is not a current issue.

As citizens of the United States, we have been granted peace and freedom as never before experienced in the history of the world. We need to pray earnestly for our government leaders and cooperate with them as much as possible. Since the mid-1900s, the government of the United States has allowed us exemption from any involvement in the military. Are we grateful enough for this privilege?

Each of us owes a debt. Never in a lifetime can we repay the debt we owe to God, who has showered us with rich blessings. Our youth need to be encouraged to serve in kingdom work today. They need Biblical truths that will build in their hearts a conviction for nonresistant living in all areas of life. None of us knows what the future will hold. World War III could break over our heads without warning. We must lean on God's strength and grace for the trials of today. Only a vibrant walk with Jesus in day-to-day living and unwavering obedience to God's Word will prepare us for future testing and suffering. May He find us faithful!

—Shanda Good

ADDENDUM III

Serving Christ by Serving Others

"It is more blessed to give than to receive!" The words of Jesus still resound in our hearts today. Service opportunities abound for youth to serve in missions: in cities, foreign countries, Christian schools, rest homes, disaster response, rebuilding projects, and more. Developed by men of vision, these programs offer the potential for spiritual growth and fellowship. While serving Christ by serving others, many youth have discerned God's direction for their lives, and have made tremendous contributions to the kingdom of heaven.

Political tension and worldwide unrest appear to be escalating, which increases the possibility of young men being drafted into military service. With an eye to the future and a commitment to God's people, Christian Aid Ministries formed the Conservative Anabaptist Service Program in 2005. CASP works with church constituencies to provide an opportunity for young men to serve, regardless of what the government presently requires. In the event of a draft, CASP projects are already in place and have been approved by the United States Selective Service System as an alternative to military service. Selective Service Board delegates have encouraged CAM to continue the development of CASP.

Is God speaking to your heart? As church leaders, you can assist and encourage your young people in such a venture. To the young person, will you consider giving a portion of your youth in service? In Matthew 25 Jesus said, "Inasmuch as ye have done it unto one of the least of these my brethren, ye have done it unto me."

—Johnny Miller

What CASP volunteers have said:

- The four weeks I spent with CASP was time well spent. It was spiritually uplifting, and I especially treasure our Bible studies and the interesting discussions about "Rules of a Godly Life." Recreation and visiting youth and ministers were also a blessing. I appreciated the encouragement, correction, and stability of the project leaders. I am thankful to all who made this possible. —N. from IL

- The work was well organized and abundant. I am not a carpenter, but I learned a lot about construction in a short time. I am thankful to the Lord for bringing us together in His family and making this experience possible. If other young men are considering CASP, I say it will be worth your time, and you will receive more than you give. I was blessed and inspired. —S. from IL

- It was especially moving to hear a local man tell of losing his wife to the flood. We sang and prayed with the local residents, and we were touched by the inspiration and gratefulness they expressed for our labors in rebuilding their homes. I thank God for the blessings of working these four weeks with likeminded brethren. —A. from IL

- I was impressed by the eighteen young men who made up my CASP crew. We became much like a large family during our time together. Their diligence in working for the Lord will continue to build God's kingdom. God has a purpose for each of them. Thank you, boys. All glory to God! —A. from PA

- Our crew helped frame seven houses and built two wheelchair ramps during the four weeks I served. One day we needed to direct 300 volunteers who worked together on this project! Although the work was not easy, I thoroughly enjoyed working with our crew and crew leader. We made lots of memories, and the experience was very worthwhile. I would encourage anyone to go if you have the opportunity. —S. from NC

What a CASP recipient said:

- "This property has been in our family for a hundred years, and we didn't want to leave. But when our trailer flooded, we finally left in one of the rescue boats. But God is good, and He sent you to build us a new house. He has blessed us soooo much! Lord, oh, bless these boys who built this new house for us!"

For more information regarding CASP, contact Christian Aid Ministries at 330.893.2428 or write to Christian Aid Ministries, P.O. Box 360, Berlin, Ohio 44610.

About the Author

Johnny Miller was born in the Mennonite community of Virginia Beach, Virginia, where his deep Biblical convictions were formed by his family and church. At fourteen, he yielded his heart to Christ, was baptized, and became a member of Kempsville Mennonite Church. At nineteen, he was drafted by the Selective Service.

In 1967, Johnny married Ruth Overholt of Minerva, Ohio. God blessed them with six children, and Johnny established a plumbing, heating, and air-conditioning business to provide for their family and interact with the community.

Johnny's busy life of ministry included two years of teaching at Minerva Christian School and two years of living in Belize, where he helped establish Cayo Christian Fellowship. In 1983, he was ordained as a deacon in the Christian Fellowship Church at Minerva.

The Millers moved to Suceava, Romania, in 1997, where they served ten years at Nathaniel Christian Orphanage under Christian Aid Ministries. Upon their return to Minerva, Johnny authored *HeartBridge* and *A Heart to Belong* to relate their touching experiences with the hurting children of the Nathaniel Christian Orphanage. These books have inspired many readers.

Johnny remains passionate about teaching godly values through preaching and writing. For the past ten years, he has also answered spiritual questions from callers responding to CAM's Gospel billboard messages displayed across America.

Johnny appreciates hearing from his readers and can be contacted at johnny@emypeople.net or in care of Christian Aid Ministries, P.O. Box 360, Berlin, Ohio 44610.

About Christian Aid Ministries

Christian Aid Ministries was founded in 1981 as a nonprofit, tax-exempt 501(c)(3) organization. Its primary purpose is to provide a trustworthy and efficient channel for Amish, Mennonite, and other conservative Anabaptist groups and individuals to minister to physical and spiritual needs around the world. This is in response to the command to ". . . do good unto all men, especially unto them who are of the household of faith" (Galatians 6:10).

Each year, CAM supporters provide 15–20 million pounds of food, clothing, medicines, seeds, Bibles, Bible story books, and other Christian literature for needy people. Most of the aid goes to orphans and Christian families. Supporters' funds also help to clean up and rebuild for natural disaster victims, put up Gospel billboards in the U.S., support several church-planting efforts, operate two medical clinics, and provide resources for needy families to make their own living. CAM's main purposes for providing aid are to help and encourage God's people and bring the Gospel to a lost and dying world.

CAM has staff, warehouses, and distribution networks in Romania, Moldova, Ukraine, Haiti, Nicaragua, Liberia, Israel, and Kenya. Aside from management, supervisory personnel, and bookkeeping operations, volunteers do most of the work at CAM locations. Each year, volunteers at our warehouses, field bases, Disaster Response Services projects, and other locations donate over 200,000 hours of work.

CAM's ultimate purpose is to glorify God and help enlarge His kingdom. ". . . whatsoever ye do, do all to the glory of God" (1 Corinthians 10:31).

The Way to God and Peace

We live in a world contaminated by sin. Sin is anything that goes against God's holy standards. When we do not follow the guidelines that God our Creator gave us, we are guilty of sin. Sin separates us from God, the source of life.

Since the time when the first man and woman, Adam and Eve, sinned in the Garden of Eden, sin has been universal. The Bible says that we all have "sinned and come short of the glory of God" (Romans 3:23). It also says that the natural consequence for that sin is eternal death, or punishment in an eternal hell: "Then when lust hath conceived, it bringeth forth sin: and sin, when it is finished, bringeth forth death" (James 1:15).

But we do not have to suffer eternal death in hell. God provided a sacrifice for our sins through the gift of His only Son, Jesus Christ. "For God so loved the world that he gave his only begotten Son, that whosoever believeth in him should not perish, but have everlasting life" (John 3:16).

A sacrifice is something given to benefit someone else. It costs the giver greatly. Jesus was God's sacrifice. Jesus' death takes away the penalty of sin for all those who accept this sacrifice and truly repent of their sins. To repent of sins means to be truly sorry for and turn away from the things we have done that have violated God's standards (Acts 2:38; 3:19).

Jesus died, but He did not remain dead. After three days, God's Spirit miraculously raised Him to life again. God's Spirit does something similar in us. When we receive Jesus as our sacrifice and repent of our sins, our hearts are changed. We become spiritually alive! We develop new desires and attitudes (2 Corinthians 5:17). We begin to make choices that please God (1 John 3:9). If we do fail and commit sins, we can ask God for forgiveness. "If we confess our sins, he is faithful and just to forgive us our sins, and to cleanse us from all unrighteousness" (1 John 1:9).

Once our hearts have been changed, we want to continue growing spiritually. We will be happy to let Jesus be the Master of our lives and will want to become more like Him. To do this, we must meditate on God's Word and commune with God in prayer. We will testify to others of this change by being baptized and sharing the good news of God's victory over sin and death. Fellowship with a faithful group of believers will strengthen our walk with God (1 John 1:7).